Children's Online Language and Interaction

Children spend a significant amount of time interacting online rather than face to face. Yet we know very little about the language they use during interaction, whether they are gaming or texting. Drawing on cutting edge research, this timely book applies conversation analysis (CA) techniques to investigate children's online language and interaction. Tudini provides a step-by-step analysis of authentic posts made by children on social media, messaging apps and gaming platforms, highlighting linguistic and interactional features. The book addresses the risks inherent in children's online interaction and the role of protective adults, yet also celebrates children's linguistic creativity and ability to adapt to new forms of communication. It also provides principled advice on how to support children in integrating online interaction into their lives productively and safely, to assist caregivers and teachers. Addressing a highly topical area, it is essential reading for students and researchers of applied linguistics, communication, education and sociology.

VINCENZA TUDINI lectures in Italian and Applied Linguistics at the University of South Australia. She has published various book chapters, journal articles and monographs, including *Online Second Language Acquisition* (Bloomsbury, 2010).

Children's Online Language and Interaction

Vincenza Tudini

University of South Australia

 CAMBRIDGE
UNIVERSITY PRESS

Shaftesbury Road, Cambridge CB2 8EA, United Kingdom

One Liberty Plaza, 20th Floor, New York, NY 10006, USA

477 Williamstown Road, Port Melbourne, VIC 3207, Australia

314–321, 3rd Floor, Plot 3, Splendor Forum, Jasola District Centre,
New Delhi – 110025, India

103 Penang Road, #05–06/07, Visioncrest Commercial, Singapore 238467

Cambridge University Press is part of Cambridge University Press & Assessment,
a department of the University of Cambridge.

We share the University's mission to contribute to society through the pursuit of
education, learning and research at the highest international levels of excellence.

www.cambridge.org
Information on this title: www.cambridge.org/9781316519684

DOI: 10.1017/9781009024969

First published 2025

A catalogue record for this publication is available from the British Library.

*A Cataloging-in-Publication data record for this book is available from the
Library of Congress*

ISBN 978-1-316-51968-4 Hardback
ISBN 978-1-009-01087-0 Paperback

To my son Marco

Contents

Figures and Tables

Figures

Tables

Preface

Any book on children's language and online interaction needs to consider its risks, since online spaces are fraught with dangers to children. Some of the main concerns include unsolicited pornography, bullying and encounters with either disclosed or undisclosed paedophiles. This book is dedicated to understanding children's online language and interaction in general rather than the issue of child safety and protection. My original intention was to focus on one specific safety issue, on how paedophiles use language and interactional resources to groom children online, focusing on a single previously published chat sequence (Chapter 7). However, the analysis of *Club Penguin* data (Chapter 3) yielded unexpected findings related to safety arising from users' deployment of ambiguous vocabulary, despite *Club Penguin*'s linguistic safety mechanisms designed to protect children from inappropriate language. This is because conversation analysis yields insights that go beyond surface understandings, often even beyond the understandings of users who are under the time pressures of real time interaction. This is especially true for children whose linguistic and interactional abilities are still developing. Researchers who apply conversation analysis methodology also have the advantage of examining the details of talk after it has occurred, with time to analyse and understand the mechanisms of interaction. The visibility of data used in conversation analytic investigations is in fact one of the strengths of this research methodology, unlike methodologies which hide the shape of interaction in coding categories. Thus, conversation analysis allows the content of conversations to remain intact and open to researchers and readers. It reveals and considers intricate details about online interaction, even apparently innocuous interactional behaviours, which contribute to our understanding of children's online social action as expressed in written conversation.

On the issue of children's safety, there are inevitable risks for children when they engage with the internet. Hence, safety is a recurrent concern in this book. For example, as I wrote Chapter 6, which is dedicated to comments on child celebrities' YouTube videos, a scandal erupted due to identification of paedophile activity in the comments sections of videos featuring children (Shaban, 2019, February 23). Hence, YouTube decided to disable all comments on such

YouTube videos for safety reasons in 2020 (Wikitubia Fandom, 2013, August 28). In fact, one of the YouTube sites from which comments are derived for this chapter has had comments disabled since data collection occurred (EthanGamer, 2015, February 20), while the other continues to permit posting of comments (EthanGamer, 2020, February 17). Thankfully no such activity was encountered during YouTube comment data collection for this book, which were derived from selected Ethan Gamer YouTube videos.

Other original YouTube videos used for this book feature only video game screens and/or animations rather than children (e.g. CookieSwirlC, 2020, December 13). As a consequence of the dangers which sadly seem to permeate children's online activities, issues related to children's safety crop up in at least three chapters. This is also true of bullying and exclusion, which feature in one section of the chapter on *Club Penguin*. These topics merit separate in-depth research which is beyond the scope of this book, though they are identified as an incidental issue related to children's interaction on the internet.

One further consideration is that children of all ages are engaged in online interaction, through chats in a multiplicity of apps and video games, especially during the Covid-19 pandemic. So, choices needed to be made regarding which video game and chat contexts to focus on for this book, with children sometimes interacting with other children and/or with adults. The ages of the children also vary considerably, as video games and public online spaces such as YouTube attract children, and sometimes adults, of all ages, though a broad age demographic is provided for each online context investigated. Furthermore, while we need to be cautious about generalizing children's talk across all online contexts due to the numerous variables, such as affordances of the different devices used, we can at least formulate some generalizations about children's talk in one specific online interactional context at a time. The findings of the emoji chapter should, however, be generalizable across platforms. Where the analysis of one context reveals interactional similarities with another, this is noted in the analysis. I trust that the chosen online interaction tools and contexts provide at the very least a snapshot of how children of various ages 'talk' online in a variety of settings, though further work remains to be done.

Acknowledgements

This book would not have seen the light of day without the support of a number of people. First of all, I wish to thank Joe for being there for me and for enduring my long absences in the study. Thank you to my son Marco for providing his expert advice on some mysterious chat acronyms and *Minecraft*. I am grateful to Rebecca Taylor at Cambridge University Press for believing in this project and to Isabel Collins, also at Cambridge University Press, for her patience and constant support throughout the ups and downs of the writing process, including some complex moments regarding copyright. Catherine Daniel, the University of South Australia Library Copyright and Licensing Coordinator, was an especially significant resource who supported me consistently in the writing of this book. Her wealth of knowledge helped me navigate changing copyright requirements especially in regard to publicly available online interactions. Her suggestion to contact the Australian Copyright Council was especially insightful as it allowed me to gain nuanced and detailed legal advice in this area. A special thank you, therefore, also goes to the Australian Copyright Council for their thorough professional advice. I am extremely grateful to my three anonymous reviewers for their detailed comments and advice, especially in regard to methodology. Thank you also to the Centre for Research on Educational and Social Inclusion (CRESI) at the University of South Australia for their support and Therese Lovett for her invaluable suggestions on children's online gaming resources. A special thanks goes to Kevin of EthanGamerTV for providing permission to write about selected YouTube video productions and related comments. I am especially grateful to David Crystal for his support and our long-distance correspondence regarding the chat transcript analysed in Chapter 7. I wish also to express my gratitude to Disney Corporation for permitting use of screenshots of *Club Penguin*. And finally, thank you to the children and families who permitted use of SMS and WhatsApp interactions in Chapter 2.

Twemoji Attribution: Emojis used under a creative commons licence, © X Corp. Full details: Copyright [2024] X Corp and other contributors.

All emojis designed by OpenMoji – the open-source emoji and icon project. License: CC BY-SA 4.0.

Transcription Conventions

Chapter 4

.	falling intonation
,	level or slightly rising intonation
?	rising intonation
-	word is cut off
↑	change in pitch height: higher than preceding speech (not square)
↓	change in pitch height: lower than preceding speech
> <	faster tempo than surrounding talk
< >	slower tempo than surrounding talk
:	sound stretch (prior sound is prolonged e.g. li::ke)
<u>Really</u>	stressed syllable underlined
CAPITALS	loud voice
° °	quiet voice
#	creaky voice
$	laughing voice
@ @	animated voice
(.)	pause, less than 0.3 s
(0.5)	length of pause
hh .hh	out-breath/in-breath
j(h)oo	laughing production
[ ]	overlap
=	latching of turns
+ +	timing of non-verbal activity in relation to talk
()	empty parentheses indicate that the word(s) could not be worked out
(())	indicates transcriber's verbal descriptions – for example, ((sits down))
'a'	indicates that a letter of the alphabet has been named

↔   action occurring during a gap in talk – for example,
            (3.0)↔((watching screen))

Adapted from cited authors (Piirainen-Marsh
& Tainio, 2014; Davidson, 2012a)

Chapter 4 Multimodal Transcription Conventions

www.lorenzamondada.net/multimodal-transcription

Chapter 5 Transcription Conventions

https://universitytranscriptions.co.uk/jefferson-transcription-system-a-guide-to-the-symbols/

1   What Is Talk and Why Do Children Need It?

Introduction

Online text chat is *written* social interaction, a unique and constrained form of talk. Children appear to have no difficulties adapting to it, as evidenced by their presence on social media. They are clearly undeterred by chat's constraints and drawn to its affordances. This volume focuses on how children interact online when using social media and video games, where written interaction is a component. Their language and interactional behaviours inevitably change as they creatively adapt to new forms of interaction. Written interaction is also more likely than spoken interaction to compromise children's safety, given the anonymity it provides to online predators. Despite these concerns, interaction by textual means remains the most popular form of interaction for young people.[1]

To understand written talk, we need first to understand face-to-face talk and the role of language, as children draw on knowledge of their first mode of interaction in the online context. The resources that we need for successful interaction differ according to whether our talk occurs face-to-face, on the telephone or online. This is where conversation analysis can assist us in appreciating how talk differs according to the interactional medium and setting. Conversation analysis techniques have been used since the 1960s to reveal how speakers organize their talk as a social achievement, which they construct jointly with other speakers. The first landmark publications by Harvey Sacks, Emanuel Schegloff and Gail Jefferson, founders of conversation analysis, have had enormous impact in applied linguistics and in research more generally.[2] These now highly influential analytical techniques were originally developed

---

[1] The Statista website indicates that Snapchat was the most popular social media tool for US teenagers in 2017, though this varies across countries (Statista, 2021c). In Germany, WhatsApp was the most popular tool among ten- to eighteen-year-olds in 2019, with Instagram and Snapchat, the next most popular (Statista, 2020). A survey of teenagers by the Pew Research Center identified YouTube, Instragram and Snapchat as the most popular social media tools (Anderson & Jiang, 2018).

[2] Published in *Language* in 1974 and entitled 'A simplest systematics for the organization of turn-taking for conversation', it is the most cited and downloaded in the history of the journal according to Joseph, B. D. (2003). The editor's department: Reviewing our contents. *Language*, 79(3), 461–463.

to examine face-to-face and phone conversation but have since been applied in a variety of contexts, from business meetings to online social exchanges. Their recent application to various children's online interaction contexts has also provided important insights into young participants' interactional design and how they adapt linguistically to online interaction (e.g. Danby et al., 2018a; Davidson, 2012b).

Some recent investigations of social media communication by Turkle (2015) and Twenge (2017) have sought the opinion of users and experts directly, through surveys and interviews. Other researchers use quantitative methods and tests to explore connections between a type of social media activity and its impact on children's language and cognitive functions (e.g. van Dijk et al., 2016). This volume turns to the interactions themselves to look for patterns and answers. Conversation analysis can reveal how children of different ages produce, organize and interpret online talk to achieve specific conversational actions which may not be obvious to them. This study will provide us with a snapshot of children's online interaction through analysis of posts by children of various ages. Hence, the study will not tell us about how individual children change and learn over time, which would require a different type of study. However, we gain insights into how children of different ages and linguistic/cultural backgrounds interact online with other children and adults and what the implications are for their development. Children have the capacity to learn all the time and in any context, including informal digital contexts. So, it is urgent that we pay closer analytical attention to the language they use online and the constraints and affordances for learning of these contexts.

Screen Time Concerns

Children's digital contexts receive regular attention in the media and research, with conflicting reports on whether 'screen time' is good or bad for children. Social media, video games and television, on mobile devices, game consoles, computers or television sets, are often all considered part of the mix of 'screen time'. However, to understand the impact of these various devices on children's development, a focus on how language can be used by children in digital interaction, within specific media and interactional contexts, is required.

This volume focuses on the most 'interactive' forms of screen time, which involve children interacting socially with others as an integral part of the online activity. Social media interaction is obviously one of these and so are many video games. By exploring the unique language and architecture of social media and video game interaction, one of this volume's objectives is to assist readers in identifying the most beneficial online resources and technological-interactional configurations (Tudini, 2020) for children. By focusing on children's online chat, we gain a snapshot of the language that they use during interaction in a multiplicity of online environments, including how they adapt to written interaction. For example, how children manage online predators' grooming behaviours linguistically and interactionally in chat has received scant attention in research, despite the exponential rise in child abuse imagery on the internet (Internet Watch Foundation, 2015; WeProtect Global Alliance, 2019). Detailed analysis of children's language use when encountering online grooming behaviours by paedophiles is therefore attended to in this volume, mainly in Chapter 7.

Video game language and interaction is a focus of this volume because it is often a dominant part of children's social life. For example, children and caregivers are under considerable pressure to purchase a game console or other device which allows gaming or interaction via social media. Recent statistics in fact show that approximately nine out of ten of Australian homes have computer games, with children playing an average 100 minutes per day (Brand et al., 2019). This is despite concerns about video games' impact on children's physical, cognitive[3] and psychological well-being. Cognitive development of children goes hand in hand with their linguistic development. The Australian Department of Health recommends that children under the age of two not engage in any screen time at all. This recommendation is based on advice from experts, including paediatricians and speech pathologists, due to numerous concerns, such as evidence suggesting that television before the age of two contributes to language delays in children. There is also research that links increased use of handheld devices to speech delays in children under two (American Academy of Pediatrics, 2017, May 4). Specifically, there is evidence that the more time children under two years old spend playing with smartphones, tablets and other handheld screens, the more likely they are to begin talking later. A recent study used magnetic resonance imaging to compare children's resting-state connectivity between the left visual word form area and other brain regions, with screen time and reading time applied as predictors. It found that time spent reading was positively correlated with higher functional connectivity with left-sided language, visual and cognitive control regions while screen time was related to lower connectivity with these regions. Based on these findings, researchers thus emphasized the importance of children reading to support healthy brain development and literacy and limiting screen time (Horowitz-Kraus & Hutton, 2018).

Other concerns relate to how children's gaze is disrupted in video interaction. Screen interaction is at best a two-dimensional form of communication, which deprives children of experience in reading others' faces, voices and

---

[3] Cognitive development is defined by the online Oxford Dictionary as 'The mental action or process of acquiring knowledge and understanding through thought, experience, and the senses.' www.oxforddictionaries.com/definition/english/cognition.

bodies directly, as occurs in three-dimensional face-to-face interaction. Computer and smartphone video conversations would appear to provide access to eye gaze, an important component of interaction. However, the way that the screen constructs gaze is not direct, as it is mediated and disrupted by the technology. Users are unable to look each other directly in the eye, for example, especially in a group setting, where users often resort to waving to get inter-locutors' attention. Video interaction is therefore likely to alter children's perception and misrepresent interlocutors' gaze on screen, with possible consequences for their developing language and social abilities.

The sharing of context and body language by geographically distanced users during video interaction is also problematic as it is usually only partial and reliant on what is accessible on the screen and mediated by the technology. While it is true that participants' on-screen contexts are being shared, Malinowski and Kramsch (2014) note that the computer screen 'fixes the user in disembodied, spectatorial relation to a removed "scene" on the other side' (p. 159), which alters children's perceptions and interactional possibilities.

Other more serious repercussions for excessive screen time have been identified by research studies in France, UK and Australia, which have found that excessive screen time, including television, could hinder children's development (Hinchliffe, 2017, September 26). It also deprives them of the actual physical world which they access through their five senses and which is so important in their linguistic development. It is therefore unsurprising that some of the developmental problems identified by these studies include an inability to read facial expressions, which leads to reduced social abilities and poorer friendships. These problems are also features of Autism Spectrum Disorder, which has lead French researchers to consider developmental delays in children up to the age of four as a form of 'virtual autism' (Cabut & Santi, 2017, June 27), due to excessive screen time and insufficient contact with human beings in the real world, but see Strouse (2019) for a review of research on early childhood language learning through digital media.

Despite these red flags from health experts and the media, video games and social media are a significant part of family leisure time, for both young and old. There are also countless studies by education experts which suggest that children's engagement with digital devices is beneficial (e.g. Danby et al., 2018b; Gee, 2003). Most families are therefore unlikely to ban these resources, but some guidance on how best to use them, in a principled way, is urgently needed. By analysing how children engage with online interaction, including its affordances and constraints, this book may assist families and teachers to integrate technology into children's leisure time more knowledgeably, avoiding its pitfalls while harnessing its riches. Classification boards also have a fundamental role in supporting the community in this task.

Beyond Ratings

While many of us enjoy gaming, both adults and children, the gaming landscape changes constantly. Our decisions on video game purchases and subscriptions are sometimes based on reviews and ratings. However, word-of-mouth recommendations are likely to be the most common reasons children choose specific video games and social media chat softwares. Adults are more likely than children to make use of security and classification categories produced by government bodies, which relate mainly to game themes, violence, sex, language, drug use and nudity[4]. The Australian Council on Children and the Media (ACCM) also provides detailed reviews of gaming apps and films by child development experts (Children and Media Australia, n.d. b). Interestingly, this same organization's recent analysis of national laws showed that children's privacy when using websites and apps is not protected (Children and Media Australia, n.d. a). Despite these resources, children's tastes may however stray from available guidelines under pressure from peers. Without caregivers' and teachers' intervention and guidance, video game ratings and guidelines are not necessarily taken seriously by young users, with under-age video game players frequently taking on R-rated games such as *Grand Theft Auto* or popular MA 15+ games such as *Assassin's Creed*. Additionally, online safety and digital addiction issues are not addressed by ratings. For example, in its submission to the Australian Federal Government's recent review of the National Classification Scheme, independent think-tank Australia Institute recommended that an R 18+ rating be applied to 'games that replicate the psychological elements of gambling', including in-game incentives and rewards (Biegler, 2020). This is due to concerns with digital addiction and young people's use of smartphones for gambling.

While gamers are most likely to select their interaction and gaming tools according to their entertainment value and word-of-mouth recommendations, it is possible to evaluate these tools based on their language and interactional features. It is only by knowing what online interaction *is* that we acquire

---

[4] See Australian classification board (www.classification.gov.au/Public/Resources/Pages/Parents .aspx#6) and British Board of Film Classification (http://www.bbfc.co.uk/). The Classification Board assessments also tend to be limited to commercial game packages rather than internet-based games, which are regulated by separate bodies (e.g. the Broadcasting Services Act (BSA) administered by the Australian Communications and Media Authority (ACMA)). The Virtual Global Taskforce (VGT) (nationalcrimeagency.gov.uk/virtual-global-taskforce) is a global initiative involving numerous countries for the protection of children from online abuse. There are also national government bodies such as the Office of the Children's e-Safety Commissioner (esafety.gov.au/esafety-information/games-apps-and-social-networking), which as the name suggests, provides general guidelines and support on staying safe on the internet, with information on popular games, social media and applications. Another significant children's cybersecurity website for caregivers and children is ThinkUKnow in UK (www.thinkuknow.co.uk/) and Australia (www.thinkuknow.org.au).

a better sense of the place of social media and video games in children's ever-crowded lives. We are also better equipped to identify the titles and inter-actional settings which are likely to provide the most beneficial and safest experience for children. Written interaction is the dominant social interaction mode in social media, whether in Snapchat, Facebook or other social media tools. It is therefore important to know how chat works before we can assess its place in children's lives. Given children's regular use of social media and games, there is a gap in our knowledge of the nature of language and interaction in these environments which classifications and e-safety websites alone cannot fill.

Is Chat Speech or Writing?

When the first text chat tools were introduced, people described chat interaction as conversation in slow motion (Beauvois, 1992), or to use David Crystal's (2006) term, 'netspeak', suggesting that it is a form of speech. In fact, it is neither speech or writing and varies both interactionally and linguistically, according to whether two or more people are chatting or whether the chat occurs in real or delayed, quasi-synchronous time (see Garcia & Jacobs, 1999). Chat adopts the conventions of writing, such as script and punctuation, while borrowing heavily from the language of spoken conversation. When children interact online, they do so mainly in writing, through various forms of text chat, including video game chat.

Despite the availability of semiotic resources such as images and emojis, which are unique to the social media chat context, written interaction is significantly more constrained than spoken face-to-face or telephone inter-action. In face-to-face interaction we have access to voice, facial expression, body language, touch and physical context to achieve understanding. We can broadly distinguish the conversational resources which are accessible in spoken face-to-face communication as kinesic and prosodic. Kinesic resources include various aspects of visual communication and space sharing such as gesture, posture, stance, touch, facial expression, eye contact and gaze. Prosodic elements of spoken interaction include accent, stress, volume, pitch, intonation and rhythm. Furthermore, from a conversation analytic point of view, the presence of pauses and sound stretches also contributes to the prosodic richness and meaning-making of spoken interaction, including on the phone. In phone conversation we at least have access to all the resources related to voice. In written interaction we have none of these interactional resources. We rely almost entirely on text and an online context which may be supported by emoticons, emojis, hyperlinks, images and videoclips to achieve understanding. And yet, written interaction, especially texting, is becoming the dominant form of social interaction, especially among teenagers. Twenge

(2017) reports that based on national US surveys, high school seniors spent an average 2¼ hours and eighth graders 1½ hours per day texting on their mobile phone. Teenagers are more likely to organize dates, social events or collaborative schoolwork using written online communication rather than face-to-face or phone interaction, as previous generations would have done. This has huge implications for how children are growing up in this brave, new, always connected world. To appreciate the implications more fully, some widely known practices and learning theories will assist us in understanding why face-to-face social interaction is so important for the linguistic and cognitive development of children.

Why Children Need Face-to-Face Interaction

Social interaction through talk begins at birth. Even though babies are unable to speak when they are born, they can distinguish speech from non-speech and communicate by producing sounds, including crying. Parents and others instinctively talk to babies and babies respond to people's voices and faces. In addition to reading and emotional attachment, talk is in fact widely accepted as the foundation for children's language development and learning, whether this occurs in informal settings like the home or in the classroom. The centrality of talk for children's development is reinforced by cases of children who were raised in isolated conditions (Curtiss, 1978; 1989; Lenneberg, 1967). These children exhibited irreversible abnormal language development and other serious physical and psychological health problems. The author's observations of a two-year-old family member show how important listening, observing and imitating adults' conversations is for children's language development. Specific words and phrases are singled out and used by toddlers when they become relevant or interesting to them (see Saxton, 2017, for a review of research on the role of imitation/repetition in children's linguistic development). Play has also received considerable attention from researchers for its role in children's development during interaction with adults and peers.

How Children's Play Promotes Learning and Development: Vygotsky's ZPD

Soviet psychologist Lev Vygotsky (1896–1934) introduced the concept of the Zone of Proximal Development or ZPD, which became widely known in educational circles in the West. The notion of ZPD was originally based on children's learning and development during interaction with adults and other children. ZPD is exhibited especially during play, where children perform beyond their current abilities, as explained by Vygotsky (1978):

We propose that an essential feature of learning is that it creates the zone of proximal development; that is, learning awakens a variety of internal and developmental processes that are able to operate only when the child is interacting with people in his environment and in cooperation with his peers. (p. 90)

Vygotsky and other experts observed that interactions with people stretch children's abilities to accomplish tasks beyond what they can achieve alone. The concept of ZPD also gave rise to the notion of 'scaffolding' or assistance by a teacher or more competent peer. Scaffolding allows people to adapt their support to children's individual learning needs, at the appropriate level, thus generating ZPD. For example, when toddlers notice a new relevant word or phrase in adult talk, they may repeat it. This may be followed by adults' repetition and use of the new vocabulary item, to reinforce and approve the child's learning. This repetition is sometimes a form of indirect correction[5] of the child's pronunciation, as a form of linguistic scaffolding which is appropriate and relevant to the child at that specific moment.

Vygotsky specifically notes the importance of play as contributing to children's development, which is relevant to our discussion of digital games:

play creates a zone of proximal development of the child. In play a child always behaves beyond his average age, above his daily behaviour; in play it is as though he were a head taller than himself. (p. 102)

Vygotsky's insights have been applied and further elaborated in a variety of contexts, especially in classroom contexts. Vygotsky's principles suggest that the best games are those that involve talk. It comes as no surprise that interaction through talk gives children the opportunity to develop their language, interpersonal skills and interactional competence, a fundamental life skill. Studies have shown how, at an early age, children develop their interpersonal and interactional competence through talk with their peers. This includes the ability to negotiate, resolve conflicts, teach one another and develop socially as human beings. Such behaviour is conducted using language; hence, talk is a visible way in which children develop socially, linguistically and culturally.

Reading aloud to children, from the youngest age, is also known to promote learning and ZPD (see Antonacci, 2000; Fox, 2001), especially around language. In addition to the vocabulary and linguistic structures children acquire through reading, caregivers have the opportunity to provide their undivided attention and affection towards their children, while using the language of books as the basis for interaction and linguistic development. However,

---

[5] Correction is one type of repair which is both initiated and completed by the recipient (other-initiated other repair) in CA terminology.

research on the link between language, interaction, play and ZPD that might occur during video game and social media interaction is still in its infancy.

According to Gee (2007) and other researchers (e.g. Marone, 2016), there is evidence that ZPD occurs during game tutorials, when gamers help each other and when the game requires gamer acquisition of specific skills prior to progressing to the next level. As gaming interactions between peers generally occur in real time, Vygotsky's theories appear relevant since they were developed in relation to real time face-to-face interaction and the ability for feedback and scaffolding by more knowledgeable others to occur at the appropriate time. The application of conversation analysis (CA) to online interactions sheds light on how scaffolding and ZPD are achieved through microanalysis of learning behaviours. Specifically, the analysis will consider how interactional resources associated with learning, such as repair and question-answer adjacency pairs, are deployed by users to scaffold one another and promote ZPD, in selected online social contexts, both synchronous and asynchronous. Repair and questions are the most obvious indicators of learning behaviours but others are likely to become evident. While the contexts under examination are social, not institutional or educational, children are known to be learning all the time, including in online contexts.

Evidence also suggests that expert-novice roles and scaffolding behaviours are especially relevant to interaction between gamers, as some children tend to be more experienced at the same game than others, including adults. This is true also of virtual worlds such as *Club Penguin*. Expert-novice roles are therefore interchangeable between peers, or between children and adults, where children have greater expertise than adults. Some children may also watch expert gamer peers' YouTube videos to gain further knowledge (see Chapters 5 and 6 on the Ethan Gamer YouTube setting). Findings from the analytical chapters will determine whether there is evidence of children making expert-novice roles and peer scaffolding relevant by supporting one another and co-constructing their knowledge of the game or social media context, by deploying conversational repair, questions and other interactional resources. The analysis is focused on interaction between children but will take 'heterogeneity of expertise' (Thorne & Hellermann, 2015, p. 282) and interchangeability of roles into consideration, as level of expertise is likely to vary according to participants and interactional context.

It may, however, be difficult to see the relevance of Vygotsky's theories and CA to asynchronous online interactions, given that there are sometimes significant delays between posts. Chapter 6 will therefore consider whether asynchronous interaction softwares such as YouTube comments show evidence of learning behaviours despite the time delay between posts in these contexts.

How Children Learn Their First Language and the Role of Conversational Repair

We take it for granted that young children learn to talk from an early age. Parents' and other people's input is crucial to the process of learning to talk, from infancy onwards. This input comes in many forms and includes thinking out loud while engaging with the child, talking and interacting directly with the child, repetition of relevant key words and phrases, reading, singing and countless other interactive activities. Facial expression, voice, gesture and body language are key elements of children's interaction with adults and other children. As noted earlier, without face-to-face social interaction with adults, infants' intellectual and emotional development risks being held back, as they would lack opportunities to engage with other human beings and develop their language.

Adults' talk is a model for children. As discussed earlier, children use and experiment with new language they hear from their parents, other adults and peers. As children develop their language beyond the preverbal stage, adults engage directly with children's talk through the process of conversational repair. Repair takes many forms, including correction of a specific item in the child's talk or allowing the child to correct themselves by signalling a problem in their talk. For example, the parent may repeat a problem item in the child's talk in the correct way, which allows the child to notice a difference between what she said and what the parent said. The child may repeat the problem item in the correct form if it causes problems in the progress of the conversation. Otherwise, she may simply proceed with the conversation and remember the suggested item for another occasion. Example 1.1 shows how this form of conversational repair (correction) occurs in a face-to-face context.

> Example 1.1
>
> 1 Alex: I had all my breakfast and I **drinked** up all the milk
> 2 Matthew: You **drank** the whole bowl?
>
> (Saxton, 2017, p. 105)

In Example 1.1, the father Matthew's act of correcting the verb 'drinked' in his son's speech (turn 2) is not obvious, as it is embedded in the conversation (see Jefferson, 1987). The conversation in fact appears to continue without further interruptions, with the father simply seeking confirmation from the child that he drank the whole bowl, without openly drawing attention to the grammatical error. In this case, the child may not notice the correction as it does not interrupt the conversation. Or if he does notice it, there is a chance that the correct form of the verb 'drank' will be included in his speech on a future occasion.

In Example 1.2, the correction is once again about language, but also about interacting politely; hence, it is a pragmatic issue (Kasper & Rose, 2001). In this correction the mother makes it clear that the child's request that she turn on the toilet light is inadequate.

> Example 1.2
>
> Jo/age 4
> Child has just taken off her recording jacket and gone through to toilet; she
>   than calls to her mother:
> Ch: ↑Put on the li::ght.
> (.9)
> M: Pa:rdo:n?
> (.)
> Ch: Put on the light please
> (.)
> M: () better ((then M puts on the light))

(Wootton, 2017, p. 173)[6]

In this example, the mother initiates repair on the child's request, as there is a missing element, 'please', which she evidently wishes the child to incorporate in her talk, to learn how to produce requests politely. Unlike the previous example where the conversation went ahead despite the embedded correction, in this case the conversation cannot proceed until the child provides the missing element 'please'. Furthermore, by using this repair initiation strategy, the mother is also withholding turning on the light, until the child uses 'please'. The repair processes presented in Examples 1.1 and 1.2 mirror to some extent what occurs in Western classrooms when children interact with teachers or at home with parents and are an important venue for ZPD and adult scaffolding of children's development of their language and talk. There are countless ways for children to learn the language required for social interaction from adults and there is a substantial body of knowledge which indicates that this also occurs with peers in face-to-face contexts. Conversational repair during face-to-face interaction is just one of the most audible and visible ways in which learning is promoted, though children may not necessarily always alter their language immediately. It is a fundamental tool for human beings to achieve understanding and for young children to develop their language and social abilities.

Repair and Learning in Online Chat

The fact that text chat leaves a permanent record on the computer screen, with notable exceptions such as Snapchat and *Club Penguin*, has linguistic, social and learning advantages. The conversation suddenly becomes visible and can be reviewed by users, including children. So, for example, they can pick up an

---

[6] For additional examples, see also Wootton (1997).

earlier section of the conversation with greater ease than if they were engaged in voice conversation, which fades once each word or turn are pronounced. The author's own research has shown that this makes text chat especially suitable for foreign language learning (Tudini, 2010; 2013). The 'visibility' or 'visual saliency' of written conversation allows adult participants to review, make sense of and make adjustments later in the conversation where needed, to get their message across. This may lead to different types of conversational repair, which we know is conducive to learning. In Example 1.3 we see very clearly that written conversation between speakers of Italian as, respectively, a first (L1) and second language (L2), may move into a more pedagogical (learning) orientation when correction occurs.

> Example 1.3
> Dorothy: che ha successo
> *what happened* (with incorrect auxiliary verb 'ha')
> Giovanni: **che è successo**
> *what happened* (with correct auxiliary 'è')
> Giovanni: era caduta la linea
> *the line had gone dead*
> Giovanni: nn lo so perchè
> *I don't know why* (with chat abbreviation of non)
> Dorothy: ☺
> ☺
> Dorothy: sai forse devo venire piu spesso qui sopra a parlare con te cosi mi imparo per bene
> *you know I have to come here more often to talk to you so I learn properly*

During their conversation about losing the connection, the L1 speaker of Italian Giovanni notices that Dorothy's question includes the wrong auxiliary verb in 'che ha successo' (post 1). He provides the correct version in line 2, without any explanation, and then continues the social-technical conversation about the lost connection. Dorothy's smiley face in line 5 acknowledges and expresses appreciation for the correction. Dorothy in fact follows this with further recognition that interaction with the L1 speaker in the chat environment enhances learning when she states, 'so I learn properly'. In this case, the correction occurs immediately after the correctible item. However, given the visibility and reviewability of the conversation, corrections often occur many posts later without disruption.

While we have plenty of evidence that written conversation tends to promote language and intercultural learning during one-to-one adult interaction (e.g. Tudini, 2007), there is a paucity of research on the language children use during social media and game interaction. Additionally, research has found that text chat can be an equalizer, which is especially relevant to children who are developing their social abilities. It apparently can provide greater empowerment to shy learners, who tend to participate in conversation more actively than if they were in a face-to-face conversation, where confident speakers tend to take over (Kern, 1995; Warschauer, 1996). This may in part explain the high level of children's engagement with social media and video games, despite the many risks.

We know that children learn all the time and that certain video games may present all manner of beneficial cognitive challenges. However, combining games with social interaction is likely to enhance the gaming experience for them. Evidence suggests that as long as children are engaging in spoken or written talk, they are more likely to learn something new from others, including online. As we have seen, in addition to promoting their cognitive development, interaction promotes their development as human beings. We do need to be aware, however, that where only text interaction is involved, children need to adapt to a new environment and find unique resources for socializing and playing with other children. For example, they do not have access to non-verbal resources such as body, gaze and voice which are fundamental elements in children's interaction, socialization (Goodwin, 2017) and language development.

Non-Verbals as an Interactional Resource for Children

As noted earlier when distinguishing kinesic from prosodic features of conversation, interacting with others face-to-face is a complex task which involves much more than just words. Whether we talk or remain silent, we use our faces, voices, hands, body and surroundings to communicate with other human beings (Streeck, Goodwin & LeBaron, 2013). Children learn how to use all of these physical interactional resources through regular contact with adults and other children from birth onwards. Conversation analytic studies have in fact revealed that from the age of twelve months onwards, gesture, vocalizations and laughter are an integral component of children's interactions (see Filipi, 2009; Walker, 2017). However, these resources, some of which are discussed in the next section, are unavailable to them in text chat.

Facial Expression

The face is particularly important in conveying (or hiding!) how we feel about a topic during talk. It may also reinforce what we are saying through the way we use our eyes, eyebrows and mouth, for example. Children are acutely aware of facial expressions of adults and peers during face-to-face interaction. Smiles or frowns are the most common examples of how the face expresses emotions and were among the first emoticons to be developed by online chat users, who used punctuation marks to create the frown :(and smile :). It is of course no coincidence that the term 'emoticon' is composed of two words 'emotion' and 'icon'.

The eyes are a crucial element of gaze, without which turn-taking in face-to-face conversation would be compromised. It is common for speakers to look directly at their interlocutors at the point when they have finished talking, in expectation of a response. Gaze may also determine who speaks or is targeted in group conversation, when members of the group turn to look and suggest that a specific person take the conversational floor. Gaze may thus be co-ordinated with the whole or some parts of the body, especially posture, in these circumstances. Twitter users adapted to the absence of gaze and other non-verbals in group chat by introducing the @ symbol combined with a nickname at the start of a post to clarify the intended addressee of a tweet. In *Club Penguin* too, users tend to use one another's nicknames or real life names where a specific person is being addressed, to avoid confusion and promote conversational coherence in group chat.

Another one of the most frequent uses of gaze is to show the speaker that you are paying attention to what they are saying, to avoid seeming impolite. Avoiding eye contact with an interlocutor during talk may be problematic and subject to a number of interpretations, depending on the topic of discussion and relationship between speakers. For many it may indicate shyness or a lack of sincerity, confidence and respect on the part of the speaker. Speakers may also avoid looking at individuals in a group situation as an indirect way of excluding them from the conversation. Similarly, since gaze is unavailable as a resource, lack of responsiveness by chat users may be seen as impolite and needs to be accounted for by unresponsive recipients. This concern promotes the posting of short posts if the software does not indicate that a message is in the process of being composed, as permitted by WhatsApp.[7]

Readers are sure to think of many other functions of the face, especially eyes and gaze, in conversation, based on their own interactions and how we deal with lack of gaze in online contexts. Researchers such as Lorenza Mondada, Charles Goodwin, Marjorie Goodwin and others, have pioneered important research on the role of gaze, the body and the physical environment in face-to-face interaction, including among children (C. Goodwin, 1981; M. H. Goodwin, 2017; M. H. Goodwin & Kyratzis, 2007; Mondada, 2012).

Gesture

Hands and arms are used in face-to-face interaction to communicate meaning through gesture. While gestures may be used differently across cultures, they are another important element of face-to-face interaction,

---

[7] For further findings on chat users' adaptation to missing non-verbals see Tudini, 2015.

especially young children (Filipi, 2009). For example, they may be used intentionally or unintentionally, to reinforce a speaker's excitement, anger or other emotion. Gestures which involve the fingers allow young speakers to point to a relevant item in their immediate physical space, to promote meaningful talk. The way people use their hands and arms during talk may also signal their awkwardness or lack of confidence, through erratic movements, for example. And, of course, these bodily actions work in tandem with other actions involving voice and face. Again, social media chat users need to adapt to the invisibility of their hands and arms by using other, usually linguistic means. In adult online interaction this may be achieved through deixis, a type of linguistic pointing to both a physical or virtual context through pronouns such as 'here' or 'there', 'you' or 'me', or through the use of emojis. Depending on the age of the child, these linguistic resources may also permit children to adapt to the missing non-verbals of chat.

Voice

Voice, including breathing, is one of the most important components of face-to-face talk, as without it, communication could only occur through facial expressions, gaze and gestures, as in sign language. Together with the body, voice provides us with information about the likely gender, age and cultural background of the speaker. This has safety implications for children interacting online, as without access to voice, they are unable to work out the age of other users or identify online predators if they meet one. How a speaker breathes during or between talk may reveal information about their state of mind. Silences and pauses in a conversation may also provide information about how speakers feel about the conversational topic, as may intonation, how fast they talk and the volume of their voices. For example, anger or disagreement may be expressed with a rise in volume. Without access to voice we are unable to hear speakers laughing or crying, though online users attempt to express these emotions through emojis and emoticons.

Intonation is also an element of voice and it does more than provide information about speakers' feelings on the topic of conversation. When combined with gaze, it assists in allocating turns, so that speakers avoid talking over each other. Specifically, in English and other languages, a lowering of intonation at the end of a turn is often used to indicate that another speaker has the chance to take a turn at talk. So, lack of access to voice requires social media chat users to adapt to this absence through language.

Turn-Taking and Sequence Organization as Readers and Writers

Since the invention of text chat in 1973 at the University of Illinois, human beings have taken to and adapted to this constrained environment where they become readers and writers of conversation rather than speakers and listeners. The fact that we are readers and writers fundamentally alters how we interact online, especially the turn-taking system, and the way turns are organized into sequences. Part of children's development as social beings, especially in their younger years, requires them to learn to talk. This includes the management of turn-taking in conversation. How do they manage or learn turn-taking as readers and writers of conversation, as required in text chat? Sacks (1992) noted that children need to learn to become socialized, which entails learning the ability to interact. One interactional problem for children, identified by Sacks, is working out how to start a conversation, which requires them to gain the conversational floor from adults. One strategy is to ask the question, 'Do you know what?', to which the required response is 'What?'. This question is part of a pre-sequence which makes an answer by the child relevant and gains her the conversational floor. While question-answer adjacency pairs are features of online text chat, whether this occurs synchronously (in real time) or asynchronously, such inter-actional negotiations to gain the floor are not required, because turn-taking occurs differently in this environment (cf. Garcia & Jacobs, 1999), with permission from other users to post on text chat not required, though participants still adhere to turn-taking rules to promote coherent conversation. Hence, it would appear from this example that while children are likely to acquire the ability to interact in the *written* conversation environment, the offline world has very different interactional requirements.

Conversation in general has been found by conversation analysts to be an orderly process with a set of rules which human beings deliberately adhere to though they may not be conscious of the mechanisms at play. One of the key building blocks of conversation for organizing turns into coherent sequences and the achievement of understanding is the adjacency pair, as discovered by the conversation analysis research of Schegloff and Sacks (1973). After examining countless conversations, these pioneer researchers found that conversation is organized around clusters, with the base unit being the adjacency pair and one part of the pair following the other. This base cluster is composed of a first pair part and a second pair part which are related to each other in meaning. Examples of these include summons-answer presequences, question-answer adjacency pairs, greetings or 'how are you' sequences. For example, if a speaker asks a question (first pair part), an answer (second pair part) is expected and usually obtained from the other speaker (recipient of the question). The same is true of greetings or 'how are you' questions, where a specific response is expected, in the interests of functional conversation.

Example 1.4 illustrates a parent and child interaction, where the adult poses a question-greeting after getting the young child's attention in a summons-answer presequence.

Example 1.4

```
1  Richard :      cassie?
2  Cassandra:     (0.5) ((Looks at Richard.))
3  Richard:   →   how ya ↑ doing¿ (first pair part)
4             →           (1.1)
5             →   m{m?
6  Cassandra      {((looks away))
```

(Filipi, 2009, p. 67)

Cassandra is ten months old and while she responds to her father's summons ('cassie?') by looking at him (turn 2), she does not respond to his question and eventually looks away rather than providing the expected second pair part answer, despite her father's repair initiation ('m{m?') which attempts to prompt a reply. Filipi (2009, p. 91) argues that adults may pursue answers from young children persistently in 'working on the child's abilities to produce a response'. This reinforces the notion that a second pair part response to first pair parts such as summons or questions are expected in conversation. Children eventually become sensitive to the need to produce answers to questions, at an early age, and may use non-verbal resources such as gesture and laughter to provide a response (Filipi, 2009; Walker, 2017). As noted by Liu (2022), adult-child conversations provide children with the opportunity to learn about language and the social world, under adult guidance. They acquire turn-taking skills, grammar and pragmatics, and when dealing with questions, conversations with adults socialize them into both when and how they respond. In summary, turn-taking requires them to understand how sequences are organized, how to project a response from their interlocutors and how to respond to them. However, Stivers et al. (2018) indicate that responses to questions by children by the age of eight are still less frequent and more delayed than those of adults. Social interaction with adults and peers is therefore one important site for children to be socialized by learning the required skills and values to function as competent members of their society.

The interactional mechanisms which are at play in spoken conversation are to some extent mirrored in written interaction, though the absence of non-verbal aspects of interaction requires that users adapt to this unique environment to understand and be understood. Allocation of turns is therefore affected, as without non-verbal elements such as gaze and intonation, users do not observe the same turn-taking rules as in face-to-face interaction. For example, when talking to friends in face-to-face mode, the current speaker's intonation and facial expression generally indicate when they are about to finish their turn, so that the next speaker may respond and take their turn. This allows the conversation to make sense and proceed successfully, with one turn following another, though repairs and overlaps often occur, especially when speakers dominate the floor. Part of this functionality of adjacency pairs in terms of meaning-making is due to the fact that second pair parts are generally intended to occur next to, or immediately following the first pair part. Adjacency or 'nextness' is therefore an important principle of turn-taking in spoken conversation, given its rapid fade quality.

While online conversationalists may continue to aim for adjacency, their intentions may be thwarted by the turn-taking system of written interaction during text chat. In particular, there is a delay in posting contributions due to the need to *write and post* rather than simply *speak* their contributions. The adjacency pair is therefore altered in written interaction, with intended second pair parts of adjacency pairs not necessarily appearing on screen as planned. A disrupted question-answer sequence is evident in Example 1.5, derived from a public *Minecraft* group chat extract.[8]

> Example 1.5
>
> →1 Player 1: hey *Player 9* did you upload a video of that weird glitch?
> 2 Player 2: whew
> 3 Player 3: you guys stay
> 4 Player 4: bring raw wood
> 5 Player 5: it totally is
> 6 Player 6: wuz bored
> 7 Player 7: me?
> 8 Player 8: someone please come to aqua city and save me
> →9 Player 9: into mod forums/bug reports, yes

The affirmative response by Player 9 to Player 1's question in post 1 occurs eight posts later than the first pair part, as intervening posts by other players disrupt the adjacency of the question-answer pair initiated by Player 1. This type of disruption leads to what researchers have identified as 'disrupted turn adjacency' (Smith, 2003, p. 42), where first and second pair parts do not necessarily appear next to each other, as generally occurs in spoken conversation sequences. This is, however, not an issue, as even young users are accustomed to reconstructing the pairs through a process of reading the conversation. Herring (2013) has also shown that group chat users may playfully disregard the principle of adjacency on purpose, creating unlikely and nonsensical pairs to promote a sense of fun and belonging in online interaction.

In group chat, where many posts appear on screen at about the same time, users may also mistakenly construe first and second pair parts as adjacency pairs when they are not intended as such by posters. These have been titled

---

[8] https://bit.ly/4ckeB1O.

'phantom' adjacency pairs (Garcia & Jacobs, 1999) because while they make sense together, they are unintentional, and posters may interpret them as relevant to one another nonetheless. For example, an expression of appreciation such as 'thanks' may be seen as relevant to a post where a user flatters another, when it is actually intended to thank a different user for another reason. This is more likely in group than one-on-one written interaction, as the addressee or intended recipient is not always clear. In group chat, users therefore tend to avoid phantom adjacency pairs and possible misunderstanding by naming the intended recipient of the post or using the @ symbol together with their nick. The author has recently observed this practice even in work emails where there is more than one recipient.

If we backtrack to when the first form of technologically mediated interpersonal interaction, the telephone, was introduced, we find that users had to adapt linguistically, even though voice was available as an interactional resource. In fact, this medium flourished despite speakers being deprived of access to each other's faces and bodies as resources to achieve meaningful interaction. Hence, it is a good example of how human beings addressed invisibility of interlocutors, as with text chat.

How Phone Users Adapted to Speakers' Invisibility

Phone conversation is the first form of real time interpersonal interaction mediated by technology. In phone conversations, speakers' voices, but not their images, are transmitted long distance to permit communication between people who are not 'co-present' or in the same physical space. Similar to social media, the fact that speakers are not in the same physical space means that their bodies are not visible to one another. They are therefore unable to identify one another using sight. This changes the language they use when they interact, especially at the start of their conversation. The conversation in fact begins once a speaker answers the ring of the telephone, which summons them to respond to a caller. In the early days, an identification routine became necessary as part of the opening sequence of the phone conversation, unless speakers' voices were familiar to one another (see Schegloff, 1979). This routine has changed in modern days due to the evolution of phone technology.

The identification routine varies somewhat and is superfluous in phones where the caller's name and phone number are already in the phone's contact list. Where required, it may proceed as follows: 1) Summons-answer with or without self-identification. This entails the ringing of telephone (summons) by a caller, which if successful, is followed by the recipient's accepting the call and using voice to both provide a greeting and indicate readiness to talk. In English, 'hello' is the usual response, which may or may not be followed by self-identification (e.g. Mary speaking). Phone greetings vary across languages, with the Italian greeting '*pronto*', literally meaning 'ready', emphasizing readiness to talk and a go-ahead signal to the caller. The Japanese also have a special polite phone greeting, 'moshi moshi', which is used when they answer the phone. This literally means 'speaking speaking', which in a sense signals a transition from machine (phone ringing) to human voice communication.

After the recipient answers the phone and greets the caller, the caller will usually proceed with a reciprocal greeting and self-identification. Quite often, the recipient of the call will then indicate that they either recognize the caller or encourage them to state their business, with a simple 'Yes' with rising intonation and/or other go-ahead statement. For example, the go-ahead statement might typically be 'what's up' in informal conversation, or 'what can I do for you' in formal talk. Readers would be aware of many more variations to this routine, based on the circumstances of the telephone call. As noted earlier, the self-identification stage may be bypassed altogether where both callers and recipients are identifiable through contact lists. This is also true of digital voice communication applications and softwares such as Skype and WhatsApp, where the conversational routines and language are affected by the communication software.

After these introductory phases of the telephone conversation, speakers are reliant entirely on voice, as mediated by the telephone equipment, to achieve understanding. Similar to online text chat, speakers have no access to one another's physical spaces or bodies as resources in conversation, as they are usually dispersed in different locations. Text chat users on the other hand do not have the advantage of voice as an interactional resource, but they do have access to their keyboards and screens. There is usually also a 'virtual' context which chat users construct together (co-construct) as part of their written talk. Social media interaction tools such as Facebook, WhatsApp and Twitter also provide access to resources such as images, including emojis, hyperlinks, voice and video recordings, which are unavailable in phone conversation. As previously mentioned, the permanence of posts on screen provides a scaffold which is unavailable to phone users because the visibility of conversations as text promotes understanding compared to rapid fade voice conversations. However, interaction through text reduces children's ability to recognize the voices of adult strangers online, which exposes them to risks.

In conclusion to this section, when social media users are unable to see or hear one another during talk and can rely only on profile pictures and software resources, it is likely that certain linguistic adaptations need to be made to achieve understanding, in the same way that phone users created new language and conversational sequences to open and close conversations (see Tudini & Liddicoat, 2017). Adaptations to text only conversation therefore inevitably become an element of their written language, which children are also likely to deploy online and which this volume will examine.

Research Challenges

Research into children's online language and interaction presents numerous challenges to researchers. This is partly because conversation analysis requires the use of naturalistic online data, which has neither been elicited or affected by the actions of researchers and would have occurred anyway. Hence, this research does not recruit participants or set up experimental contexts for analysis. It relies on existing natural contexts where online interaction involving children occurs.

In naturalistic settings where original online data involving children are used, appropriate ethics clearances, informed consent and anonymization are required for private interactions, as in the mother-son data used in Chapter 2[9]. Ethics guidelines do however permit the use of public online interactions such as YouTube comments without consent as they are considered public information and can be accessed by anyone. This approach is supported by ethics guidelines of the Association of Internet Researchers and upheld by Nissenbaum's (2009) framework of 'contextual integrity'. In keeping with this framework, which supports *appropriate* flow of information without restricting it entirely (p. 2), all participants' nicknames and information on geographical locations have been anonymized. Any images associated with nicks and public profiles are also omitted and described only where relevant to the analysis, without revealing participants' identities. This is in keeping with Zimmer's (2010) concerns on the ethics of sourcing public data from Facebook, which are also relevant to other public social media. The author copied all posts from the conversation verbatim, including original emoticons, emojis, abbreviations, acronyms, spelling and grammatical errors.

Gaining consent would nonetheless not be possible where public YouTube comments are concerned, where there are posts by multiple children whose contact details are unavailable. And while ethics requirements permit the use of public interactions involving children, the identity issue is significant. Firstly, as will be seen in the analysis, identity becomes a relevant topic to participants in public interactions on YouTube (see Chapters 2 and 6) where it is clear that many children feel obliged to declare their ages because they use parents' and carers' accounts to be able to access the comments function. Public profile pictures of users in the data often present images of adults, so many children wish to clarify to both their YouTube celebrity and other users that they are children and that their presence is legitimate in a context which is designed for them. However, one of the drawbacks of using public data from social media is that users are permitted to interact anonymously, using profile names, gamer

---

[9] Where required, participants gave written informed consent in accordance with University of South Australia Human Research Ethics Committee (HREC) requirements. The use of public online interactions is also in accordance with university HREC guidelines as at the time of writing.

tags and nicknames. So we have no guarantee that participants are children, though their developing language may betray the age of some users, as will be discussed in Chapter 6. Young adults also openly reveal their age when they are long-term fans who engage in nostalgic viewing of Ethan Gamer's later YouTube videos and participate in comments.

Gender is seldom revealed in the profile names in the YouTube comments context. However, when they do indicate a gender, relevant gendered pronouns such as 'he' or 'she' are used in the analysis for clarity. Where gender is unclear, as often occurred in Chapter 6, feminine pronouns are adopted in place of neutral 'they', since the latter option, though more inclusive, was found to be confusing in the analysis.

While content creators and users have the support of YouTube's AI filters and moderators to remove inappropriate content in comments, we have no way of knowing for certain whether apparent child users are in fact paedophiles, as pretending to be a child is one of the tactics used by paedophiles to groom children (Chiang & Grant, 2019). Some paedophiles are, however, quite open about their presence, as confirmed by the fact that comments on YouTube videos featuring minors were disabled in February 2019 and became unavailable to users due to the posting of predatory comments (Alexander, 2019, February 24). This action included Ethan Gamer's YouTube comments, some of which had been collected for this research, but did not affect those where animations or video game screens are featured[10].

Another challenge when writing this book is the speed of technological change. While some platforms and resources examined in this book may still be available in ten years' time, they will most likely become more sophisticated and/or change quite dramatically, as will the devices used to access them. Hence, the affordances and constraints for children's language and interaction are likely to change as well, though the basic interactional framework is likely to remain intact. Analysis of children's online interaction is therefore a moving target, as even currently, children in the same location or across the globe are likely to be using different devices. This will cause variability in levels and quality of access to the various tools and resources. For example, this variability is one reason why frequency counts and attempts to generalize children's frequency of use of resources such as emoticons are irrelevant in this study, as different devices provide different resources, with the newer ones providing the greatest choice and ease of access to users who own them across platforms. This issue will be addressed in greater detail in relation to interaction on specific platforms.

---

[10] Some Ethan Gamer YouTube comments were collected for this project prior to this action, however, there are no predatory comments in the data collected (see Chapter 6). The predatory comments had targeted perceived compromising physical positions of child YouTube video creators, which are not accessible in animations.

Copyright is also a complex issue when conducting research on online resources, regardless of whether these are available publicly or privately. First of all, the graphical component of interactions is owned by the companies that created the software, which is why copyright clearance needed to be obtained for analysis of *Club Penguin*, as the graphics are an important dimension of children's interaction. Therefore, analysis which is based on review of previous literature often lacks graphics, for which authors are able to substitute only a description. Chapter 3 on *Club Penguin* also required a rigorous copyright clearance process with the creators, Disney Corporation. The most complex copyright clearance was related to YouTube comments (Chapter 6), as YouTube did not provide a clear process; hence, advice was provided by experts in copyright law at the University of South Australia, who recommended that clearance be obtained directly from the YouTube video content creators themselves. In this case copyright clearance was not required for any of the graphical components, which were excluded to protect participants' privacy, but for the comments themselves. As they were de-identified public comments, the Human Research Ethics Committee at the University of South Australia approved their use; however, possible copyright matters needed to be addressed through the content creators as owners of the relevant YouTube videos and with legal advice from the Australian Copyright Council.

Children's use of emojis in interaction also raised complex copyright issues as they are owned by many different creators and companies according to the device and platform in which they are available. This was especially problematic in Chapter 2, which is focused on emojis in children's interaction. The issue was circumvented by substitution of original emojis with free emojis for private and commercial use (Wikimedia Commons, 2021), though they may not always correspond exactly to the originals.

In keeping with principles of CA methodology, 'proof-procedure' will be applied in the analysis, whereby recipients' responses assist in interpreting how a prior turn was understood (Sacks et al., 1974; Reeves et al., 2017). As noted by Sacks et al. (1974):

... while understandings of other turns' talk are displayed to co-participants they are available as well to professional analysts, who are thereby afforded a proof criterion (and a search procedure) for the analysis of what a turn's talk is occupied with. Since it is the parties' understandings of prior turns' talk that is relevant for their construction of next turns, it is their understandings that are wanted for analysis. The display of those understandings in the talk of subsequent turns affords both a resource for the analysis of prior turns and a proof procedure for professional analyses of prior turns – resources intrinsic to the data themselves. (p. 729)

There are, however, instances where responses to single posts are atypical, as in the YouTube main comments strand or in some multi-party chat. Research by Farina (2018) on Facebook interaction has revealed that adult users are most likely to respond to first rather than subsequent posts in a strand and this also seems to be the pattern in children's YouTube main comments interaction (see Chapter 6) where users prioritize interaction with the YouTube producer rather than with other users. Hence, use of such instances is limited and comments substrands are preferred, due to the stronger probability of obtaining a response from the YouTube celebrity or other users.

Implications

Despite fundamental differences between spoken and written conversation, the reader might rightly assume that digital activities where social interaction is the main activity, as occurs on social media and certain games, have the potential to provide some benefits to children, even if they are not face-to-face. What might Vygotsky think of social media interaction, which is conducted mainly through writing? There are many unanswered questions which will guide this study, as follows.

1. Given the significant amount of time many children spend online, how are learning behaviours such as conversational repair deployed, and scaffolding and ZPD achieved during online interaction, which occurs mainly between peers, without the support of non-verbal interactional resources or guidance from adults?
2. What is the language of children's online interaction like, lexically, syntactically and pragmatically?
3. What is the place of certain video games which isolate children and do not include interaction with human beings and language-rich environments?
4. How does children's interaction unfold in the vast array of video games and social media tools that are available on the market?
5. How do children manage chat's unique turn-taking system and sequence organization, given that these are developing abilities in children's younger years?
6. How can we foster quality interactional experiences for children so that their online recreation is conducive to learning and language development?
7. Is it possible to identify interactional configurations which maximize children's learning while interacting online?
8. Is it possible to identify the most interactive games, not in the technical sense, but in the sense that they involve talk and interaction with human beings?
9. How does online interaction compromise children's safety?

This volume seeks answers to these questions to provide the reader with a guide to selecting and setting up the best video games and social media tools for children. Chapter 8, the final chapter, therefore returns to these questions to examine how the study has addressed them.

In Summary

- Children's online language and interaction is a neglected area of research despite the popularity of social media and video games.
- Screen time has been linked to language delays, obesity and virtual autism.
- Chat is a unique hybrid form of social written interaction.
- Play and face-to-face interaction are essential to children's development.
- The body is a key resource in face-to-face interaction.
- New language and interactional routines were invented with the advent of the telephone, as is occurring now with new media.
- In chat, we interact as readers and writers, not speakers and hearers.
- Invisibility and unavailability of users' voice have implications for children's safety.
- Current ratings are an inadequate guide to video games as guidance on level of linguistic and social interactivity and learning potential is also required.
- Research challenges in investigating children's online language and inter-action from a CA perspective using naturalistic data include the issue of identity and ethics in public online interactions, speed of technological change and copyright restrictions related to software graphics and emojis.

About This Book

Chapter 2 examines children's use of emoticons and emojis, to assist us in understanding an extensive range of their conversational functions as the basis for interactional analysis in subsequent chapters. Chapter 3 then turns to massively multiplayer online game/chat software *Club Penguin* that was popular with children until the desktop version was closed down in 2018. The chapter considers how children adapt linguistically to unique features of *Club Penguin* chat in a range of interactional environments. Chapter 4 instead reviews previous research to examine the interactional structure of video game interaction, differentiating between offline and online gaming interaction between children or between children and adults. Chapter 5 applies the analytical framework developed in Chapter 4 to public *Minecraft* interaction between Ethan Gamer and his fans, focusing mainly on the role of in-game chat during a public gaming session. Chapter 6 deals with children's asynchronous chat interaction on YouTube comments, to explore linguistic and interactional resources available to them, the nature of comments interaction and how they manage such an interactionally constrained medium using substrand rather than main strand comments to promote collaboration between users. Chapter 7 turns to online grooming language and interaction in text chat, by examining one published example of chat interaction between an identified offender and his young teenage victim. The analysis provides insights on how paedophiles use language to negotiate children's trust in the early non-sexual stages of online relationships and how children are likely to respond interactionally. Chapter 8 summarizes findings and reviews the implications of previous chapters. It also provides suggestions for conducting further research in this area.

As detailed in the Appendix: Data Table, data for this book are derived from various mostly publicly available online contexts. Chapter 2, in particular, is based on data from multiple media sources involving children of a variety of ages, genders and cultural backgrounds, to provide a representative sample of how children use emojis. These include private SMS and WhatsApp messages between a mother and son aged between fourteen and sixteen years, which were not specifically collected for the study as they were naturalistic exchanges. University of South Australia Human Research Ethics committee requirements were followed to gain permission for use of these data. In addition to WhatsApp and SMS messages, publicly available YouTube comments from Ethan Gamer (2015, February 20; 2020, February 17), Cookie Swirl (2020, December 13) and Guinness World Records (2018, December 15) are also part of Chapter 2's data set. Chapter 3 data are instead derived from *Club Penguin* chat data available online or in publications. Specifically, the online chat data were sourced from *Club Penguin Rewritten* (2020, April; 2021), *Club Penguin Reunion* (2016, August) and *Club Penguin Wiki* (2018, February). Other chat exchanges were derived from Burley (2010) and Marsh (2013). Chapter 4 gaming data is based on reviewed publications, including Mondada (2012), Piirainen-Marsh & Tainio (2014), Hung (2011), Davidson (2012a) and Chien (2019). Chapter 5 gaming and chat data is based entirely on a public YouTube video gaming session between Ethan Gamer and his fans (EthanGamer, 2019, May 28), as a single case analysis. Chapter 6 YouTube comments data is derived mainly from Ethan Gamer (2015, February 20; 2020, February 17) substrand comments while data used in the analysis for Chapter 7 is from Crystal (2011).

2   Beyond Emotions: Emoji Talk

Introduction

Emoticons and emojis are an integral part of written social interaction across most social media platforms. Emojis are especially varied and easy to access through the keyboards of smartphones and other mobile devices. The latest smartphones include a dizzying array of emojis when compared with early models and some recent models even allow users to create animated emojis based on a scan of their own face and a recording of their voice. This representation is known as an 'animoji', a word composed of 'animated' and 'emoji'. This function would in theory permit greater precision in conveying users' facial expressions through a 3D animated image, which is then used in online communication. However, the animoji does not represent users' faces exactly but superimposes their facial expressions, including dimples, onto an image of selected cartoonlike animals or aliens.

The animoji example illustrates mobile phone producers' preoccupation with developing new conversational resources which convey users' meaning more precisely and in a more entertaining way than fixed emojis. Nonetheless, emojis have been widely adopted because they fulfil numerous functions in chat interactions, such as assisting users to convey meaning, achieve understanding and build relationships in an otherwise faceless, voiceless, bodiless online context. This chapter reviews and draws upon relevant research on the multiple functions of emoticons and emojis in adult online interaction, the focus of most of the research so far, for the analysis of children's use of emoticons and emojis.

Data for this chapter are derived from a variety of children's social media interactions (see Appendix: Data Table[1]). There was significant variation in the amount and type of emojis or emoticons used by the participants, according to the user and the device used. This variation is partly because access to emojis varies according to the device, application or software used by the participants; hence, the number and type of emojis used is likely to vary accordingly. For

---

[1] The data table in the Appendix provides details of all the data used in this book, including sources of examples used in this chapter.

example, some technologies provide easier access to emojis than others, with new emojis added to current collections over time. Smartphones in particular are known to provide readier access to emojis than computers by incorporating emojis in their keyboard, rather than requiring additional steps such as a Google search. This feature has improved over the years, with the typing of relevant text automatically producing an image which may either replace the text or be added to it for visual reinforcement and other purposes. The use of emojis in YouTube comments on desktop computers requires users to take more steps than on smartphones and this impacts emoji accessibility (see Din Vision, 2020, April 20). Hence, the type and quantity of emojis in the dataset is influenced by these factors.

Children's age is also likely to impact on how they use emojis, as they tend to become increasingly confident with language in general, social media and digital interaction by the time they reach adolescence. According to Howard (2018, June 22), in the US, 23 per cent of children aged eight to twelve have a social media account, compared with 80 per cent of children aged thirteen to eighteen. Younger children who are still learning to express themselves verbally may in fact prefer emojis over text as an appealing, playful mode of self-expression online, if ease of access is not an issue. Hence, the analysis considers all types of emojis and emoticons, to gain a snapshot of the uses to which children put these interactional resources in a variety of contexts. To start with, the following section provides a methodological premise on ambiguous emojis[2] and possible intergenerational differences in their interpretation in the constrained text chat environment.

Misunderstanding Emojis

The process of understanding emojis can be unreliable in some cases, as emojis are not always clear, even as visual representations of emotions. However, children and young people seem to be much more conversant with emoji meanings than adults. This is evident both from my personal experience and in the following case where a daughter corrects her father for misinterpreting the laughing with tears emoji as a crying emoji. He had attempted to express his sympathy over the anniversary of the death of a relative, Uncle Todd (Nagi, 2015).

(Photo) User 1

@User 1: Love my dad but this is why parents shouldn't text or use emojis

---

[2] The Wikimedia Commons (2021) guide to copyright-free emojis is an important reference to provide generally accepted descriptions and interpretations of emojis; however, these need to be adapted to a naturalistic online context. All original emojis in the data have been replaced by these copyright-free ones.

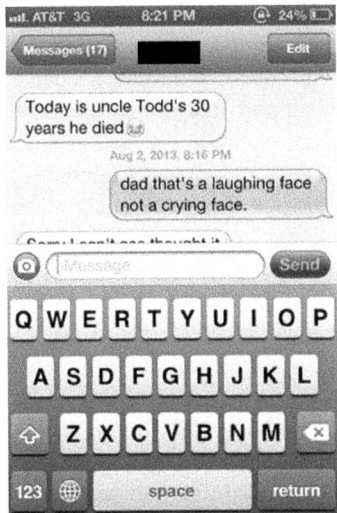

Figure 2.1 Laughing emoji misinterpretation and correction.

In Figure 2.1, what was intended as an expression of sympathy became a social blunder due to misinterpretation of the crying (tear) component of the emoji. The daughter corrected the error but though this message was apparently intended for private use, she posted it on the internet for public view on a website for seventeen-year-old users. The internet is peppered with errors of interpretation of the laughing with tears emoji and others. These errors have even been profiled for entertainment in a series of examples of emoji 'fails' in tabloid newspapers (Roberts, 2017, July 18). Errors of interpretation by users are inevitable in constrained written conversation environments, though clearly some emojis are more ambiguous than others. Gibson et al.'s (2018) analysis of the hand covering face emoji suggests that users' reported interpretive ambiguity of emojis may in fact be a 'recurring feature of emoji use, as the various associations that people have of them may not fit with the other communicative actions being undertaken' (p. 97). This same study emphasizes the role of other textual actions and the interlocutor in understanding the communicative function of emojis. In the Chinese data examined, the study reveals a variety of interpretations of the same emoji, including 'emphasizing that an utterance was ironic, that a question was rhetorical, or that a certain word or phrase was "accountable"' (p. 97). Clearly, the interactional context is fundamental in promoting user understanding of emojis given the multiple possible interpretations.

The proliferation of emoji 'fails' and Gibson et al.'s (2018) research raise an important methodological issue for analysis of emojis, as the expression of meaning through images is connected to the surrounding text and the recipients of that text, who assist our analysis by providing an interpretation. Thus, while errors of interpretation by children are infrequent in the data used in this study, contextual cues and recipient responses support analysts' own interpretation of ambiguous emojis where they occur. For example, the sad crying emoji 😪 discussed in Example 2.14 is described in Wikimedia Commons (2021) as a 'sleepy face', whereas the context of the post suggested other interpretations. Hence, careful linguistic and interactional analysis is required to provide nuanced perspectives on this social practice. When available, participant responses assist in providing correct emoji interpretations.

Review of previous research and analysis of children's use of emojis will provide an initial framework to understand how children use them in online interaction in subsequent chapters. Emoji functions identified in the analysis include expressing affective states, humour and identity but also promoting politeness, enhancing meaning, recontextualizing and engaging in playful behaviours, many of which are intended to build rapport with other users. It will, however, become evident that the functions of individual emojis often overlap within the same interactional context, even when deployed by single users. I should first note briefly the original difference in meaning between the terms 'emoji' and 'emoticon', though this differentiation has somewhat blurred over time.

Difference between Emoticon and Emoji

Before emojis became available, users accessed and used emoticons in emails and chat. These symbols continue to be used today and are created mainly using punctuation marks in text-only communication such as email. These days, however, operating systems may automatically convert smiley faces or frowns derived from punctuation marks into a type of pictogram, similar to the emoji. For example :) becomes ☺ on most keyboards. From 2011, mobile phone operating systems and applications instead provided users with easy access to an array of emojis, pictograms which were originally created in Japan and portray not just facial expressions but other images as well (Pardes, 2018). Access is so easy on recent model smartphones these days that if there is an emoji that can replace a word or phrase, the phone system prompts users with the relevant emoji in the message they are constructing. It thus becomes easy for users to either adopt or reject the emoji in their texts, which may lead to the use of previously unintended emojis. This is because it is sometimes quicker to accept rather than reject the emoji if the system automatically replaces a word while writing posts.

Emoticons and emojis have a variety of interactional functions in written exchanges which go beyond portraying the user's mood. When social media users are reliant exclusively on written text, that text acquires a significant weighting in conveying users' meaning, as it is unsupported by the usual conversational resources available in spoken conversation. Emojis and emoticons therefore potentially lessen that reliance on text for user-readers by providing pictorial elements to communicate additional, more nuanced meanings where written language is the principal mode of interaction. With a little more effort, users may nowadays opt to use GIFs, memes and memoji to express their feelings more humorously. Graphics Interchange Formats (GIFs) are typically brief animated images which are taken from movies or television series and loop continuously. Memes on the other hand are typically static images with text captions. One of the interactional functions of the mobile phone animoji tool described earlier is providing access to recent facial expressions and the voice of the user, within a written conversation. Specifically, the animoji extends an existing function of fixed emojis, namely that users choose a pictorial image of an exaggerated facial expression that best reflects how they are feeling. In the case of animojis, one might expect a more realistic and nuanced facial expression, though how they are actually used in interaction remains to be seen once the number of users of up-to-date mobile phones increases and relevant data becomes available. My own experimentation with the recent memoji, which are like animoji but with enhancements such as stickers and text, suggests they might be used in a similar way to the popular 'memes' for entertainment and expression of emotion in a playful personalized manner during written interaction between friends and family, rather than less intimate interlocutors (but see Herring et al., 2020 on gender differences). The later operating systems of mobile phones provide easy access to unanimated memes and other interactional resources through the keypad, which explains their recent popularity.

Both GIFs and memes are used mainly for comic effect in online social interaction. They have become popular in social media interaction and may be used in place of emojis for expressing feelings or responding to other users' posts because they tend to be more entertaining than emojis in certain situations. They do, however, require a greater effort to deploy in written interaction than emojis and occupy an entire post. Hence, emojis tend to be the dominant practice in most social media, unless interaction is based on the posting of images rather than text, as in the case of Instagram. Children's group chats may potentially also show a preference for GIFs and memes over emojis where they prioritize play and entertainment in their interactions. However, this focus requires further investigation which is beyond the scope of this study.

From this point on, for the sake of brevity, I adopt 'emoji' to refer to most of these elements, with some exceptions. Let us now consider the sophisticated uses children put emojis to in written interaction, as a basis for understanding the diversity of children's uses in later chapters.

Attendant Activities and Politeness

In a landmark study, Gail Jefferson (1987) observed that in face-to-face interaction conversationalists engage in a variety of 'attendant activities' around 'dispreferred' actions such as correction. These activities promote politeness in talk, though correction is only one of many dispreferred actions in talk. So to understand how emojis are a form of attendant activity, it is necessary to delve into the notion of 'preference' in conversation, especially the difference between preferred and dispreferred conversational actions, which are of course also evident in children's online talk. The best way to illustrate this is through the example of an invitation. The invitation 'would you like to come to the cinema on Friday afternoon?' typically allows for two responses, namely, acceptance or refusal. Acceptance is straightforward and is usually done without delay. This is in fact the *preferred* response to an invitation. The other possible but *dispreferred* response is refusal. This may cause delay in talk and could even be seen as rude, if additional conversational work is not done. Typically, this might involve explaining why the invitation cannot be accepted. In the following example from Burley (2010, p. 7), Penguin 2 (P2) invites the other children to be her friend in a *Club Penguin* room, but her invitation is met with a dispreferred response:

> Example 2.1
> 1 P2: Anybody wanna be my friend?
> 2 P2: Please. I like your outfit, you are so cool, wanna be friends.
> 3 P1: I don't like your hair. [Walks away]

Clearly, P1's response in post 3 is dispreferred, as her actions, both verbal and non-verbal, constitute a refusal to be P2's friend. The conversational work which accounts for her refusal is also inappropriate and impolite, as it is a negative evaluation of P2's appearance, for which P1 is eventually chastised by the other children.[3] She also draws on *Club Penguin* interactional resources to walk her Penguin avatar away, thus reinforcing her refusal of P2's friendship with a virtual physical rather than verbal action.

Correction may also be treated as dispreferred in spoken and online interaction. Groundbreaking research by Schegloff et al. (1977) showed that people who are engaged in conversation will give the speaker making a mistake the opportunity to correct themselves rather than pointing out and correcting their mistake openly. This is likely to be less risky socially than open or 'exposed' correction. Jefferson (1987) differentiates 'exposed' correction from 'embedded' correction, which is deployed without drawing speakers' attention to the error and allowing the conversation to continue on the same topic. We saw an

---

[3] See full discussion in Chapter 3 of this volume.

example of this in Chapter 1, where the father continued talk on the topic of his son's drink while at the same time including the correct item in his response, without verbally drawing attention to the missing verb in the child's talk. This form of correction also permits the exchange to proceed without disruption of an existing conversational trajectory.

When exposed correction does occur, Jefferson notes that there are 'attendant' activities that accompany the correction. These activities do the conversational work of accounting for the dispreferred act of correcting and may include instructing, complaining, admitting and so on. Accounting for open correction diminishes the possibility of being considered impolite, as well as having other consequences for the relationship. In written conversation, emojis may fulfil a similar function where dispreferred conversational actions occur.

Emojis as Attendant Activities

In previous research on text chat between speakers of Italian and English as either a first or second language, I observed a great deal of exposed correction, accompanied by emojis, mainly by participants noting linguistic errors (Tudini, 2010). In these interactions, there were two frequent attendant activities when correcting, one was instructing and the other was the use of emoticons, to mitigate dispreferred actions such as correction or refusal. Example 2.2 is an example of instructing, correcting and emoji use in the same post, in chat interactions between university students.

> Example 2.2 Winking emoji in chat correction sequence.
>
> 1 Lis: ti piace cuocere?
> *do you like to cook?*
> 2 Gianluca: si, mi piace
> *yes, I like it*
> 3 Gianluca: a te?
> *and you?*
> → 4 Gianluca: si dice cucinare … 😉
> *you're meant to say cucinare*

In Example 2.2 Lis used the wrong Italian term for cooking, as 'cuocere' in Italian means to cook in a passive sense, as when a meal cooks, not when a person does the cooking of the meal. Gianluca's use of 'you're meant to say …' frames an instruction to Lis, followed by the correct alternate word 'cucinare'. This instruction-correction is terminated by a winking emoji, which has the function of softening the preceding dispreferred conversational action. The emoji may be intended to express collaboration and support to Lis, to avoid appearing impolite. It is actually part of the same post; hence, it is intended to be seen as belonging with the instruction-correction component of the post.

While the winking emoji in Example 2.2 was positioned within the correction post, many other emojis and emoticons in the same study were positioned either in the preceding or subsequent post, visually adjacent to the correction post.

Emoticons and emojis clearly constitute a significant attendant activity that allow users to deal politely with linguistic and interactional problems in chat. The role of emoticons in mitigating potentially face-threatening corrective feedback was in fact also highlighted as an affordance of L2 chat by González-Lloret (2015). These findings point to emoticons' affordances for politeness, and hence pragmatic function, in an otherwise constrained L2 discourse environment. Mitigation of corrective feedback through emoticons performs an important social function in chat between L1 and L2 speakers where exposed correction is common, though it is socially dispreferred and therefore rare in spoken L1 conversation (Schegloff et al., 1977).

While research has shown that emoticons assist in softening the impact of potentially face-threatening online behaviours such as correction, refusal or other dispreferred conversational actions, thus avoiding the disruption of new or established relationships, we know very little about how children mitigate potentially impolite behaviour online and the role that emojis play in that. Polite conversational actions are taught explicitly to children by adults, as they grow up, as we saw in the 'please' example in Chapter 1 (Example 1.2), where the mother encouraged the child to use 'please' in her request. Online politeness and netiquette also need to be spelled out to children once they start using social media to assist them in promoting positive relationships online or in recognizing unacceptable behaviour of other chat users. A focus on the role of emojis as attendant activities in potentially face-threatening and risky online situations is appropriate to prepare children for prosocial and safe written interaction online. However, based on chat interaction data collected for this study, children are less likely to correct other children's language when compared to adult expert-novice speaker chats (exemplified in Example 2.2) or some of the brutal exchanges involving adult 'trolls' which are common on the internet. Conversational repair, especially linguistic correction (other-initiated other repair), was found to be a feature of adult L1–L2 environments in previous research; hence, affiliative emojis make a correspondingly frequent appearance where differential language expertise is at play (Liddicoat & Tudini, 2013). The children's chats examined for this study involve children using mainly their first language; hence, linguistic corrections of other children's language are not a feature, despite the presence of misspellings and typographical errors. Group chat environments such as YouTube comments, in particular, are less likely to include language correction activity given its face-threatening nature, which is amplified by the public nature of the group chat context. However, some instances of emoji use as attendant activities to mitigate dispreferred actions and promote politeness were found in various children's online contexts. For example, one of the most frequent uses of emojis was to mitigate potentially face-threatening posts. This is not to say that mitigation always occurs in such instances. Examples of face-threatening behaviours without emojis or other attendant activities are plentiful in children's dyadic and group chat. This is especially true where the discussion is relatively private, such as in a YouTube substrand and/or where there are negative evaluations of a YouTube star's gameplaying performance. Users may in such cases be openly critical and sometimes use emojis to reinforce their disapproval. In the substrand[4] discussion in Example 2.3, users deploy negative assessments to question the merit of Stampy Cat's record-breaking feat in a videoclip where he plays *Minecraft* (Guinness World Records, 2018, December 15).

> Example 2.3
>
> 1 User A: Guinness World Records he cheated and you guys dont even care . . .
> 2 User B: He didn't really do it tho! He had spawn eggs and all the items prepared! For it to count he should ACTUALLY start in survival! And u can't get spawn eggs in survival only in creative! So I hope this is a joke!
> 3 User C: THE DUMBEST RECORD EVER I MADE 20 CAKES IN 5 MINS IN BEDROCK EDITION IN SURVIVAL WHITEOUT [WITHOUT intended] SPAWN EGGS WHY DON'T YOU GIVE RECORD I DID FASTER
> 4 User D: I could do it faster
> 5 User E: @User C but the guy make 10 cake in 3 minute
> 6 User F: This is cheating he was supposed to open up an infinite world in survival THEN make the cakes. Instead, he went into CREATIVE mode, took the resources out of his inventory and then made the fake record. I don't even know that why you are allowing people to cheat. 😦😦😦😦 👤 👤 😊 👺👺👺👺👺👺👺👺👺👺
> 7 User G: I think I can defeat him
> 8 User H: Minecraft awesome
> 9 User F: @User H I'm the first one to see your comment

While in general emojis tend to soften dispreferred actions, in this case the emojis in post 6 *reinforce* a normally dispreferred action, a negative assessment. In contrast with many children's YouTube celebrity comments spaces, which abound in positive assessments, negative assessments which express disapproval are the main activity in this substrand with some exceptions (see for example posts 5 and 8). Such negative assessments are directed at the YouTube star and his apparently controversial achievement of a Guinness World Record while

---

[4] Only a limited number of main thread YouTube comments have been included in the data for this chapter because while they are a relevant form of online interaction for children, they rarely receive replies to assist researchers in interpreting posts. Posts which receive replies, such as Example 2.3 from a substrand, are therefore preferred in most cases where YouTube data is used, to ensure that the analysis of emojis considers recipient responses.

playing *Minecraft*, which was filmed and posted online. Most participants had similar opinions and in this case they mostly disapproved of the award. In post 6, User F justifies and accounts for his negative assessment by explaining why the star is supposedly 'cheating'. As stated previously, accounting is a type of conversational work which accompanies a dispreferred action, similar to an attendant activity. Accounting for the dispreferred action is nonetheless still part of the complaint, which concludes with a series of emojis depicting displeasure and disagreement. These include angry faces, persons gesturing no/ forbidden, unamused faces and finally twelve thumbs down emojis to complete the strong negative assessment. It is interesting that the other participants in this substrand also display strong competitive orientations with the star and other participants regarding *Minecraft* activities. This substrand is quite different to the interactions in other children's YouTube comments where positive assessments of the YouTube stars are the predominant online activity, as in Example 2.4 (CookieSwirlC, 2020, December 13).

> Example 2.4 So cool.
>
> 1 User A: Omg that is so cool
> 2 User B: 😍 😍 😍 😍 😍 😍 😍 😘 😘 😗 😗 😙

In Example 2.4, in addition to providing verbal positive assessments such as 'that is so cool' (post 1), participants use emojis to express their praise and appreciation for the YouTube video actions of star Cookie SwirlC. Specifically, post 2 is taken up entirely by emojis, with no text. It includes seven smiling faces with heart eyes, face blowing a kiss, kissing face, kissing face with smiling eyes. The display of stand-alone strings of emojis is a common practice in children's online spaces, mainly to provide positive assessments of their interlocutors, including YouTube stars.

The post in Example 2.5 instead provides an example of emojis used for the mitigation of a potentially face-threatening comment towards the star of the video (EthanGamer, 2015, February 20); hence, they can be considered an attendant activity which recipients are expected to associate with the poster and their message. The emojis may be a tactful attempt to mitigate the user's comment about Ethan's adoption of glasses, which could be construed as impolite because it regards the star's physical appearance. The participant uses a sequence of three different emojis as part of their comment.

> Example 2.5 Mitigating emojis.
>
> User A: Ummm, I know it's been awhile, but SINCE WHEN DID YOU HAVE GLASSES?! 😅 😆 😳

User A displays a hesitation marker 'Ummm' and hedges his subsequent comment about Ethan Gamer's glasses with the statement, 'I know it's been awhile', to justify why a change in appearance may otherwise be acceptable. The potentially face-threatening component of the comment on the YouTube star's glasses is 'shouted' through use of capital letters, to reinforce his surprise at this change, as he did not apparently wear glasses in his YouTube videos as a younger child. This post ends with a question mark, to denote a rhetorical question, and an exclamation mark to further reinforce his surprise. The three emojis are in the following sequence: (1) laughing with tears; (2) grinning with sweat and (3) shocked, mind blown. While the first laughing emoji reinforces the face-threatening nature of the post, the grinning with sweat emoji may signal the poster's fear and awareness that he is going too far with his comment; hence, it may be interpreted as an attempt at mitigation of a dispreferred act, in this case the reference to his glasses and ensuing laughing emoji. The mind blown emoji playfully reinforces his verbal expression of surprise at Ethan Gamer's adoption of glasses. So, there are a variety of functions at play here.

The playful but potentially inflammatory post in Example 2.5 did not receive a response from other posters because this comment is addressed to Ethan Gamer, as denoted by the use of the personal pronoun 'YOU' and contextual information (video of Ethan with glasses). As a matter of fact, most comments in the main YouTube comments thread are addressed to the star in the videoclip rather than to other commenters (see the discussion of YouTube comments in Chapter 6). Like many YouTube stars, Ethan Gamer only responds occasionally and briefly to his many fans' comments and the likelihood of other commenters responding is low from an interactional point of view in the YouTube environment, unless the interaction is in a more private substrand. Therefore, we do not have the benefit of a response to this, though the fact that no offence was subsequently expressed by Ethan and no defensive posts enacted in a substrand by his fans suggests that the playful mitigative function of the emojis may have achieved its goal. It is not unusual for children to intervene when another child is criticized or mistreated online (see Chapter 3, Example 3.7); hence, the intervention of other children would have been an expected and pre-ferred option. So, it is possible that the emojis successfully mitigated this comment for other participants.

In summary, I have identified emoji use both to mitigate and reinforce dispreferred actions in YouTube main and substrands. The reinforcement of dispreferred actions using emojis is, however, not common in the data, but is a likely practice where there is conflict and disagreement among users. Where gaming is involved dispreferred actions such as negative assessments may display the competitive behaviours of gamers when interacting in public spaces such as YouTube.

Expressions of Emotion: Face

While expression of mood and feelings is only one of many emoji functions in online interaction, it is worth examining further, from a conversation analysis perspective. As Prior (2019, p. 518) notes, 'it is through language (and other multisemiotic resources) that emotions are made relevant and meaningful', which is especially relevant to children's use of emojis.

In the *Club Penguin* environment, especially where large numbers of users are in a virtual room, smiling emojis are often visible, without any accompanying text, in speech bubbles (see Chapter 3). These emoji posts are likely first and second pair parts, though the sequencing is not visible in the *Club Penguin* environment and may be used in both small and large group 'conversations'. These images are often a humorous exaggeration of reality, but they suggest that the user is happy to be there and available to interact. Hence, it is an affiliative, prosocial action. Given that other users post the same emojis in response, this interpretation seems appropriate. Similar actions occur in the YouTube environment:

> Example 2.6
> 1 User 1: Hi 😄
> 2 User 2: Hi! :D

In the Cookie SwirlC YouTube comments chat depicted in Example 2.6 (from CookieSwirlC, 2020, December 13), it is common for participants to post greetings with smiley emojis or emoticons, which may be addressed to either the star or other children. If users do not address other participants using the @ symbol and/or their names, it is unclear whom the addressee is in multi-user environments such as YouTube comments.

But how do recipients actually process these emoji-based conversational actions? It is likely that when users view the image, they associate the emoji's expression with the face of the imagined, actual user, to gain an impression of their mood during the interaction. Similarly, if a chat user announces that they are very well, combined with a smiling face with smiling eyes emoji, recipients do a mental mapping of the expression of the emoji on to the poster's imagined face, as might occur in Example 2.7 (CookieSwirlC, 2020, December 13).[5]

> Example 2.7
> 1 User A: Hi cookie how are you doing I'm going great 😄 [main strand comment]

---

[5] Applying speech act theory, Dresner and Herring (2010) distinguish three ways in which emoticons function: (a) emotion, mapped directly onto facial expression (e.g. happy or sad); (b) non-emotional meaning, mapped conventionally onto facial expression (e.g. a wink as indicating joking intent; an anxious smile); and (c) illocutionary force indicators that do not map conventionally onto facial expression (e.g. a smile as downgrading a complaint to a simple assertion) (p. 263).

2 User B [CookieSwirlC]: Awesome :D [substrand response]

3 User A: @CookieSwirlC OMG IT MADE MY DAY THAT YOU REPLIED OMG AHH

In Example 2.7, the participant deploys a smiley face with smiling eyes to conclude her greeting and 'how are you' to the YouTube star, to reinforce that she is 'going great'. In this instance, the star actually replies privately, using the substrand as a resource to connect with her fan. Her expression 'awesome' could be interpreted as either a routine reply to User A's 'how are you', to denote how well she is, or it could be a response to User A's positive situation ('I'm going great 😊). She concludes her post with a smiling emoticon using simple keyboard symbols ':D', which represents a happy face. User A's response orients to the unexpected nature of User B's response in post 3, as she expresses her enthusiasm in capital letters to draw attention to her reply (a practice known as shouting) and includes a couple of 'OMG' interjections. In this case both the emoji and the emoticon are likely to be associated with the posters' faces and moods, to promote understanding and prosocial behaviours. And where there is a textual component as part of the post, recipients of emojis in general are likely to associate the text content of the post with the emoji representation of the poster's happy face and feelings.

Depending on context, recipients may do the same when a sad face is displayed by users as part of a post including text. Recipients' responses are helpful to interpret emojis appropriately, though some emojis may potentially be misunderstood by inexperienced users during written interaction (see 'Misunderstanding Emojis'). Misinterpretation of certain emojis is unlikely, however, as can be seen in Example 2.8 (from CookieSwirlC, 2020, December 13).

Example 2.8

1 User A: I have no robux 😩 😩 😩 😩 😩 😩 😩 😩 😩 😩 😩 😩 😩 😩 😩 😩 😩 😩

2 User B: which game in roblox

In this case User A expresses sadness at not having any of the Roblox in-game currency. She does this by combining her statement with a series of eighteen loudly crying face emojis, as denoted by the open mouth. Without the addition of crying emojis, the textual component of the message on its own would have been open to interpretation and the user's request for robux inadequately conveyed. User B repairs User A's statement with a request for clarification on which of the many Roblox games she is playing, possibly to provide assistance. User A provides no follow-up post to this request.

In summary, it is unsurprising that the established role of emojis to express social media users' emotions to promote meaning is also a feature of children's online interactions.

Expressions of Emotion: Body

Clearly, we use emojis to convey non-linguistic information which is available to us in face-to-face interaction through voice, facial expression and the body. Given the range of emojis at our fingertips, we do not limit ourselves to using only facial expressions. There are other ways of expressing affective states, by using images of the body doing a variety of things. For example, in announcing good news online women may deploy a female dancer emoji to suggest that they are in a sense 'dancing with joy', which they may or may not physically be doing in real life in real time. A study by Al Rashdi (2018) reveals that a group of Omani women use this emoji to welcome the entry of a new member into their female-only WhatsApp group.

> Example 2.9 Female dancing emojis.
> 10. 7/4, 10:07:41 PM: Deema: 💃💃💃💃💃💃🙌👏👏👏👏 🗨🗨🗨
> 11. 7/4, 10:07:58 PM: Deema: The group has just lit up
> 12. 7/4, 10:08:14 PM: Nada: 🎉🎉🎉🎉🎉🎉🎉🎉🎉🎉🎉🎉🎉🎉🎉
> 13. 7/4/13, 10:09:19 PM: Arwa:
> 🎉🎉💃💃💃👏👏👏🙌🎈🎈🗨🗨🗨👏👏👏👏👏🎉🎉🎉🎉🎉🎉

The repetition of the dancing and other celebratory emojis, including hands clapping, confetti ball, party poppers and balloons, is interpreted by the author as sending a 'metamessage of excitement and enthusiasm' (p. 122) which a smaller number of emojis would not have achieved so effectively.

While the dancing emoji is not present in the data, children frequently use other types of emojis, including emojis which involve a part of the body, to express their excitement and enthusiasm online. This is especially the case in public settings such as YouTube comments where the main interactional activity is to provide assessments of the YouTube star and their video, often in the hope of gaining their attention. Repetition of emojis with or without text is often used in this setting, as we saw in Example 2.8 (crying emoji) earlier. In Example 2.10 the male child, as denoted by his nick, deploys one of the most frequently used emojis, a thumbs up, to express his enthusiastic positive assessment of Ethan Gamer (from EthanGamer, 2015, February 20).

> Example 2.10 Thumbs up as positive assessment.
> User 1: 👍👍👍👍👍👍👍 best Youtuber ever

The thumbs up emoji is posted seven times and is followed by a superlative descriptor of Ethan Gamer 'best', reinforced by 'ever'. Similarly, Ethan's 'coolness' is accentuated with emojis and superlatives by another user in Example 2.11 (from EthanGamer, 2015, February 20).

Example 2.11

User 1:

♥♥♥ 🤘 🤘 🤘 ♥♥♥♥♥♥♥♥ 🤘 🤘 🤘 🤘 🤘 🤘 🤘 ♥♥♥♥♥
♥♥ 😎 😎 😎 😎 😎 😎 😎 😎 best Ethan ever super cool amazing
extremely cool

The male child alternates multiple hearts with 'horns' hands, which can also be interpreted as 'rock on' hands, and smiling emojis with sunglasses. These reinforce the enthusiastic positive textual assessment of Ethan as 'supercool', 'amazing' and 'extremely cool' while conveying the user's love and admiration.

Another frequently used emoji which represents a part of the body to express emotion is the folded hands emoji, which has multiple functions and meanings according to context. In Example 2.12, S appears to be on his way home and is taking longer than usual. He uses a folded hands emoji to reinforce his frustration, as part of a prayer/interjection to the Madonna.[6]

Example 2.12

1 M: Arrivi all'1.30?
Are you arriving at 1.30?
2 S: Si sto per arrivare
Yes I'm almost there
3 S: Madonna Santa 🙏🙏

The child responds affirmatively to the mother's question about his expected time of arrival home. In post 2 he follows this with an interjection-profanity 'Madonna Santa' which is commonly used by children (and adults) in the Veneto region of Italy where this bilingual child had previously completed some schooling. This post is concluded with two folded hands emojis which suggest the act of prayer, to reinforce the frustration expressed by the prior interjection and a note of humour. This same emoji has a politeness function when the same child uses it to reinforce his expression of appreciation to his mother (see Example 2.22). Additionally, in Example 2.23, another child uses this emoji to reinforce their pleading as part of a request to a YouTube celebrity. So, children are likely to deploy the same folded hands emoji for multiple functions, to express themselves in online contexts. Unlike the laughing with tears emoji, which has a limited meaning, gesture emojis appear to be used more flexibly by children in online interaction. Their affordances for meaningful interaction are therefore recognized and used creatively by children.

The clenched oncoming fist emoji is another favourite symbol of affiliation among children in online spaces such as YouTube. In Example 2.13, it is used

---

[6] From mother–son SMS phone messages (see Appendix). Henceforth, M is used in place of 'mother' and S for 'son'.

as part of a text message of thanks with a grinning face emoji from YouTube star Ethan Gamer when he engages privately with his fans in a substrand (EthanGamer, 2015, February 20).

> Example 2.13
>
> 1 A: I've been watching you since 2016 and your videos are amazing! You are the only YouTuber that is epic! (main strand)
> 2 Ethan: Tysm! 😁 😮 (substrand)
> 3 A: Your welcome :)
> 4 A: Keep on making amazing videos

The clenched oncoming fist emoji is Ethan Gamer's substrand response to a fan's positive assessment of the star and his videos in post 1. It is commonly interpreted in the data and most online contexts as a prosocial virtual fist bump to express affiliation, rather than as a punch. The recipient in Example 2.13 (post 3) provides an appropriate polite response 'your welcome' to the star's expressions of appreciation 'Tysm' (Thank you so much) and in post 4 he both encourages Ethan Gamer to 'keep on making' YouTube videos and provides another positive assessment ('amazing videos') in the same post.

In Example 2.14 Ethan Gamer again deploys a clenched fist bump gesture emoji as part of his expression of appreciation 'ty for the support😮' when he uses the more private substrand to respond to User A's post in the main strand (EthanGamer, 2015, February 20).

> Example 2.14
>
> 1 A: Anyone here in 2020 I loved this series u helped me when I was younger u where my childhood i know you won't respond but I want to tell u that you are amazing amd u have grew up a lot 😔.
> 2 Ethan: Ty for the support! 😮
> 3 B: Just like me.
> 4 C[7]: Ethan!!!!!!!!!!!!

User A's profile picture (not reproduced here) suggests he is male. He fits multiple actions into a long unpunctuated post which reflects speech, in a type of online monologue. Lack of punctuation is common in the data and online spaces generally. This is contrary to findings from adult interaction where users may use punctuation as an interactional resource to indicate to their interlocutor when they have finished and it is their turn to post (Tudini, 2015). This post first addresses other users ('Anyone here in 2020') who are viewing the post at the same time as he writes (2020) rather than when the YouTube video was created (2015), as the asynchronous chat permits. The post then (a) provides a positive

---

[7] This participant's nick includes the title 'Dr' and a profile picture of a female adult, though they are probably a child. Chapter 6 shows that it is a common practice for children to use a parent or carer's account to access the comments function.

assessment of the YouTube series using past tense ('I loved this series'); (b) shifts his attention from other users to Ethan Gamer ('u') declaring how helpful the series was to him and how he represented his childhood ('u where (were intended) my childhood'); (c) suggests that Ethan won't respond to his post, which may be interpreted as an indirect request for a response; (d) provides a positive evaluation of the star ('you are amazing'); and (e) concludes with a reflection that Ethan has grown up, together with a final sad crying face emoji. This emoji expresses an affective state (sadness) and is associated with the user's nostalgic mood regarding his own and Ethan's lost childhood. Contrary to User A's expectations, Ethan Gamer actually does respond to this post and reinforces his expression of appreciation with a prosocial fist punch emoji, which he uses frequently when engaging with fans. User B's response 'Just like me' most likely expresses agreement with User A rather than Ethan, as users mostly orient to first posts in online threads rather than subsequent posts (Farina, 2018). User C however concludes this substrand by calling out to Ethan rather than User A and expresses excitement at his presence in the substrand, as denoted by the multiple exclamation marks.

In contrast to the affiliative conversational work of emojis which represent facial expressions and gestures to express various affective states, as discussed so far, we also noted earlier in Example 2.3 the use of the thumbs down and other emojis to express disapproval of a YouTube star's achievement. While negative assessments are unusual in the children's online spaces under examination, as they are generally prosocial and friendly towards other users, in this particular case most participants felt the same way. So, while these comments and emojis were unfriendly towards the YouTube star, they promoted affiliation between the group, within a relatively private substrand.

In summary, children adapt to the textual environments of online chat by deploying emojis to represent a variety of affective states, mostly to promote affiliation towards their interlocutors. In the analysis so far, we have seen children's inclination to use face and gesture emojis in particular to replace the missing non-verbal dimension of text chat and communicate their feelings and stance more clearly to interlocutors.

Emojis as Meaning Enhancers: Irony

The smiley and frowny face were suggested by computer scientist Scott Fahlman at Carnegie Mellon University in 1982 to signal that something was a joke (or not) in a computer science discussion forum (Krohn, 2004). Even without knowing this fact, we would be very much aware of using emojis in this way in our own online communication. Example 2.15 is an email invitation to friends living abroad to stay in the author's home when they visit. It illustrates how an emoticon (not an emoji in this case) can express the opposite of the literal meaning of the text, to convey irony.

Example 2.15

Glad I'll be seeing both you and Richard in November. Our five star accommodation is available to you :).

The second sentence in this example constitutes an invitation to stay in the author's home when the friends visit. However, the home is referred to as 'five star accommodation', which is intended as an exaggeration, as it suggests a high degree of luxury. To ensure that this reference was not taken seriously, a smiling emoticon was added to the invitation, constructed from punctuation marks, to indicate that the writer was joking about the level of luxuriousness of the home. The emoticon therefore allowed the recipients to see the statement as ironic, by suggesting that the opposite of what was expressed in the textual component of the message was true. This prevented the writer from being taken literally and thus potentially appearing immodest. A suitably placed winking emoji in other contexts may have has a similar function of suggesting that the user is joking about the written component of the message.

Unsurprisingly, children also avail themselves of the ironic function of emojis in online interaction at times, as studies have shown that they understand irony in face-to-face interaction from the age of four (Recchia et al., 2010). There is evidence of the use of irony even when interacting online, despite the constrained interactional environment. For example, they may deploy emojis for irony when playfully teasing other children and YouTubers. Example 2.16 is a comment on a YouTube video addressed to the star Cookie SwirlC (CookieSwirlC, 2020, December 13). The video is dedicated to the construction of a gingerbread house for Christmas.

Example 2.16 Gingerbread house.

User 1: Lol I ended up eating your bread house 😂 😂 😂

The comment starts with 'Lol', the abbreviation for laugh out loud, which sets the tone of the comment as playful or joking. Hence, the statement that the commenter ate Cookie SwirlC's gingerbread house is unlikely to be intended to be taken seriously, especially because it concludes with three grinning emojis, and it is unlikely that the user has physical access to Cookie's virtual environment. There is no response to this post, as it is addressed to Cookie rather than the fans, but it provides a note of irony and humour while also contributing to the general feeling of joy related to the upcoming Christmas period. At the same time, it expresses this commenter's love of sweets.

In a long-distance WhatsApp exchange between a mother and her fifteen-year-old son, a tongue poking out emoticon :P is used to mitigate a potentially insulting sexual reference through the use of irony.

Example 2.17

1 M: La pianta sul balcone di Anita e Derek. Vedi se papa la riconosce!
The plant on Anita and Derek's balcony. See if dad recognizes it!
2 S: Mmmmm dove [dov'è intended] la foto
Mmmmm where [where's intended] *the photo*
3 A: [first photo of prickly pear]
4 S: Dad says its a Fico d'india fiorentino . . . [tr. Florentine prickly pear] Not very manly :P
5 M: [second photo of prickly pear]

The poking out tongue emoticon at the end of post 4 allows the poster to signal to his mother, who is with mutual friends in Italy, that he is joking about the exaggeratedly provocative sexist comment on the prickly pear as an 'unmanly' sexual organ. The statement that the prickly pear is Florentine suggests that the friends' city (Florence) is associated with 'unmanliness'. In this conversation, the son appears to be reporting his father's comments and his use of a poking out tongue emoticon removes any doubt about the playful ironic nature of the comments about the friends' plant.

In their study of how Ecuadorian teenage girls respond to compliments on Instagram, Placencia and Powell (2020) note the ironic function of emojis in one user's response, shown in Example 2.18.

Example 2.18

1 F4's photo 13
2 A: Jajajaja eres tan sexy vales!!!!♥♥♥ 😳 😳 😂
'Hahahaha you're so sexy Vales [modified from Valeria]'
3 F4: Jajaj (sexy) dice! Jajaj eso solo lo aprendi de ti ♥ 😊
Hahah (sexy) she says! Hahaa that's only something I learned from you
4 A: a si Bueno tienes razón
'Oh yes okay you are right'

(p. 115)

As the authors note, the preferred and predominant response to these teenage girls' posted photographs of themselves is compliments from other members of the group, as is evident in post 2 where A uses multiple heart and heart eye emojis to reinforce her positive assessment of F4's photo. In her response to A's assessment that she is 'sexy', F4 responds by downgrading this positive assessment of herself with a weak self-deprecating disagreement accentuated by laughter tokens in the first part of this post ('Jajaj (sexy) dice!'). This self-mocking assessment is followed in the second part of the same post with acceptance of the assessment within a reciprocal compliment which suggests that the positive assessment is relevant to both of them ('Jajaj eso solo lo aprendi de ti ♥ 😊'). The concluding heart and smirking face emojis, combined with the initial laughter tokens, suggest irony and that the comment is in jest. A responds with agreement in the subsequent post, given the joking tone of the previous post and its indirect positive assessment of both of them. Therefore, agreement is a socially preferred response in this case, since self-praise is combined with praise of the other (see Pomerantz, 1978).

In summary, children may use emojis as an interactional resource to express irony, even in written interaction, to mitigate problematic posts by expressing the opposite of the literal meaning, to promote understanding and affiliation.

Emojis as Meaning Enhancers: Gesture

As noted in the discussion earlier on emojis as expressions of emotion, the body and gesture, in particular, are important interactional resources for children online. In addition to expressing emotions, they also assist in enhancing the meaning of textual components of their posts. One example of the meaning-enhancing function of gesture and the body through emojis is when children use the thumbs up emoji 👍. While it can be used to reinforce a positive assessment and express approval (see Example 2.10), it can also be used to express agreement with a previous post or as reinforcement of a previous statement, as in Example 2.19.[8]

> Example 2.19
> 1 S: Non ti preoccupare sono sul X30 👍
> *Don't worry I'm on the X30*
> 2 S: Non prende le persone dopo la mia fermata
> *It doesn't take people after my bus stop*
> 3 S: Stop 8
> 4 M: Perfetto! Che conveniente!
> *Perfect! How convenient!*

In this SMS exchange the child uses the thumbs up emoji to express his satisfaction at being on the right bus and reassure his mother, with the thumbs up emoji reinforcing the textual message ('Non ti preoccupare').

In contrast with the function of the thumbs up emoji in Example 2.19, in Example 2.3 we saw that the thumbs down emoji was used to reinforce a negative evaluation of a YouTube star's Guinness Book of Records award for the speed with which he completed specific *Minecraft* tasks. The arms crossed emoji also reinforced his disapproval, to provide a non-verbal enhancement of his textual negative assessment using gesture.

The recipients of the message and the level of formality of the relationship are likely to dictate whether or not a user adopts an emoji in place of the text. However, children often use emojis to replace standard text to reinforce emotions online. In Example 2.20, an online fan mixes emojis with text to

---

[8] SMS collection mother–son (see Appendix).

express his enthusiasm for Ethan Gamer's YouTube channel on the main strand (from EthanGamer, 2020, February 17).

Example 2.20

1 A: I

u 🍦 🍦 🍦 🍦 🍦 🍦 🍦 🍦 🍦 🍦 🍦 Ethan gamer TV

2 B: ☺

This playful post mixes heart and thumbs up emojis with text to provide a stronger version than the textual version of 'I love u' would have provided. While the heart symbol is not strictly a gesture, the post shows the meaning-enhancement function of emojis in personal online texts, especially when combined with text to promote understanding. Users may also find the extra effort required to reconstruct the text which has been replaced by emojis engaging.

In Example 2.21, from a more private YouTube substrand, fans of Cookie SwirlC seem to be in a race to be first in this online space (from CookieSwirlC, 2020, December 13).

Example 2.21

1 User A: 1st (main strand)
2 User A: Yuhh (substrand)
3 User B: 2nt
4 User C: @ [User B] :)
5 User A: @ User C 👁 👅 👁

In Example 2.21, User A responds to her[9] own main strand comment '1st' with 'Yuhh' in a substrand. This is an affirmative colloquial response in place of 'Yes' which reinforces her main strand comment in post 1. User B responds by stating that she is '2nt', probably intending '2nd', though it is also possible that the misspelling is a playful rendition of how 'second' might be pronounced in spoken English in some areas of the world. User C subsequently proffers a smiley emoticon, addressing the first poster User A ('@ [User B] :)') by using the @ symbol, to which User A responds with a more complex emoji, also using the @ symbol to ensure the correct user knows that she is being addressed. This emoji combines two eyes with tongue poking out in the middle; hence, recipients are likely to receive this as a face poking out a tongue. Depending on how it is received and the relationship between the two users, this emoticon is likely to be interpreted as either playful or unfriendly, given the competitive nature of this social activity. The substrand interaction stops at this point and there are no further relevant responses from these participants even in

---

[9] Profile pictures and names on this site suggest that most of the participants are female; hence, feminine pronouns are used unless there is clear evidence of a male participant.

the main strand. It is therefore unclear which interpretation is correct, though the lack of continuity suggests it may have been interpreted as unfriendly.

To summarize, there is evidence that children deploy gesture emojis such as thumbs up to reinforce the meaning of the textual component of their posts. They may sometimes also use gesture emojis created by a combination of stand-alone emojis, such as poking out tongue in a single post, to reinforce the competitive feelings around their online social activity.

Pragmatic, Not Emotional

The blending of emoticons and emojis with text leads linguists to suggest that the primary function of these interactional resources is to convey pragmatic rather than affective (emotional) meaning, and that they should be understood in linguistic rather than non-linguistic terms. A pragmatic interpretation of emojis is based on the context of utterances, which in the current case consists of text chat posts which are directed at specific recipients. Specifically, according to Dresner and Herring (2010), we need to look not just at the literal meaning of these posts but also at the writer's intention, known as illocutionary force. So while in spoken language an utterance may constitute the literal speech act of advising, complaining or enquiring, the speaker may in actual fact have a different intention. For example, if in a lecture theatre the professor interrupts her lecture to complain about the heat, this literal speech act of complaining may correctly be interpreted by hearers in that particular context as an indirect request to turn on the air conditioning. In summary, emojis are important supports in conveying subtle meanings in a constrained interactional context where multiple conversational resources are unavailable. They help users to express what they actually mean when they post speech acts as written utterances online, as we saw with the prickly pear example (Example 2.17). Or they might help to indicate a joke, as in the case of Example 2.5, where a fan comments on Ethan Gamer's use of glasses. Whether they are a component of a written post or posted on their own with no accompanying text, they clarify and enhance the literal meaning of preceding or sometimes subsequent utterances, including to express politeness. This is especially clear in the following SMS text exchange between a mother and young son, where the folded hands emoji reinforces his polite textual expression of appreciation for being offered a lift from the bus stop.[10]

> Example 2.22
>
> 1 M: Papa viene alla fermata 8
> *Dad is coming to stop 8*
> 2 S: Ciao siamo arrivati

---

[10] Mother–child SMS messages (see Appendix).

Hi we've arrived
3 M: Quando pensi di tornare?
When do you think you're returning home?
4 S: Ma tutto bene
But it's all ok
5 S: Tutto bene la valigia e a posto
All ok the suitcase is packed
6 S: Non lo so haha
I don't know haha
7 S: Si sono quasi a (name of suburb)
Yes I'm nearly in . . .
8 S: Grazie 🙏
Thanks 🙏

In this asynchronous SMS exchange the child is on his way home from school. There are at least two examples of split adjacency pairs, where responses to information or questions are not posted or do not appear immediately after the utterance that requires a response but quite a few posts later. For example, the response to post 1 ('Papa viene alla fermata 8') occurs after another intervening exchange, at post 8 'Grazie 🙏 'where the child uses a joined hands emoji to reinforce his appreciation at receiving a lift. User 1 in Example 2.23 enacts a similar function.

Example 2.23

User 1: could I join please 🙏🙏🙏🙏🙏🙏🙏

The series of joined hands emojis is part of a request to join in the video game being played and showcased by Ethan Gamer (2020, February 17). These fulfil an important politeness function in the absence of users' facial expressions and the prosody connected with pleading.

To conclude this section on the pragmatic function of emojis used by children, there is evidence that the various pragmatic functions of emojis discussed so far reinforce politeness in interaction, which in turn exhibits the prosocial intent of users who deploy these symbols in online written interaction.

Expressing Prosocial Behaviours

We have seen that while emojis are important meaning enhancers and pragmatic devices in online written interaction, as with all linguistic devices in talk, they also have a social impact, with users deploying them to show their prosocial intent. Children in *Club Penguin* regularly use smiley face emojis in speech bubbles to display their presence in a particular virtual room and their availability to interact and play with other participants (see Chapter 3). These posts are frequently posted without text and may constitute a first pair part greeting which invites an appropriate answer, such as an emoji or text greeting, from other users. We have seen in the previous discussion that both children and adults use emojis in myriad ways, mainly to express and reinforce prosocial friendly interactions. This may be achieved through subtle meaning-enhancing behaviours, representations of mood, but there may at the same time be elements of play, humour and entertainment. The playful, prosocial element of emojis is also evident when users deploy them to express irony, as described earlier.

As Pomerantz (1985) notes in her analysis of responses to assessments, agreement with positive assessments is preferred while disagreement is a dispreferred response, with the exception of negative assessments of oneself, where disagreement is expected to avoid seeming critical of the speaker. Even children interacting online seem to mostly adhere to these rules of interaction, with emojis supporting agreeable behaviours. As Pomerantz (1985) points out:

conversants orient to agreeing with one another as comfortable, supportive, reinforcing, perhaps as being sociable and as showing that they are like-minded. This phenomenon seems to hold whether persons are talking about the weather, a neighborhood dog, or a film that they just saw. (p. 77)

However, Pomerantz' study found that disagreeing has the opposite effect and is mostly oriented to as 'uncomfortable, unpleasant, difficult, risking threat, insult, or offense'. This is also true of children's online interaction overall, where being sociable is the main objective, to the point where antisocial excluding behaviours may even be chastised by other children (see Chapter 3, Example 3.7). We have also seen in Example 2.3 that agreement with negative assessments of YouTube celebrities' achievements may be oriented to as preferred by some groups, despite the controversy.

Emojis are also used playfully and prosocially when children wish other users their good wishes or congratulations for a special occasion such as a birthday or Christmas celebrations. The CookieSwirlC (2020, December 13) Christmas YouTube comments, including the substrand, display a range of emojis which were posted to the star and other users. On these occasions, the most common emojis in the YouTube interactions are 'blowing a kiss' or 'heart eyes' emojis, which confirm their function of expressing emotion and reinforcing a positive evaluation. Emojis at post 4 in Example 2.24 occupy an entire post, as a stand-alone string of emojis.

Example 2.24

1 User 1: Omg that was funny that she ate both houses
2 User 2: Omg that is so coool
3 User 2: 😛😛😛😛😛😛😛😗😗🙂🙂🙂🙂

User 2 responds with another positive assessment ('Omg that is so coool') to User 1's positive assessment of the humorous scene which unfolded in Cookie's YouTube video. She then follows post 2 with a separate post which displays a series of emojis, including seven heart eyes emojis, two face blowing a kiss emojis, two kissing face emojis and one kissing face with closed eyes emoji. This string of emojis clearly derives its meaning from User 2's preceding post, as a type of online increment (Tudini, 2015) which is added to and latches on to post 2 to enhance the positive assessment and provide an enthusiastic appreciation of Cookie's actions in the video. So, while post 2 appears to be complete, post 3 with the series of emojis provides further information which is interactionally relevant to post 2. In Example 2.25, the emojis also have the function of enhancing a prior positive assessment of both the video's introduction and the star herself, but in this case, they are posted with the text in the same post.

Example 2.25

1 User 1: I LOVE YOU
2 User 2: And I love your new intro its so cute and your sooo sweet and cute 😘 😘 😘

Three face blowing kiss emojis are deployed to reinforce User 2's enthusiastic assessment, which is expressed both textually and visually with the three emojis. The positive textual assessment is achieved in post 2 with (a) the use of the verb 'love' in 'I love', which is stronger than 'like'; and (b) the descriptor 'cute' which is used both in reference to the video's introduction ('its so cute') and Cookie ('your sooo sweet and cute'). The adverbs 'so' and 'sooo' with an elongated 'o' provide additional superlative enhancement of the adjectives 'cute' and 'sweet' in place of 'very'. It should also be noted that User 2's use of 'And' at the start of her post suggests she is collaboratively incrementing or building on the previous user's comment 'I LOVE YOU' as 'And' latches on to this prior comment from a syntactical point of view and at the same time implies agreement with User 1's positive assessment. It also adds an additional item to 'love' ('And I love your new intro …').

The analysis of children's prosocial deployment of emojis in this section has identified mainly face emojis. There are, however, other emoji interactional resources which children use prosocially in a different way, by recontextualizing the real into the virtual world.

Playful Recontextualizations

While emojis have multiple functions, they are also conversational resources that allow social media participants to convert their real life experiences and language into digital texts. Certain emojis make this function clearer than others. While referring principally to the practice of sharing digital photographs and videos, Jones (2009) identifies the 'technologies of entextualization' which permit young people to entextualize social and other activities, which may then be republished as new units of text in the online context. Androutsopoulos (2014) notes that Jones' (2009) approach extends the original definition of entextualization 'from transcription (i.e. transformation of spoken into written linguistic signs) to semiotic representations of social activity that are produced by means of digital technologies, then recontextualized and interactively negotiated with an audience' (p. 5). One of the functions of emojis in text chat is to permit users to recontextualize the real world, including their own real life feelings and experiences, to the digital conversational context, often playfully. As noted earlier, these emoji recontextualizations during online interaction are subject to recipients' interpretation.

Example 2.26 from a WhatsApp exchange between a mother and her fourteen-year-old son shows a combination of a photo post and text post with an emoji.

Example 2.26

1 S: [06/01/14, 12:24:48 PM]:
2 S: [06/01/14, 12:25:22 PM]: Il mio taglio 👹
My haircut
3 M: Azz! 6 proprio naziskin!
Fudge! You're such a skinhead!

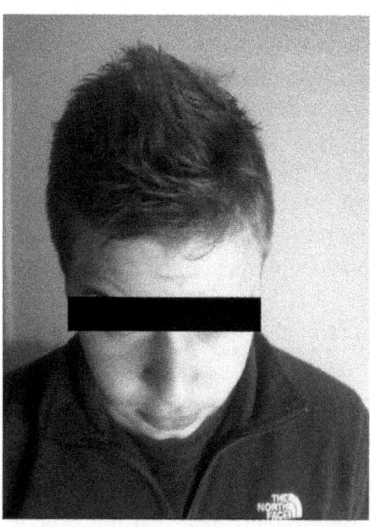

Figure 2.2 Mobile phone photo of young man showing haircut.

In this exchange the son posts a photo of himself to his mother, after receiving a haircut with a short crest. He presents himself with the crest pointing towards the smartphone camera and a raised eyebrow. Based on the time stamp available on WhatsApp data, the mother does not immediately respond, as is to be expected in asynchronous/synchronous chat software, so after thirty-four seconds, the son follows post 1 with another post. This second post is a repair which appears to explain his prior post by indicating his haircut ('il mio taglio'), suggesting that his mother look at it. This post is concluded with a mind blown emoji, which also appears to have a type of crest. The mother replies with an interjection ('Azz!'), which is also a euphemism for a profane interjection in Italian, to express the expected astonishment at the haircut. The second part of this post suggests the haircut resembles that of fascist skinheads. So, despite the use of a photo which clearly displays the child's haircut and brings a real life event (the radical haircut) into the child's digital world (online interaction with his mother), he deems further explanation to be required via text and the emoji that most resembles his haircut, to obtain the appropriate response.

Example 2.27 is a repair sequence in a YouTube substrand interaction between three female gamers, where a pile of poo (cow pat) emoji is used for comic effect (EthanGamer, 2015, February 20).

Example 2.27
1 User 1 (main strand): he said cow it's mushroom
2 User 2 (reply to User 1):
+ User 1
It's mooshroom
3 User 3: It's a type of cow …

In this sequence there are two repairs, with User 1 noting that Ethan Gamer should be using 'mushroom' rather than 'cow' when referring to the relevant virtual animal in *Minecraft*. User 2 follows up with a correction of User 1, addressed clearly as +User 1, who apparently should use the correct *Minecraft* term 'mooshroom'. These two corrections respectively by User 1 and 2 are followed by an explanation by User 3 that a mooshroom is a type of cow. This explanation contributes and clarifies the repair for Users 1 and 2. To promote understanding and add an element of humour, a pile of poo emoji representing cow dung concludes post 2. As cow dung is associated with cows, this emoji recontextualizes the real life and virtual *Minecraft* animal to the chat, even though cow dung does not feature in *Minecraft*.

Example 2.28 instead provides instances of a common practice of deploying images of objects which are associated with celebration, in this case Christmas (CookieSwirlC, 2020, December 13).

Example 2.28

1 User 1: ♥🌀🍪🍪🍪🍪🍪🍪🍪🍪🍪🍪🍪🍪🍪🍪🍪🍪🍪🍪🍪🍪🍪
🍪🍪🍪🍪🍪🍪🍪🍪🍪🍪🍪🍪🍪🍪🍪🍪🍪🍪🌲🌲🌲🌲🌲🌲
🌲🌲🌲🌲🌲🌲🌲🌲🌲🌲🌲🎁🎁🎁🎁🎁🎁🎁
🎁🎁🎁🎁🎁🎁🎁🎁🎁🎁🎁🎁🎁🎁🎁🎁🎁🎁🎁
2 User 2:
I love your candy cane wings! Merry early Christmas, I hope you have a nice
Christmas! ♥😊🍪🌲🎁

User 1 deploys a stand-alone string of emojis, including nineteen Christmas trees
and twenty-six gifts, without any text. Given that the Cookie SwirlC YouTube
video is on the Christmas theme, these emojis recontextualize typical real life and
video activities related to Christmas. User 2 continues on the same theme but she
includes text comments which express appreciation for one of the edible items in
the video ('candy cane wings') and Christmas greetings. These comments are
followed in the same post by emojis which express appreciation (heart, smiling face
with hearts and cookie symbol) and celebration (Christmas tree and gift). Given the
multiple meanings of the rainbow symbol it is unclear without a response by
another user to understand whether User 1's string of rainbow emojis is an
expression of sexual orientation, as is often the practice in recent times, or simply
an expression of happiness. The latter is the most likely interpretation given the
Christmas theme of the video and the subsequent emojis in this post. Hence, these
types of emojis have the role of connecting users with an imaginary celebration
context, in this case Christmas, as intended by the YouTube creator.

Stand-alone strings of emojis without words, as in Example 2.28, are quite
common especially in the YouTube comments. They rarely receive a response
from other users, possibly because they are not easy to decipher from an
interactional point of view without a text to frame them. These wordless strings
of emojis, which connect users' real life worlds to the virtual world, are likely to
have a prosocial and entertainment function, as in Example 2.29 (CookieSwirlC,
2020, December 13).

Example 2.29 Chocolate bar emojis.

1 User 1: 🍫 🍫 🍫 🍫 🍫

In this case a stand-alone string of chocolate bars is deployed by User 1, with
no accompanying text. It suggests that the child is offering these items to other
users or to the YouTube star and reflects children's preoccupation with food in
this gingerbread house context. The repetition of chocolate bar emojis is a type of
exaggeration most likely intended to playfully suggest excitement over sweets.

There is no limit to this kind of playful linking and virtual recontextualization through emojis and this is one of the features of children's emoji use in the
dataset.

Expressing Identity

Mobile phone operating systems are constantly updated to reflect users' different ethnic, gender and religious backgrounds. Surprisingly, a series of 'woman with hijab' emojis and gender-neutral emojis were only recently added to the emoji collection by Apple, approved by the Unicode Consortium. The headscarf emoji was created in response to the Hijab Emoji Project initiated by a fifteen-year-old Austrian teenager, who pointed out that there was no emoji to represent Muslim women who wear hijabs (Hijab Emoji Project, 2016). These and other new pictorial images are evidence that emojis fill an important gap in expressing users' identity in online interaction. They do this by transferring representations of identity in the physical world to virtual contexts. The work of emoji faces in expressing users' identities, affective states and interactional intentions has become much more sophisticated and representative of the diversity of our societies.

Despite these promising trends, in the dataset for this study children do not enact their identities through emojis. While the online contexts investigated are culturally diverse, this diversity is more likely to be expressed through language used in the posts and especially through profile pictures and names in YouTube comments. While children from many countries and many cultural and religious backgrounds participate in YouTube comments spaces, they use only standard emojis to express themselves in the dataset examined. This may, however, be an issue of access to all the emoji options. Children's most common identity markers in the data will be discussed in separate chapters, especially Chapter 6 on YouTube, where they are on public display.

Conclusion: Emoji Social Functions

We have seen that children use emojis as interactional resources in a variety of different ways, mostly to make up for the absence of the physical world, including the body and context. The following list summarizes the interactional functions discussed in this chapter:
• Attendant activities with dispreferred actions
• Expressing affective states
• Pragmatic: enhancing/modifying meaning of accompanying text (e.g. polite, ironic, prosocial and antisocial behaviours)
• Play, humour and entertainment
• Recontextualizing physical contexts online

Many of these functions may of course overlap. For example, the posting of a stand-alone string of chocolate bar emojis has at least four functions: expressing an affective state (the user's love of chocolate), recontextualizing physical contexts online, showing playfulness in online interaction and exhibiting prosocial friendly behaviour. Additionally, we have seen that the same emoji may be used for multiple functions in different contexts, as in the folded hands emoji (Examples 2.12, 2.22 and 2.23) which was used to express an affective state (frustration) and as a politeness marker to reinforce an expression of appreciation and pleading (please) as part of a request.

Clearly emoji use, both in terms of quantity and quality, is likely to vary not just across age groups but also across cultures. Politeness is an especially interesting research area in this regard. For example, Bruce Kavanagh (2016) found that those writing comments in Japanese blogs used significantly more emoticons to highlight polite intention than their American counterparts, especially to express solidarity and gratitude. Such differences are likely to reflect face-to-face strategies; hence, culture and context determine their role in online interaction as well. Children of different age groups are also likely to use emojis as politeness markers differently, possibly reflecting their social development in face-to-face interaction.

Children's use of emojis to express a range of conversational behaviours in written talk requires further attention. While researchers consider the role of these devices in promoting successful, creative and safe written interaction online, it is clear that there is still a great deal of work to do in understanding how children of different ages use them and whether children of different cultures and genders (see Pearce, 2017) will enact their interactional functions differently. This chapter therefore provides an initial framework for further research in that direction.

In Summary

- Emoticons and emojis are a human adaptation to text chat and an attempt to fill the gap left by fundamental non-verbal, voice and contextual resources which are available to speakers in phone and face-to-face interaction.
- Emojis have a key role to play in promoting understanding and politeness between young chat users, with likely variation across ages and cultures, possibly also across genders. They may also be deployed to constructively critique others.
- Emoji meaning is negotiated with interlocutors in interaction and is subject to (mis)interpretation and repair.
- Emojis have multiple, often overlapping, interactional functions and meanings for users across platforms. Children identify the affordances for meaningful interaction of the more flexible emojis and deploy them creatively.
- Users deploy emojis to provide a bridge between the virtual and physical world through recontextualization; they are, however, reliant on recipients' linguistic and social skills, correct interpretation and contextual information created by the surrounding digital text or real world context.

3   Penguin Talk

Club Penguin: Designing Language for Child Safety

The original desktop version of *Club Penguin* was a unique experiment in language for children's online interaction, especially in terms of chat safety provisions. It was very popular with children because it combined a cartoon-like interface, games and real time social chat for six- to fourteen-year-olds across the globe, with a reported 330 million users at its peak. It was in fact so popular that *Club Penguin Rewritten* (2021) was created by volunteers once the desktop version *Club Penguin* and application *Club Penguin Island* were shut down respectively in 2017 and 2018 (Kelly, 2020, May 15).[1]

Club Penguin probably owes its popularity to the fact that children were able to take on the identity of a penguin or other animal character and interact with other participants by producing comic book style speech bubbles each time they posted a turn in their written talk. The resources provided by the software allowed them to create an appealing cartoon-like character for written inter-action with other users. While many activities were possible, including games and problem-solving tasks, the social networking component was one of the biggest attractions for children who wished to stay in touch with friends after school or make new virtual friends. Given its focus on social interaction with peers, this software had the potential to promote children's scaffolded language development through ZPD and other learning activities. Marsh's (2014) study, based on observational and interview data, identifies multiple purposes for literacy in her investigation of children's language and literacy practices when engaging with *Club Penguin*. These include literacy for (a) establishing and maintaining relationships, (b) pleasure and/or self-expression, (c) identity construction and performance, and (d) establishing and maintaining social networks. *Club Penguin* chat software was also set up for chat in multiple languages, which attracted multilingual children both from English-speaking and other countries. Despite its potential, there were, however, some significant but necessary limitations from a linguistic and interactional perspective.

[1] An unauthorized *Club Penguin Online* was relaunched and shut down again in May 2020 due to safety and copyright issues after accruing up to eight million users.

Linguistic restrictions in *Club Penguin* promoted child safety, as language could not be freely composed by users due to filters. In the two main chat modes Standard Safe Chat and Ultimate Safe Chat users had access to a 'set phrases' feature similar to the predictor function on smartphones, but no numbers, and a limited number of questions and exclamation marks (*Club Penguin Wiki* 2018, February). Thus, in order to chat safely in *Club Penguin*, children selected from set phrases and words (see Figure 3.1). In the more open Standard Safe chat, users were likely to be banned for using profanities and other words, such as 'love'. Moderators also actively monitored chat activity and users were encouraged to report linguistic and other rule violations, similar to Habbo.com (Oy, 2004) and other virtual worlds, where children often have access to moderator help twenty-four hours per day (Sadler, 2020).

It is notable that many of these safety features were included in the new volunteer run *Club Penguin Rewritten* (2021), though a legal disclaimer emphasizes the role of parents in keeping children safe:

The Club Penguin Rewritten team does it's [sic!] best to filter out inappropriate words and players, and we moderate the website 24/7 to take action against inappropriate players, however, some players will continue to attempt and break the rules. It is the parents [sic!] responsibility to moderate their children to ensure safety. If you are concerned about your child's safety, you may go to servers with 'Safe Chat' where players have access to words approved by our team. (Club Penguin Rewritten, 2020, April)

Of course linguistic restrictions did not prevent offensive language being insinuated. This could be achieved through use of stylistic devices such as rhyming words which resembled the offensive word in question, euphemisms and other tricks based on available linguistic resources. Connelly (2013) notes also that Barbiegirls.com players are able to circumvent linguistic restrictions by deliberately misspelling words which the software's internal dictionary is unable to detect, but which recipients understand thanks to their awareness of the code. As we shall see in the analysis of a café role-play, certain euphemisms for inappropriate content may be ambiguous due to their multiple meanings. Hence, the role of moderators and vigilant parents and carers is crucial.

Evanescent Language

The turn-taking system of *Club Penguin* chat is closer to that of Snapchat than Facebook Messenger or WhatsApp, as posts do not remain on screen. This may interfere with children's understanding of interactions, as the temporariness of each post means they are unable to review previous messages. It also changes the turn-taking structure of their interactions, as they are unable to read and respond to many of the posts that are posted prior to the most recent one. In most permanent 'quasi-synchronous' chats, users are able to review and reconstruct conversations by reading them, prior to posting their responses. In *Club Penguin* chat, however, this is not possible as participants' contributions are not arranged chronologically, as they appear on screen. The posts become visible in speech bubbles and then disappear, a little like what occurs in the rapid fade of spoken language, but without the advantage of prosody and other non-verbal cues, which assist listeners in understanding speech. Contributions are therefore temporary and users may often miss a post where large numbers of participants are in a room. Posts do not have the advantage of permanency and reviewability that is common to most chats and which promotes understanding of the conversation through a reading process. Additionally, while participants are aware of timing of posts in real time, it is more challenging to understand the timing of the posts retrospectively, to know which post appeared first and how to match first and second pair parts of adjacency pairs to reconstruct sequences. The automated post-sequencing resource which is available in most chats is unavailable in *Club Penguin*, which complicates interaction further. However, judging by the popularity of 'evanescent' chats like *Club Penguin* and Snapchat, these constraints do not deter children, in fact they are likely to be considered an affordance. One can only speculate that *Club Penguin* and Snapchat users are drawn to this type of chat as they avoid the risks associated with leaving permanent conversations online for public view.

When relying solely on screenshots, researchers of evanescent chat interaction are required to reconstruct written conversational sequences retrospectively, by basing their reconstructions on logical first and second pair parts of adjacency pairs. This approach is not methodologically foolproof and may lead to the creation of 'phantom' adjacency pairs and sequences, both for researchers and participants. The sequencing of posts in *Club Penguin* is also complicated by the fact that we are often dealing with multi-party chat, where many participants may be present in the same chatroom. It is much easier to reconstruct a conversation where there are only two participants, rather than many. Screen-capture software would permit researchers to record timing and sequencing of posts, as well as the composition process (Meredith, 2017). However, in her study of permanent dyadic chat, Berglund (2009) notes that it is possible to analyse meaning-making by gaining access to the same information which is at the disposal of participants in interaction when they make sense of each other's utterances. So, she argues that in the chat context it is not essential to have access to recordings of participants computer screens because 'this information is not available to the other participant in interaction either, but instead it is possible to rely on log files only for analytical purposes' (p. 10). The analysis of *Club Penguin* interactions based on screenshots of evanescent chat logs is thus an acceptable methodological approach in online conversation analysis, especially when this is all that researchers have at their disposal, given the subsequent closure of this chat tool. It should also be noted that while researchers do not have access to the exact timing of each post due to absence of a timestamp, *Club Penguin* users would be very aware of the need to submit posts in a timely fashion, in response to chat partners' posts. This requires them to reconstruct the timing of each post, as well as which posts are meant to go together, based on what makes sense to them as they follow the 'conversation'. This is similar to what we do in plain text chat, though most chat software at least presents the posts in the order in which they were posted.

In a sense, we might consider the exercise of reconstructing a coherent written interaction in *Club Penguin* environments to be a form of linguistic and literacy exercise for younger children, within the limitations imposed by the software. Some children may however be overwhelmed by the reconstruction requirement, given the evanescent posts and unavailability of automatic sequencing, especially if they are inexperienced users and readers.

Adapting to Long-Distance Written Interaction

Unlike console-based games such as *FIFA*, which children use mainly for interaction in the same physical location with other players or on their own, *Club Penguin* is devised for children's interaction long distance. Interaction in the same physical space would however technically be possible where children are chatting on separate mobile devices together. This is not an uncommon scenario as many readers will know!

As the dominant form of interaction in *Club Penguin* environments is achieved through writing, there are none of the non-verbal cues which are available to children in face-to-face or even phone interaction. This means that children cannot use or access one another's voices, facial expressions, gaze and body language. As we saw in Chapter 1, these elements of human communication are fundamental to achieve understanding. Both voice and facial expressions convey the conversational intentions of a speaker, yet human beings have adapted to the constrained written communication medium regardless. As we have seen, emoticons and emojis are one of these adaptations. While they have limitations, they allow social media and video game users to convey some of the subtleties in meaning which are usually provided by non-verbal and contextual cues in real life conversation. We have seen that they also have functions which are unique to the written chat environment, which in some cases are unrelated to non-verbal cues, as they are unavailable in face-to-face interaction. This is also true of many *Club Penguin* emojis.

Another adaptation to *Club Penguin* interaction is the use of virtual context as a resource for interaction. The various rooms and tools provided by the software influence the kind of language that is used, much in the same way as occurs in real life, where physical context of the interaction plays a key role in promoting understanding between speakers. So, when users are in a representation of a *Club*

Penguin café, their chat is based on that particular virtual context and is likely to revolve around food and drink. Interaction may also involve avatars playing with *Club Penguin* games and other virtual resources.

Having introduced general interactional features of *Club Penguin*, the following analysis examines the constrained language of Ultimate Safe Chat mode before proceeding to analyse the different ways that children structure and enact online language and conversation in this environment.

The Safe Language of Online Friendship

Club Penguin users are constrained in their linguistic choices and vocabulary due to safety features of the chat and more so in the safe chat modes. For example, in *Ultimate safe chat* mode in *Club Penguin* only a predefined choice of phrases, emoticons and actions are available to choose from. Figure 3.1 is a screenshot of the ultimate safe mode menu where children can make their choice from the drop-down menus.

The language in Figure 3.1 provides restricted linguistic and interactional options for children to express themselves while sustaining a safe and friendly conversation online. This does not include hidden words and phrases which

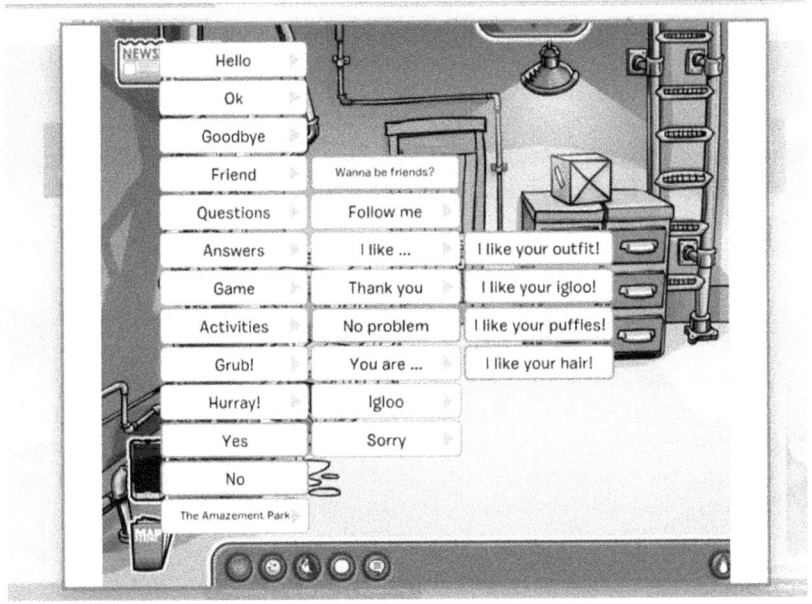

Figure 3.1 *Club Penguin* main safe language menu. Source: © Disney

would have been available to children in the drop-down menus, but which are no longer available for research. We have only the Ultimate Safe Chat Mode information page at our disposal (Club Penguin Wiki, 2018, February). Nonetheless, if we focus solely on the visible screenshot language, we see that there are brief but complete written turns which constitute first or second pair parts of adjacency pairs, the building blocks of conversation. To start with, in the left-hand column greetings 'Hello' and 'Goodbye' and affirmative answers or expressions of acceptance such as 'OK' are available. Obviously, words such as 'OK' have a variety of uses in conversation, according to context and language (Betz et al., 2021). For example, in addition to providing an affirmative answer or expression of acceptance, it is used at the start of an announcement or question to attract interlocutors' attention, as in, 'OK, anyone want a drink?' The affirmative answer 'Yes' can also be used as an expression of enthusiasm when combined with other words and phrases, as in 'Yes! We've scored!' Given the multiple meanings, combinations and uses of words, apparently limited single words have much more conversational potential than it seems, depending on context. Whether and how children discover this in *Club Penguin* environments requires further systematic research across age groups. The drop-down menu for 'Questions' and 'Answers' in the left-hand column is no longer available online and thus not visible in Figure 3.1. However, questions and answers are a key adjacency pair we use to co-construct conversation. In the middle column, expressions of appreciation such as 'Thank you' and matching response (second pair part) 'No problem', along with apology 'sorry' are also available to users to promote harmonious relationships among users and make amends when required. Like many Figure 3.1 items, 'Sorry' also has multiple uses according to context. For example, it can promote polite conversation when people excuse themselves prior to announcing unpleasant or dispreferred news to recipients, such as disagreement or leave-taking. An example of this is 'sorry I have to go'.

Another interesting feature of the safe chat mode language is the inclusion of compliments in the right-hand column, such as 'I like your puffles' etc. Puffles are appealing furry pets which are acquired by users in *Club Penguin*. These compliments are obviously designed to promote friendship and harmony among participants, as in the invitation '*wanna be friends?*' at the top of the middle column, a favourite conversation starter for children in this environment. Many more conversation starters (not presented in Figure 3.1) are available to users, such as 'Whats up?', 'Hey there!' 'What's new?', to name a few. Example 3.1 is an extract from a *Club Penguin* chat between children (Burley, 2010) which indicates that children avail themselves of set phrases to communicate in safe mode, though they may not always obtain the affiliative response they expect.

Example 3.1
1 P2: Anybody wanna be my friend?
2 P2: Please. I like your outfit, you are so cool, wanna be friends.
3 P1: I don't like your hair. [Walks away] (p. 7)

While ultimate safe chat mode phrases presented in Figure 3.1 'I like your outfit', and 'wanna be friends' are used by participants in this conversation (post 2), it is unclear whether negatives such as 'don't' are available to participants to be combined with 'I like …' (post 3) which is visible in Figure 3.1 (middle column). Nonetheless, users have the option of selecting either ultimate chat mode or standard chat when they create their account, which may explain the negative evaluation that appears in Example 3.1. Once they choose Ultimate Safe chat, they need parent permission to move to standard chat. However, those users who enable standard chat automatically have access to Ultimate chat mode phrases.

Club Penguin Wiki (2018, February) authors note that despite reducing swearing and bullying, Ultimate Safe Mode communication can be difficult. Specifically, users need to navigate to find the right message and in some instances the list does not provide the appropriate message at all. Wiki authors cite the example of open-ended chat phrases such as 'What's your puffle's name?', which do not permit a reply unless in standard chat mode.

In any case, despite the linguistic and expressive constraints of using a limited number of set phrases in safe chat mode, there may be advantages in terms of turn-taking, both in safe and standard chat. Specifically, users may at times prefer to use set phrases instead of composing their own, in the interests of saving time in getting their message across. As other users are unable to see the message composition process in this chat, it is necessary to get the message across as quickly as possible; hence, set phrases reduce the delay in writing and posting messages, despite the time required to navigate. The set phrases and the predictor function may even promote the learning of new vocabulary to develop conversational literacy, in a meaningful context; however, this requires further investigation (see Marsh, 2014).

Penguins Speak for Themselves

The examples examined in this section are mostly screenshots or text-only transcripts of authentic speech bubble posts by users. Analysis makes the most of whatever non-verbal information is available in screenshot examples, such as the positioning of penguins, which may indicate the addressees of their posts and assist in the reconstruction of sequences. Gaze is an important element of face-to-face interaction which is missing in chat environments. So children are likely to use whatever limited resources are available to express themselves more clearly. Positioning of their penguin avatar to indicate an addressee is one of these resources, which is unavailable in text-only chat. So, in my analysis, if one post meaningfully matches another and two penguins are shown to be next to each other and/or facing one another, it is assumed that the post is intended for the nearby penguin. Users themselves are likely to use these basic non-verbal signals to communicate or interpret conversational behaviour in this environment. In group chat, however, many posts are intended for multiple recipients in the room, as will be demonstrated.

Based on available examples and *Club Penguin* activities, the analysis distinguishes between (a) open conversation (similar to ordinary conversation); (b) role-play and (c) play-oriented social interaction (constrained by game rules). The notion of open conversation is distinguished from role-play and other forms of play so that we gain a sense of the range of interactional possibilities of children's online environments. It should be said, however, that even when users are engaged in open conversation, which does not involve role-play or other forms of play, they are doing so as penguin avatars. This suggests that they are role-playing at all times. However, it is only by analysing their virtual interactions that we can identify role-play language and orientations. Clearly, virtual environments for children such as *Club Penguin* are hybrid where users combine open conversation and play in different ways. The next section first discusses large group interactions before moving to small group interactions.

Large Group Posts: Open Conversation

Users' posts in Figure 3.2 are derived from a *Club Penguin* 'reunion' website and are in standard rather than safe chat mode.[2] This website was selected because of its natural rather than intentionally humorous exchanges which constitute the bulk of *Club Penguin* screenshots published online. It was hoped in this way that the analysis would produce insights into how user exchanges in group settings are most likely to unfold, though the actual age of users is unknown. The posts are generally prosocial and directed at other penguins either as individuals or as a group, to promote interaction and play. There are at least forty penguins in the room, which includes furniture and a drink area resembling a bar or café. There are teacups on the counter. There is also a board on the left of the screen promoting a 'smoothie smash' and on the right a staircase with a *Club Penguin Times* sign at the entrance.

While there are a total of ten legible posts, let us begin with the five posts on the bottom half of the screen (Example 3.2 below). These posts are probably

---

[2] www.thecpglitch.com/2016/10/club-penguin-reunion-2016-screenshots.html (site now inactive). Legible nicknames have been covered to protect users' identities.

Figure 3.2 *Club Penguin* café chat, including small group corner conversation. Source: © Disney

intended for all penguins in the room, as posture and language suggest they are not directed at anyone in particular. The software does not allow a sequence of posts to remain visible as one single sequence – the posts appear one at a time, as each post disappears when another is posted by the same user. The order in which these contributions were posted is therefore unknown. Post numbers are however provided in the transcript for ease of reference.

> Example 3.2
>
> 1: GETTING CROWDED IN HERE
> 2: smiling emoji
> 3 smiling emoji
> 4 woof
> 5 SMILE IN

The five posts by five different penguins include a comment in capital letters 'GETTING CROWDED IN HERE', which suggests shouting in internet language. There are also two smiling emojis, a playful 'woof', and 'SMILE IN', which suggests this participant is 'smilin' and therefore in a good mood. While the smiling emojis have a similar function, this user's display of a positive emotion through a virtual text smile ('SMILE IN') is prosocial as it suggests availability to chat with other penguins. Like post 1, it too appears to be shouted, as it is in capital letters and stands out from the smiling emojis. In addition to being prosocial, this post shows linguistic skill through language play as the user makes creative use of available linguistic resources *smile* and *in* to suggest the friendly colloquial expression 'smilin' which drops the final 'g'. This phrase is unlikely to be generated by the available safe chat menu, as 'smile in' appears to be a child-generated linguistic construction of two standard English words. Like 'wanna' (Figure 3.1), 'smilin' or 'smiling' would be more likely in the safe chat system. In summary, both the emojis and the verbal smile 'SMILE IN' are an attempt to compensate for the lack of visual cues in this environment. The shouting through capital letters in post 1 may also be a strategy to draw people's attention to the user's expression of concern, as the room is in fact crowded with users. Participants are unable to be heard by raising their voices, but larger letters take up more space in the virtual room to increase visibility. The 'shouting' also reinforces the idea that no penguin in particular is being addressed; hence, it is a public post for all users in the room.

This group (Example 3.2) is not strictly involved in role-play, but the display of a happy, friendly attitude suggests availability to establish rapport with other users while accessing *Club Penguin*'s interactional resources. Some of these resources attempt to compensate for missing real world interaction resources, including the representation of voice (shouting) and smiling faces. This includes one user's shouted expression of concern about the crowded room.

Café Role-Play in a Crowded Room: Safe Language Failure?

We now focus on the conversation between five penguins in the corner of Figure 3.2, sitting on or near the couch and armchair. This constitutes a semi-private conversation within a group setting. The sequence of posts in Example 3.3 is based principally on the reconstruction of first and second pair parts of adjacency pairs displayed in Figure 3.2, as described earlier.

> Example 3.3
>
> Penguin 1 (couch) post 1: want anything?
> Penguin 2 (armchair) post 2: can I have [illegible]
> Penguin 3: (armchair) post 3: chips
> Penguin 4 (standing near couch facing forward): post 4: THAT GOOD STUFF
> Penguin 5: (standing in front of Penguin 4): post 5: !
> Penguin 6: (backless armchair near front of group) post 6: me

Given the cartoon café context of the room, it is unsurprising that the only small group conversation is a role-play about food orders. Penguin 1 appears to initiate the conversation, though her speech bubble partially covers Penguin 2's speech bubble containing post 2 'can I have ...' It is therefore possible that post 2 was posted before or at the same time as post 1, though this makes less sense.

It is thus likely that posts 2, 3, 4 and 6 are a response to post 1, the question 'want anything?' But they could also be phantom adjacency pairs, with first and second pair parts apparently belonging together though they were not intended as such. For example, it could also well be that Penguin 2 saw Penguin 1's post while composing and posting 'can I have' and an illegible item, in an attempt to start the role-play.

Post 4 is an example of ambiguous language which is potentially taboo and unsuitable for children. Penguin 4 contributes a shouted response 'THAT GOOD STUFF', in an attempt to attract participants' attention with capital letters. There are a few possible interpretations of this response, which is not unusual, as single words and phrases may have multiple meanings in different contexts and positions in interaction sequences. Firstly, post 4 is probably a direct response (second pair part) to Penguin 1's question 'want anything?' One interpretation is that Penguin 4 is simply suggesting that she desires an undefined food or drink item in the room. However, there is also another interpretation which renders the expression unsuitable for children. In English slang, 'stuff' or 'good stuff' may refer to drugs or sexual activity, as confirmed by Recktenwald (2017), who interprets this phrase as referring to drug use in a chat session linked to a livestream of the *League of Legends* game involving adults. We have no way of knowing for certain whether this is the intended meaning. Penguin 5's subsequent exclamation mark, an expression of surprise, seems to confirm this interpretation, though it may be referring to another post. If it is intended as a response to post 4, then there is a strong chance that this user interpreted the expression as taboo and should be considered unsuitable for this context.

As previously mentioned, when analysing the language used in interaction, the role of recipients' interpretation is crucial, as human beings construct interaction together, not on their own. This example shows up the limitations of language-based child safety features, though the taboo interpretation may thankfully be unfamiliar to many children, as it was to the author initially. Where euphemisms of inappropriate language are known only by certain in-groups, they may also be unknown by adults who are unfamiliar with that group's language. Young people of different age groups and fans of specific video games have their own in-group code which excludes unknowledgeable adults (and children). Of course, it is also possible that this expression is merely a positive evaluation of 'chips' and hence a response to Penguin 2's previous post. Clearly, this post is open to multiple interpretations as we do not have access to additional subsequent posts.

Regardless of the complexities of reconstructing and interpreting ephemeral written interactions such as *Club Penguin* chats, it is clear from this exchange that smaller groups of participants may construct a coherent role-play, despite the linguistic restrictions imposed by the software. The large group chat going on in the same room is quite different from the more private one occurring with the six penguins in the corner, a form of role-play that attempts to mirror what occurs in face-to-face contexts, except that in this case participants have to work to construct a coherent 'conversation' with the linguistic resources made available by the *Club Penguin* chat language system. We should also note that while the six penguins appear to be talking to one another, their talk is visible to others in the group; hence, it is not actually private. Users would be well aware of the public nature of their conversation; hence, while their posts may be intended for the small group, the large group of users are 'overhearers' in the sense that they may be reading the posts as well. There is also evidence that child safety is elusive, despite the program's restrictions on language.

Club Penguin Group Chat Celebrations: The Role of Postcards

In Figure 3.2 earlier, posts are dedicated mainly to celebrating *Club Penguin*'s eleventh anniversary. However, we also see that when one of the chat site's fictional characters turns up, the attention is focused on her (Figure 3.3).

In contrast with posts which have no specific addressees, the conversation has shifted significantly here with users directing their posts specifically at Megg, who is apparently a moderator as well as being a popular character in this environment. The well-wishing that was evident previously (not repro-duced here) is temporarily suspended to attract Megg's attention, as in the post 'megg megg megg' on the left. The excitement at Megg's arrival is also evident with the exclamation marks and posts, such as 'MEGG IS HERE' (shouted in

Figure 3.3 *Club Penguin* café chat when Megg arrives. Source: © Disney

capital letters) and 'omg' (Oh my God!). Both in this screenshot and others which include Megg, participants request a virtual postcard 'postcard me', using imperative (command) verb forms. Postcards are used mainly to enact invitations and encouragements to other participants, with some postcards related to *Club Penguin*'s theme for the month (Club Penguin Wiki, 2018, February). *Club Penguin* postcards are clearly desirable items, with standard messages sent directly to an individual penguin in their mailbox. These would otherwise need to be purchased with virtual 'coins', the main *Club Penguin* currency. It appears that users at this event know that Megg has the authority to provide these.

The value of postcards is also evident in Figure 3.4, which is again a group chat, but this time there is no specific addressee of the posts, except where someone is named.

In this screenshot of *Club Penguin*'s anniversary party, the main interactional activity is that of requesting postcards, which may be used to establish or consolidate friendships. Users do not just request them from the *Club Penguin* character Deamama, but from other penguins as well (see 'please postcard me everybody' and 'everyone postcard me please XD'). The latter post includes a simple emoji which represents laughing with eyes closed or a big grin, both of which suggest friendliness towards other users. There are only two posts where postcards are not the topic of conversation, one at the bottom left where the

Figure 3.4 *Club Penguin* café chat when Deamama arrives. Source: © Disney

penguin tries to get the attention of Penny ('hey penny') and one on the bottom right where a penguin enthusiastically expresses her support of the EPF (Elite Penguin Force), a group of penguins whose role it is to keep *Club Penguin* safe.

The exchanges in Figures 3.2, 3.3 and 3.4 examined so far are clearly a form of open conversation, mostly in large groups, with users making use of *Club Penguin* resources such as virtual postcards to establish and consolidate relationships in group chat. We also observed a small group social interaction through role-play (Figure 3.2) in a crowded room where many participants were present. The main functions of users' contributions in Figures 3.2, 3.3 and 3.4 are requesting and ordering items, expressing concern, excitement and support, well-wishing, naming and calling out to other users. The next section focuses on a small group chat where no other users are present.

Small Group Chat: Play-Oriented Social Interactions

The examples analysed in this section provide evidence of various types of interactions and language which revolve around play, including role-play. After all this is a MMORG (massively multiplayer role-playing game); hence, role-play is inherent in the assumption of the penguin avatar role. One type of playful interaction involves users exploiting the possibilities offered by the *Club Penguin* software. For example, users may make playful adjustments to the way their penguin avatar appears on screen. These adjustments are facilitated by the *Club Penguin* software and mirror children's off-screen dress-up activities.

Example 3.4 is from a study by Burley (2010) of the chats of her eight-year-old daughter, represented in the examples as D, who reportedly chose to interact as a male penguin.[3] According to the author, after choosing her clothes and colours (black penguin with green jacket), the penguin called D looks for her friends in the nightclub where there are penguins who play with colour options and dance.

> Example 3.4
>
> 1 Penguin 1 (P1)/texting: Everyone turn red and dance.
> 2 D/texting: Why?
> [Now there are 4 red, dancing penguins].
> 3 P2/texting: Omigosh, epic.
> 4 D/texting: Woo hoo!
> [She has turned red and is dancing. Now there are 6].
> 5 P1/texting: Turn red and dance. Make the dance floor red. (pp. 6–7)

Post 1 indicates that Penguin 1 has issued an order to other penguins in the room, to turn red and dance. While D questions this at first in post 2, she then joins the other penguins in turning red and dancing (see author's comment at

---

[3] Comments in square brackets are by the author, Burley (2010).

post 4). Two users P2 and D express enthusiasm for the changes in posts 3 and 4 while more penguins join the room and the activity. P1 continues to act as self-appointed leader of the group, and at post 5 issues further requests, including to make the dance floor red. The language here is typically conversational, with imperative verb forms used to perform requests 'dance', one instance of questioning 'Why?' (post 2) and expressions of enthusiasm 'Omigosh, epic' (post 3) and 'Woo hoo!' (post 4).

The language and interaction we see in Example 3.4 mirrors and simulates real life activities which may involve dominant children and dancing. The main objective of users in this room is entertainment and going along with the majority, especially the self-appointed head penguin who is issuing requests. However, there are some obvious differences that are worth noting. Firstly, dancing is not physical, only virtual, as the only part of the body involved is the children's hands on the keyboard. Hence, there are none of the beneficial effects of off-screen dancing. Secondly, we may need to be reminded that this is a voiceless world where penguins are constructing written, not spoken talk. Thirdly, the facility with which users switch colour of their penguin and the dance floor is not possible in the real world. In summary, the interaction is authentic, entertaining and prosocial but is unique to virtual environments such as *Club Penguin*, where software facilitates screen-based imaginary actions.

Example 3.5, from Marsh (2013), is also predominantly game and role-play oriented, with little space for friendship negotiations. It also shows a significant level of linguistic creativity in engaging with an imaginary ball game without a virtual ball or any physical (bodily) activity apart from hands on keyboard and possible private talk. This game is based on text and quite different from other game activities on *Club Penguin*, where users may choose to engage in specific ludic and point-scoring activities such as competitively riding a sled, without any concern for social interaction with other sled riders.

Example 3.5

1 Avatar 1: Misses
2 Avatar 2: U better
3 Avatar 1: Takes shoot
4 Avatar 3: Whacks round hed
5 Avatar 1: Heart stops
6 Avatar 2: Hands up
7 Avatar 3: Good
8 Emily's avatar: How did you turn on your TV.^
9 Avatar 1: Falls
10 Avatar 2: Waaaaaaaaa
11 Avatar 3: Catches
12 Avatar 2:1 weaving

(p. 82)

As noted by Marsh, the avatars in Example 3.5 'used the chat facility to outline their imaginary actions as they raced around the igloo'. From an interactional perspective, this ball game role-play is particularly interesting as it includes a variety of conversational actions, including imaginary emotions (post 5: 'heart stops'), imaginary physical actions (posts 1, 3, 4, 6, 9, 11, 12), positive evaluations (posts 2, 7) and excitement (10). This does not include Emily's post 8. The three avatars are so exclusively focused on constructing this game that Emily's avatar is ignored by the players when she requests assistance with the TV set up (post 8: 'How did you turn on your TV'?). According to the author, Emily eventually moves to another igloo. Providing assistance to Emily was clearly not a priority with a virtual 'ball game' under way, which suggests she was unwelcome. However, we do not know whether she would have been welcomed had she joined the activity rather than introduce a topic which was out of context in that particular group at that moment in time. The ball game players in this instance missed the opportunity to scaffold Emily in development of her technical abilities, promoting ZPD, while Emily in turn was excluded from the game and missed out on the opportunity to engage in linguistic play which is unique to environments such as *Club Penguin* and other chats. As occurs with adults, it is sometimes necessary for young users to understand and fit in with the rules and cultures of specific online contexts in order to engage appropriately and gain acceptance as participants (cf. Hanna & de Nooy, 2003). However, the reliance on text and lack of access to non-verbal social cues may make it difficult for children to make the right decisions.

Small Group Chat Play: In Summary

In summary, the games and role-plays we've examined in Examples 3.4 and 3.5 provide some idea of what play-oriented interactions look like in socially interactive environments such as *Club Penguin*. As occurs in face-to-face, these interactions are hybrid because they are at the same time play and socially oriented. They have little or no resemblance to *FIFA* or similar games where interaction is not the basis of the game. The fundamental difference is that children generally do not engage with *Club Penguin* on their own, with the computer system, as often occurs with video games. There is, however, evidence that the later *Club Penguin Island* (mobile version) appeared to be more like a video game allowing solo play due to the reduced number of users compared with the previous versions. In *Club Penguin* original version, other people are needed and creative role-plays and friendship requests mirror the same activities that occur in the playground. These may involve the search for and establishment of new friendships, creative role-plays and fictitious games that show linguistic inventiveness to create a new form of interaction. While *Club Penguin* is a written interaction environment, there is some evidence here that new and unique types of socially interactive games are possible in the *Club Penguin* system, including those which are invented by the children. The absence of the body and physical world in interaction is nonetheless a concern, especially where the beneficial activities of dancing and ball games can only be simulations of the real thing.

Small Group Chat: Open Conversation

In addition to interactions incorporating *Club Penguin* tools and games, users engage in exchanges which are entirely social, either one-to-one or in groups, where no play is actually occurring, though they may lead to play. In Example 3.6 (from Burley, 2010), two online friends organize meetings for the next play session.

> Example 3.6
> 1 P: Shall we play tomorrow
> 2 D: Maybe
> 3 P: Pls
> 4 D: What time?
> 5 P: Right now
> 6 D: Ok, meet me at Yeti Server
> 7 P: Plaza

(p. 8)

Post 1 by P is a request to play on the following day, which receives a lukewarm response from D in post 2. So P pleads with D to agree to her request by posting 'Pls'. D's response requesting information on the time of their appointment is interpreted as an affirmative answer by P, who suggests that the play session occur immediately 'Right now' rather than the next day, as originally indicated in post 1. D agrees to this request and suggests they meet at Yeti Server, though P then suggests an alternative, Plaza. To summarize, the main function of this exchange is negotiation of a play session between two users. These eight-year-olds successfully negotiate three matters in relation to this session: (a) whether to play; (b) when to play and (c) where to play. These matters need to be attended to if the play session is to occur and reflect the types of negotiations that occur in real life environments and on the phone. Given that there are only two participants, the posts appear in an orderly fashion on screen and are a form of open conversation where participants set up more interactionally constrained virtual play activities in another server.

Rejection and Punishment

The predominantly social orientation of *Club Penguin* interaction is especially clear in Example 3.7, where relationships and rejection of participants become a feature of a group of children's written talk. According to the author of this study (Burley, 2010), Penguin 2 is a new penguin who enters a room where both her daughter (D) and other children are present. Penguin 2 (P2)'s request for friendship is rejected by one penguin (P1), but taken up by D.

Example 3.7

1 P2: Anybody wanna be my friend?
2 P2: Please. I like your outfit, you are so cool, wanna be friends.
3 P1: I don't like your hair. [Walks away]
4 D [to me]: I feel bad. That was mean.
5 P2: Meanie. [Emote] Angry face.
6 D: I'll be ur friend. Hair's ok. Do u have a ponytail?
7 P2: [After a quick change to a long brown ponytail] Like this?
8 P3: Me too. All 3 of us.
9 P2: Ok
10 D: Let's go shopping. Follow me. (p. 7)

This exchange starts with Penguin 2's request for friendship in post 1. Her request is not directed at any specific penguin, as she uses the term 'anybody'. Hence, either of the three (or more, it is unclear) penguins present in the room are being addressed. The unclear addressee makes it difficult for P2 to get a response, even though this is a clear first pair part in the form of a question that requires an answer (the second pair part). It may also be interpreted as showing a lack of confidence on the part of Penguin 2, as it is quite different from 'can I join your group' or other possibilities which match the activity and people in the room. 'Anybody wanna be my friend' also suggests that she is looking for a friend in the singular, rather than participating in group activities. This may also cause a problem in the exchange as only one penguin would need to accept the friendship of this unacquainted penguin. Lack of access to body language and gaze also limit participants' ability to understand whether a specific addressee is intended. We do not have access to the graphic representation of this chat, so we do not know whether Penguin 2's avatar is positioned to talk to someone in particular.

So, the unclear addressee, possible lack of confidence and appeal to a single penguin in a group setting appear to create an interactional issue at post 1. This becomes evident when Penguin 2 is forced to carry out extra conversational work in the subsequent post (post 2) to justify her request for friendship. The extra conversational work in post 2 entails three elements: (1) pleading, (2) complimenting/positive evaluation 'I like your outfit, you are so cool' and (3) repetition of the original request 'wanna be friends'. The repetition of her request suggests that she did not receive an immediate response, as does the first element of post 2 ('Please') where she pleads with the other penguins to accept her previous offer of friendship. The example does not show this, but some considerable time, in conversational terms, is likely to have elapsed between post 1 and post 2.

Penguin 2 finally receives a response in post 3, but not the desired one, as Penguin 1 rejects her offer of friendship quite harshly. Her rejection is conveyed by expressing dislike of the way her penguin avatar appears on screen, criticizing its hair in particular: 'I don't like your hair'. Of course the actual child identifies with the Penguin avatar she creates and takes the criticism (negative evaluation) of her hair personally. At the same time Penguin 1 uses its avatar's body language to reinforce her textual criticism, as it walks away from Penguin 2. No emoticons are used at this point, the criticism-rejection is conveyed sufficiently well with words and virtual body language. There is also a suggestion here that Penguin 2 had addressed Penguin 1 in particular. This is evident when she uses the word 'outfit' in the singular, rather than plural 'outfits' in post 2.

A response to this episode, as it is under way, is conveyed privately and verbally by D to her mother in line 4 ('to me'). This response comprises two elements: (1) expression of her guilty feelings 'I feel bad' and (2) disapproval of Penguin 1's action 'That was mean'. Then in post 5, Penguin 2 accuses Penguin 1 of being a 'meanie', a derivative of 'mean', the term used privately by D in the previous post. This accusation is reinforced with an emoticon of an angry face (represented as text in the example). D follows this in post 6 with acceptance of Penguin 1's friendship 'I'll be ur friend', thus defusing the situation. Post 6 therefore comprises of three actions: (1) acceptance of Penguin 2's friendship, (2) acceptance of her hair 'Hair's ok', which contrasts with and repairs Penguin 1's criticism and (3) an indirect suggestion that she change her hair style 'Do u have a ponytail?' Penguin 2 agrees to her suggestion in post 7 and quickly changes to a long brown ponytail, followed by a request for approval of her choice 'Like this?' Penguin 3 then joins the interaction, suggesting that she too will change to the same ponytail and that the three of them should do the same. Obviously, she intends D, P2 and herself, and excludes Penguin 1, who had behaved in an unfriendly manner towards P2. This negotiation subsequently leads to a 'shopping' role-play, as indicated in D's post 10 'Let's go shopping. Follow me'. With post 10, D again takes the initiative in moving the interaction forward to another activity, apparently leaving behind the 'meanie' P1, who in this way has been penalized for her antisocial behaviour.

This episode shows a predominantly social orientation, which eventually leads to a virtual shopping role-play and a more hybrid social play-oriented interaction. This is enhanced through the use of *Club Penguin* resources, including the option to make changes to one's appearance to promote group belonging. The only instance of repair in this example is D's repair of Penguin 1's negative evaluation 'I don't like your hair' with 'Hair's OK', which has an important function of disagreeing with Penguin 1's criticism and consoling Penguin 2 for probably taking offence. This negotiation of friendships involves a group of four children and mirrors the same kinds of negotiations that might occur in the schoolyard, including exclusion and acceptance, though in a much more linguistically and interactionally constrained environment, without children's access to non-verbal and physical resources.

Reading and Writing Other than Talk

Club Penguin users are not only engaging in social interaction and collaborative play through written conversation, though this is the predominant activity. They may also engage in reading and writing more traditional written texts that are not directly a part of their online interaction. For example, they may choose to read an unknown user's profile prior to contacting them. Another activity is that of writing and sending postcards to other users. There is also the opportunity to read and contribute to the *Club Penguin Times* newspaper. Clearly, these activities are valuable for the development of children's language, though the extent to which users engage in the literacy activities is unclear. The author's own experience observing her son and the limited scholarly literature on this chat suggests that children are mainly interested in chatting with their real world or new virtual world friends.

Implications

To understand whether *Club Penguin* promotes interaction and learning through collaborative play, including role-play, further research would be needed which takes the age of children into account. While this analysis provides some insights, real time screen recordings would also enhance the accuracy of analysis and our understanding of language and interaction in *Club Penguin*. Additionally, these would provide a more complete picture of timing and sequencing of posts. Considering that this has been one of the most popular children's virtual environments, it is crucial that the community understand it or similar products better.

What we know is that despite their attractiveness to children, *Club Penguin* contexts are not real and lack the richness of face-to-face environments where human beings thrive. They are creative simulations by innovative software developers and designers for young users to make use of their creative abilities, language, hands, devices and *Club Penguin* resources to interact with others through reading, writing and virtual interaction, including various forms of play. Participants are entirely reliant on the identities and cartoon bodies that can be built around the avatars. We also saw that the language safety features are not foolproof; hence, open discussions and monitoring of children by adults are essential.

In Summary

- *Club Penguin* was an important linguistic experiment for children's safe chat interaction.
- Even *Club Penguin*'s most restricted language could be combined and adapted for creative play, vocabulary learning, interaction and inappropriate online behaviours.
- While *Club Penguin*'s evanescent unsequenced posts posed considerable challenges for researchers and for understanding, children were able to use available resources to engage in social interaction, including through role-play and play-oriented interaction, whether in pairs, small or large groups.
- While not reliable, the position of penguin avatars assists in signalling and identifying addressees of posts to facilitate analysis.
- The language used in group interaction was limited mainly to requesting, ordering, naming and calling out to other avatars, well-wishing and express-ing concern, excitement, support and availability to interact.
- Greater variety of linguistic devices and negotiations was evident in small group exchanges, including new creative forms of interaction, such as dance and ball game simulations, with accompanying textual renditions of imagin-ary emotions and physical actions. These small group exchanges included negotiations related to exclusion and acceptance of other children.
- One user's request for technical help and opportunity for ZPD was ignored by peers engaged in a ball game, which also resulted in her exclusion from the game.
- One instance of repair in small group chat was socially oriented, to express disagreement with a user's negative evaluation of another user's appearance.

4   Video Game Talk

Introduction

A recent Australian report on video game use by Brand et al. (2019) indicates that while all Australians surveyed play an average of 81 minutes daily, children play 100 minutes per day or close to 12 hours per week. According to Walker et al.'s (2018) longitudinal investigation, however, over half (52%) of Australian children use video games up to 4 hours per week (less than 1 hour per day), while the other half (48%) use them for up to 7 hours per week (or around 1 hour per day), which is significantly less than the figures reported in Brand et al.'s (2019) study. In statistics from the United Kingdom, age is noted as a factor, as gameplay increases as children grow older, from children of three to four years who spent an average 4.7 hours weekly in 2019, to twelve- to fifteen-year-old children who spent around 11.6 hours per week playing video games (Statista, 2021a). Therefore, when compared with statistics of Australian children in the same age group, twelve- to fifteen-year-old UK children spend about the same time per week as Australian children playing video games, based on Brand et al.'s (2018) figures. In Finland, instead it seems that 98 per cent of boys aged ten to fourteen and 89 per cent of girls of the same age play digital games at least once a month according to the Official Statistics of Finland (2019, cited in Kahila et al., 2021). The Pew Research Center (Lenhart et al., 2015) found significant gender differences in teens' video game play, with 84 per cent of boys and 59 per cent of girls aged thirteen to seventeen year claiming that they play video games. While statistics on children's gaming vary due to numerous factors, they reinforce the fact that video games are a significant part of children's lives. While these figures do not provide details on types of games, it is clear that many children engage with and derive pleasure from gaming. It is therefore necessary to better understand the interactional architecture and affordances of these activities for children's learning and development.

While Gee (2003; 2007) does not analyse children's interactions, his work on video games highlights the many benefits of gaming for children and adults. These advantages include the pleasure and learning that children derive from games. Learning advantages he identifies include problem-solving, literacy and learning how to work in teams, as occurs especially where gamers are working collaboratively. A conversation analytic study by Bennerstedt & Ivarsson (2010) shows how text chat is used by adult gamers who are geographically dispersed, both globally or virtually within the game, to communicate and organize team members in *The Lord of the Rings Online (LOTRO)*. The identified learning benefits of games have given rise to the notion of 'gamification' in educational and training settings, whereby game mechanics and principles are applied in non-gaming contexts such as schools, to motivate students and promote learning (e.g. Kingsley & Grabner-Hagen, 2015). As Starke et al. (2021) note however, many games do not integrate pedagogical elements in their game approach since educational content and gamification elements are unrelated. In order to achieve such an integration, they note that interdisciplinary collaboration is required between relevant education experts and game developers. There are, however, advantages in gaining a more nuanced understanding of how children interact with the plethora of games available, to be able to better apply game principles in educational contexts, where budgets for game development are likely to be considerably smaller than for commercial games.

A groundbreaking study by Walker et al. (2018) showed that Australian children of ten and eleven years, who engaged in digital play for up to 240 minutes (4 hours) per week, improved their literacy and mathematical thinking. While details on the types of digital games used by children in the sample are not provided, they also found that lower levels of play (120 mins) did not show children's achievement gains but that high levels of video game play (421 minutes) were associated with problems relating to children's self-regulation, academic performance and emotional development. Findings on achievement gains contrast with much of the literature and media reports on screen time concerns for children, but they do suggest that a balanced approach is needed in the amount of time children spend gaming. The Walker et al. (2018) study also signals the need for children to engage with quality games such as *Minecraft* (Mojang, 2009), to maximise children's collaboration and achievement. Given the addictive nature and commercial objectives of most video games, this study confirms the need for balance in terms of time spent gaming and better guidance on the most appropriate games for children.

Interacting through Point and Click or Language: How to Tell the Difference

Given the positive links between talk and learning discussed in Chapter 1, it is important for children to engage with video game environments which promote interaction through talk with adults and other children. When identifying the most 'interactive' video games for children, we need to ask ourselves: do these promote interaction through talk? Or is interaction mainly a series of points, clicks and interactions with the game system for the purpose of achieving a game goal, such as victory against a fictional game character or progressing to the next level? If there is interaction through talk, what does that talk consist of? Is it written or spoken? These are important questions to ask when choosing and assessing the most suitable video games for children. In summary, it is helpful to understand whether children are interacting mainly with human beings or the game system. This is important because no matter how complex and cognitively demanding single player games may be, they are likely to be more valuable from a learning perspective if they involve collaboration with other players through talk.

Online social interaction through talk is a feature and attraction of popular massively multiplayer online role-playing games (MMORGs), which are normally hosted on a web browser. Such games are most suitable for young children's independent play when they are designed for them, with appropriate safety features, and often require interaction through text rather than voice chat as an integral part of the software. Gillen's (2009) study on MMORG *Teen Second Life* provides an example of an 'enclosed' safe island created for interaction and role-play between young people aged thirteen to seventeen years and accredited adults. This study includes analysis of a sequence of text chat interaction between two young participants, the researcher and the *Second Life* system, which contributes to understanding the complexity and creativity of student literacy practices. Chapter 3 of this book considered the language of the MMORG *Club Penguin*, given that it was designed to be safe for children and is a prime example of online text social interaction which includes games, like the popular chat and game environment *Habbo* (Oy, 2004). The current chapter instead considers previous research on video games which are designed predominantly for gaming rather than social interaction, though they may also permit both voice and chat interaction as a component of gaming. The analytical principles developed in this chapter support analysis of a single episode of *Minecraft* gaming in Chapter 5.

Interweaving Game Actions and Various Forms of Chat

The first step in understanding gaming is to understand the multiple ways that players interact, particularly their mode of interaction. Bearing in mind that conversation is a joint (co-constructed) effort, how are children co-constructing the conversation *outside* and *inside* the game? What does the interplay between the voice or text conversations and the game actions look like? This is of course likely to vary according to the game, number of players and where they are located.

Devices used to play games may be mobile, like a smartphone, or fixed, such as computers and game consoles. When video games are played collaboratively, in the same physical space, gamers are co-located. In this case, most participants' voice interactions are off-screen verbal face-to-face, with the game screen in view and in use at the same time. Where, on the other hand, game participants are geographically dispersed, collaborative interactions may involve some online talk between participants, usually text or voice chat. These interactions are usually made possible by either an in-built game console and chat/voice chat software, or independently downloaded software such as Discord, Skype or WhatsApp.

A common gaming combination is where virtual and physical voice are combined with text interaction during gameplay. For example, two co-located gamers may be playing a game in one location and two in another location. In such a scenario there may be social interaction in the following ways:

1. spoken talk with a co-located gamer
2. gamers in one physical location engage in talk with gamers in another location using either the voice chat channel (or other voice chat software) and/or the game's text chat channel
3. non-verbal interactions (co-located)
4. 'response cries' (Aarsand & Aronsson, 2009a), a form of self-talk which is not directed at anyone in particular, via voice chat or in the same physical context

Any kind of digitally-mediated interaction may therefore involve multiple types and combinations of talk, as described in Table 4.1 below, which summarizes some of the different interactional configurations and combinations of video game interaction with game actions. This includes interaction via a single device or multiple devices, both in-game and out-of-game, off-screen and on-screen and by single players interacting with the game only.

As illustrated in Table 4.1, there are multiple variations in the way that children's video game interactions may unfold while gaming. Interactions may be one-to-one or multi-party in groups of three or more, via text, voice and face-to-face.[1] The following sections of this chapter focus on relevant research conducted on children's video game interaction, using the distinctions described in Table 4.1 as a framework. Most of the research so far has focused on off-screen voice interactions between co-located players, combined with game actions. Despite the reported surge in interest in multiplayer games during the pandemic, due to the need to replace face-to-face interaction during lockdowns (Statista 2021b), there appears to be a dearth of research on voice or

---

[1] Co-located gamers actually sit side by side though they may also turn to face one another; hence, the term 'face-to-face' in this chapter indicates physical co-location rather than the actual position of gamers.

Table 4.1 *Video game talk-in-interaction configurations, and combinations*

Spoken interactions	Written interactions	Interaction with game only
Virtual long-distance voice: via in-game voice chat channel or out-of-game communication software (e.g. Discord, Skype, WhatsApp, game console)	Virtual written: long-distance text chat between single or multiple geographically dispersed players: in game, on-screen or out-of-game (on-screen text chat communication software)	Virtual game actions only, without other player/s
Voice interaction with other co-located player/s (out-of-game, off-screen)	Virtual written (cross-modal): between long-distance and co-located players: in-game, on-screen or out-of-game (on-screen text chat communication software)	Private talk (including response cries aimed at no one in particular (oneself or device/game)
Non-verbal interactions (gaze, handshakes etc.)	Non-verbal interactions (gaze, handshakes etc.): only if co-located and combining text with voice chat and co-located gaming.	
Response cries	Response cries (including private talk if using only chat and inaudible to other game participants)	

text chat interaction between geographically dispersed young users. Nonetheless, it is worth considering available findings on children's video game interaction so far.

Text, voice or face-to-face interaction may be carried out separately or in combination, leading to increasingly complex forms of talk and the impression that children are multitasking, especially since this talk also involves interaction with the game. Mixed-mode interactions during public multi-party video chats not involving games have been described as 'cross-modal' by Rosenbaun et al. (2016) as participants may alternate between text or voice chat or respond to text chat using voice chat and vice versa. This cross-modality is a feature of gaming interactions too (see Hung, 2017). Spoken interactions may be in-game when they are available through the game software or out-of-game between co-located gamers. Written interactions and game actions are instead always on-screen as they require mediation by a device and appropriate software, whereas response cries and private talk are deployed out-of-game and off-screen, either in company (co-located) or alone. Following Goffman's (1978) definition, Aarsand and Aronsson (2009a) identified 'response cries' as 'public displays of emotions in the form of vocalizations such as self-talk, imprecations and audible surprise' (p. 1557). However, response cries may also be overheard by geographically dispersed gamers through voice communication software and may not be directed at anyone in particular. A further variation in gameplay is that users may be chatting via game console voice chat software while playing multiple games. According to Hung's (2017) study on teenage gamer voice interaction on Xbox live, they are not tied to a single game since their console permits participants to play a variety of games at the same time. In this context not all participants are actually gaming; they may be watching television or engaging in another activity before engaging with the voice inter-action and/or game. Furthermore, Hung's (2017) study indicates that participants may also interact outside the Xbox voice chat and use their phones to text each other during these 'party' sessions, often to encourage new participants to join the chat, the game or both, which confirms the cross-modality and multimodality of these interactions.

While MMORGs such as *Club Penguin* and *Habbo* involve text chat as a central interactional resource to play games, video games discussed in this chapter involve mainly voice interaction between (co-located) gamers. However, due to increased bandwidth and internet speeds, voice interaction has become the norm rather than the exception where children play these games collaboratively, whether online or on a gaming console. In fact, the Pew Research Center (Lenhart et al., 2015) found that 71 per cent of boys and only 28 per cent of girls use voice connections when playing games with others online, to collaborate and talk with other gamers. However, findings do not distinguish video games such as MMORGs, which are based predominantly on text chat interaction, from other types of video games. Geographically dispersed participants are likely to prefer voice interaction in the latter case, mediated by devices they are gaming on, so their hands are free to play rather than chat, though gaming combined with text chat is still an option (see Chapter 5).

Self-Talk during Gaming

Gamers who are either playing on their own, with the game or interacting only through text chat with game participants, may also engage in private talk to themselves, in a form of thinking aloud, as noted in Table 4.1. In an instructional rather than social online setting, Suzuki (2013) identified a student's deployment of 'private turns' through vocalization of language off-screen which was inaudible to other adult participants during a Japanese class offered via audio software. While private talk is not intended for another video game player and is possibly directed at the video game system as well as oneself, it is worthy of further investigation as Suzuki's research has shown that this form of talk is likely to promote learning during online interaction in educational settings. It should be noted, however, that teen gamers are more likely to play video games with others than on their own, with 83 per cent reported to play games with others and 75 per cent online (Lenhart et al., 2015).

A form of 'private talk' is deployed when gamers are in the company of other players, though it is difficult to distinguish what is intended for oneself or another player. Response cries are an example of this form of talk. Children in fact utter these while gaming alone or in company as they are essential interactional resources for participation in gaming, according to Aarsand and Aronsson (2009a). Piirainen-Marsh (2012) notes that these types of actions seem to orient to two participation frameworks simultaneously, that is, either the one between the players and the one between the player and the game. So gamers' actions in the material world are interwoven with those in the virtual game world, with players using both verbal or non-verbal actions (e.g. gaze, orientation of their bodies and verbal practices) to orient to one or the other. Ensslin's (2012) discourse analysis of out-of-game interactions between adults showed that response cries between two gamers playing *Worms 2* signalled enjoyment, with a variety of emotional connotations including malicious and supportive amusement, anxiety, awe, shock or bawdiness.

The Place of Text Chat in Video Game Interaction

The game's chat channel is less likely to be used if voice chat software is adopted to speed up communication; however, both channels may continue to be open. Gamers are likely to prefer voice over text chat, bandwidth permitting, to avoid game delays caused by typing of chat posts. As noted previously, written talk such as text chat, is considered a 'quasi-synchronous' form of interaction (Garcia & Jacobs, 1999). The difference between quasi-synchronous text chat and synchronous voice conversation is evident from the way that delays change the usual order of the conversational turns as they are posted on screen. Text chat users adapt to the unique conversational turn-taking mechanisms, which explains the apparently disorderly sequencing of the posts, as discussed in Chapter 1.

Although game interaction is either synchronous (voice) or quasi-synchronous (text chat), there may be instances during text chat where there are longer delays due to users not being at the game screen at the same time. This is similar to what occurs during certain types of written interaction on social media, where you have a combination of quasi-synchronous and asynchronous interaction. Facebook Messenger and WhatsApp chat are examples of software which permit variation in the timing of response posts. Video game talk therefore involves synchronous face-to-face interaction where gamers are co-located; and where they are geographically dispersed, voice or text chat permits synchronous and quasi-synchronous interaction respectively. It should also be noted that in the case of online voice talk, despite it proceeding in real time, server glitches or audio quality may cause interruptions, delays and problems with understanding (Liddicoat, 2010).

Attending to the Game and Interaction

Game actions add a layer of complexity to video game interaction, especially if gamers are proceeding simultaneously with written chat. Hence, with only two hands at their disposal, they can either attend to the chat or the game action or juggle the two activities. As mentioned above, gamers prefer voice over text chat where available, to avoid delays which slow down the usually fast pace of most games. Nonetheless, gamers have the option to hold their responses and return to the text chat after completing in-game actions or other forms of talk, if available to them. These are just a few common variations in talk which we need to be aware of and which allow game participants to construct video game interactions collaboratively. What is striking about game interactions to observers and researchers, is that despite its complexities, young users adapt linguistically to this mode of interaction and manage to achieve understanding, at times by learning from each other.

The Language of Teen Gaming

Example 4.1 from Lorenza Mondada's (2012) conversation analytic study of two French teenage gamers is derived from a gaming session where participants use out-of-game co-located talk as an interactional resource. This example shows the two main types of interactions which are occurring, (1) between the players and the game (*FIFA*) or (2) between the two players:

Example 4.1[2]

01 RAP tu le mets hein,
   you score it PART
02 luc scores the goal for Real Madrid
03 LUC huh
04 RAP bien
   good
… turns to LUC
05 LUC voi.là
   here.it is
mutual gaze and handshaking

---

[2] Transcription symbols used by reviewed authors in this chapter are available (see standard conventions) and at www.lorenzamondada.net/multimodal-transcription (multimodal).

This example captures the multifaceted nature of interaction between two apparently competent *FIFA* players who are engaged in gaming in the same room rather than at a distance, without the need for technological mediation (text or voice chat). While for the sake of brevity this example does not reproduce details of timing and photos of the two teenagers, it shows us that instructions (commands), evaluations and expressions of satisfaction are combined with game actions (e.g. goal scoring) and non-verbal face-to-face interactions (turning to one another, mutual gazes and handshaking). It is clear from Mondada's (2012) study that the two teenagers playing the *FIFA* (football) video game engage in all manner of social and linguistic activity, using both voice and their bodies. They use the position of their bodies to move in and out of the game to engage in interaction within the game space and in the physical space outside the game, at the appropriate time in key moments, for example, when scoring a goal. The gamers engage in a great deal of advice-giving, which promotes successful gameplay and shows a form of learning from each other. An important conclusion by Mondada (2012) in regard to the language used by these teenagers is that shorter, simpler language such as commands (e.g. kick the ball) is used when they are focused on the game. More complex but typical conversational language is used when they pause and turn their heads towards one another, with the main content of this exchange being positive or negative evaluations of the preceding game activity or recounting what they achieved. Some positive evaluations such as 'nice', repeated many times, occur both during and outside the gameplay, such as during breaks. Findings also suggest that the central activity of game-mediated interaction in the context Mondada (2012) describes is in fact playing the game, while the conversational work is a side activity.

Mondada's (2011) study of directives (commands) which are composed of French imperative verbs, in the same video game context as Example 4.1, reveals that they are not necessarily an impolite way to utter requests, as previous speech act theory research on indirect requests suggests. Rather, Mondada (2011) suggests that research on the use of imperative verbs needs to consider the context in which they are uttered. In the case of spoken out-of-game interaction on *FIFA*, imperative verbs are appropriate request forms for the fine-tuned co-ordination of social and game actions.[3] In her analysis of gamer language during off-screen oral conversation between adults in *Gamecorp* and *FIFA10*, Ensslin (2012) also observes that given the rule-driven nature of games, commands are common; and considering the emotional nature of gameplay, there may be expletives (swearing), interjections such as

---

[3] See also Sydorenko et al. (2021), for a summary of the various types of directives used in L1 and L2 adult gaming interactions and Davidson (2012a), on the prevalence of directives during extended and negotiated help sequences between young children.

'whoa', laughter and other expressions of emotion. As Ensslin's research involves adults rather than children, however, such linguistic activity may vary according to age.

Piirainen-Marsh (2012) focuses on teens in a multimodal analysis which considers both verbal and non-verbal actions, as they play collaboratively on *Final Fantasy X*, which is intended for single players on a game console (Sony PlayStation). The two participants achieve this collaborative gaming by taking turns in holding the control and operating the game and by planning and negotiating their choices together. The analysis shows how the game structures their interaction as the game's situations and tasks unfold, through animation, visual images and texts such as menus. The authors conclude that gamers' collaborative work with the game and each other permits them to build a shared experience, manage game tasks as joint projects and use language to build sociality. This is achieved even though they are only using a single player game, albeit collaboratively. Piirainen-Marsh and Tainio's (2014) study also involves two participants and *Final Fantasy*, but with a focus on learning over time, with the first sessions on *Fantasy IX* recorded when players were eleven and the second sessions on *Fantasy X* at age thirteen. The analysis demonstrates how the gameplay and associated interactions address knowledge asymmetries in relation to both English language and the game and contribute to learning in this multilingual setting. Findings show that while in the first gaming sessions the less experienced, novice participant is less active, he becomes more active as he develops expertise and confidence in engaging with the game, which includes improved ability to read and interpret information on the screen and independently assess the available game options. These changes are considered by the authors to constitute 'trajectories of learning to read the game and solve game-related problems through joint activity' (p. 1035). The language used by gamers in the interactions presented in this study is more diverse than that used by gamers playing *FIFA* described by Mondada (2012), which is dominated by directives and evaluations. There is evidence of repair work, including requests for clarification, in addition to response cries, positive or negative assessments and reading computer commentary aloud. Example 4.2 provides a snapshot of these interactional features between Pete (P), Kapa (K) and video game.

Example 4.2

```
3⇨P    [I can't eat until viik:er
                      weaker
       [((selects attack))
Game commands appear on screen at turn 3: Attack
                                           Jump
4      (.) [((K fires toy gun))
5 K    <n[o↑ih>]
       <th[e↑re>
```

```
6 P    [kökkö]
       [stupid]
       ((– > P continues to 'Attack'))
7      (.) ((attack ends))
8⇨K    mikä on <jumppi> (.) mitä sillä tekkee
       what's < jump > (.) what can you do with it
9      (.)
10 P   Mustard Bomb (.) vähän tuo on °hullun hyvä°
       Mustard Bomb (.) that is °so good°
11⇨K   +(              ) +Sina:ppipommi.
                 + Musta:rd bomb.
       +((points with toy gun, +fires towards the screen))
              (adapted from Piirainen-Marsh and Tainio, 2014, p. 1027⁴)
```

In turn 3, P repairs the ungrammatical language of the game character: 'I no can eat until weaker' (not reproduced here), by producing a grammatically correct version. After K's response cry (turn 5) and P's evaluation (turn 6), K requests clarification on what 'jump' can do at turn 8, which is related to knowledge of the game. However, P does not respond to this request and provides a positive assessment on the acquisition of a mustard bomb (turn 10). Hence, the language used in these interactions may occasionally reflect participants' knowledge asymmetries in relation to how to play the game, though they bring their L2 expertise into play regarding incorrect English language used by game characters.

It is possible that each of the two participants in Mondada's (2012) study had similarly high levels of gaming expertise in playing *FIFA*; hence, repair work related to the game may be less likely when compared with gamers with knowledge asymmetries presented in Example 4.2. Clearly, the language and repair work is likely to vary according to the specific context, especially according to the game and expertise of the gamers.

Sjöblom's (2008) study involving young people between eleven- and twenty-one-years old, gaming at internet cafés, shows how both on- and off-screen semiotic resources structure the gaming interaction, including how they relate to players' issuing of instructions or orienting themselves in on-screen spaces. This study also identifies a 'professional' vision of gaming, as being a competent gamer requires the ability to foresee events in the game, because 'players are continuously seeing and analyzing the ongoing on-screen and off-screen action for possible upcoming actions' (p. 154). Hung's (2011) study of video game play includes a chapter (5) which describes the off-screen inter-actions of four adolescents speaking Mandarin and Cantonese, where one of them is a complete novice both to the *Super Smash Brothers* game and the

---

⁴ Figures in the original study are not reproduced here.

Nintendo controller, while the others are experienced. The language used by participants is quite varied, similar to Piirainen-Marsh and Tainio's (2014) study where participants have knowledge asymmetries related to the game. While there is an abundance of directives from the experienced players, the novice player in particular regularly asks questions which seek clarification and assistance on how the game works so she may progress. She also deploys complaints about receiving inadequate assistance. At a certain point the language used by these participants orients to their respective 'teaching' and 'learning' role in this specific game context, as in Example 4.3.

Example 4.3

((players at the character selection screen))

1   Li(M)   *nimen you bu jiao wo*
                 you again not teach me
                 (You never teach me.)

2   Kevin   *()*

3   Andrew(M)   *jiaole ni a*
                 taught you exclamation
                 (I taught you already.)
                 (0.3)

4   Li(M)   *na   jiu   meici yizhi an*
                 Then every time keep press
                 (You always just tell me to keep pressing)

5   *a::::::*
                 exclamation

6   Andrew(M)   *ni   yao   tiao ma::::::::::::::::::*
                 you have to jump final particle
                 (You have to jump,

7   [*tiao   dao renjia   xiamian*
                 [jump to others below
                 jump underneath others.)

8   Jason(M)   [*ni   an   (zhege)* Li *an zhege*
                 [you press (this)   Li press this one
                 [(Press (this), Li, press this one to attack

9   *da   zhege an   tui   ren chuqu*
                 attacks this one press push people away
                 Press this one to push people away.

10   *haiyao an   xia   an   xia*
                 also   press down press down
                 And also press down to –)

                                            (adapted from Hung, 2011, pp. 113–114)

In turns 1, 4 and 5, Li expresses her dissatisfaction regarding her co-players lack of support, concluding with an exclamation at turn 5. The utterance 'you never teach me' (1) orients to her co-players as 'teachers' and herself as 'student'. These roles are confirmed by Andrew at turn 3 when he defends himself by claiming 'I taught you already'. Li's complaining prompts Andrew to provide instructions on the game in turns 6 and 7, followed by Jason from turns 8 to 10, who uses directives to explain what occurs in the game when certain buttons are pressed. The author notes the need for instruction and learning to be co-constructed between novices and experts, for it to be success-ful. The game actions are not available in the analysis; however, participants' interactions provide an idea of what is occurring in the game. It is also likely that the 'teaching' and 'learning' component of game interactions is rendered more complex during fast-paced video games.

Kiourti's (2019) multimodal analysis of the interactions between four Cypriot gamers aged sixteen to seventeen while playing multiplayer first-person shooter game *Counter Strike: Global Offensive (CS:GO)* indicates that rather than indicating aggression, swearing and bad language are strategies with specific social and gaming purposes. They are an attempt at (1) preventing 'individual or team-based performative face-loss when communicative viola-tions occur during gameplay' (p. 158), (2) cooling stress, (3) ensuring in-group bonding and (4) providing feedback to co-players when they do not perform. Though it breaks the rules of politeness in other contexts, in the video game context described by Kiourti (2019) bad language is deployed to promote effective gameplay while protecting and maintaining participants' positive identity as gamers. This suggests that greater flexibility is required on the part of adult family members regarding the language of teen gamers.

Researchers' multimodal research to understand gaming interaction, includ-ing both in-game and out-of-game and on-screen and off-screen activities, requires replication in multiple video game contexts involving children, given the diversity of configurations and games and variety of ages, levels and types of expertise of young gamers. This would provide a more complete scientific picture of children's language, interaction and learning during spe-cific types of video games. Given the focus so far on research involving teenage gamers, it is therefore useful to turn to research on younger children's inter-action with video games which are designed for their age group (e.g. Danby et al., 2018a; Davidson, 2010; 2012a; 2012b).

Younger Children's Gaming Talk

Davidson (2010) examines interactions between children aged four and six years old respectively and their father while playing a *Wiggles* game. In this case the father plays the role of mediator between the two children, who compete for use of the mouse. The analysis shows the complexities associated with young children completing a simple game collaboratively and the mediat-ing supportive role of adults. The authors argue that by revealing how chil-dren's engagement with the computer is socially accomplished, the study also provides insights into children's social worlds in a single player game context involving collaborative play between two players. Davidson's (2012a) conversation analytic study examines the revealing off-screen 'helping' behaviours which occur between a four-year-old child playing *Reader Rabbit* and her older seven-year-old sister. The game used in this study is an edutainment software program which purports to teach children basic reading and writing skills. While the computer screen is not visible in this analysis, both the children's linguistic and embodied actions, especially towards the computer screen, are included as turns in the analysis, as are some computer-generated commands. Given that the younger child is still acquiring the ability to read, write and play the game, the 'helping' and learning behaviours are in this particular case the dominant interactional activities. Additionally, the older child enacts the role of expert toward the younger child, who is treated as the 'less competent other' (cf. Liddicoat & Tudini, 2012). This enactment by the older child is evident both in the negative evaluations of her sister's incorrect interactions with the computer and in the complimentary language 'good girl' which is evident on two occasions when completing the required steps correctly. Example 4.4 provides examples of both types of evaluation.

Example 4.4

85 (1.0) ↔((H beside K and looks at computer screen))
86 H: o::h Kaydie [no
87 [((computer sound))
88 (0.2)
89 H: yeah delete yeah (0.2)↑good ↓girl
90 (0.4)

Turn 86 ('o::h Kaydie [no') shows the older sister's disapproval of Kaydies's action while turn 89 includes approval of both Kaydie herself and her corrective action. Overall, this study shows clearly that collaboration between novice and expert child during a computer game promotes learning and shows evidence of ZPD (Vygotsky, 1978) related to managing *Reader Rabbit* software and language.

Another study by Davidson (2012b) focuses on the disputes that arise between the same two sisters described above, while playing the single player game *Animal Links*. The mother designates the four-year-old as the main player and the six-year-old as the 'teacher', however, the analysis shows that the children persistently renegotiate the designated roles to avoid dispute. This is achieved through complex social interactions which include their active monitoring of each others' actions and accounting for their actions both through talk and physical moves in the game as an ongoing aspect of orderly gameplaying. This study provides compelling evidence of children learning to negotiate and manage disputes around a video game, as part of their off-screen out-of-game talk around a single-player game and their designated roles. The value of this type of interaction for children's social development is clear, though disputes are inevitable.

Danby et al.'s (2018a) conversation analytic study across various age groups (three to eight years) in three countries and game contexts, including *Minecraft*, provides detailed descriptions of young children's collaborative actions and talk around digital gameplay. The study finds that digital games promote social interaction and collaboration to problem solve, share strategies, participate in games and learn from peers. Contrary to suggestions that children's gaming is a solitary activity, the study also notes that digital games are used interchangeably with toys and that they can be used by children as resources for playground games.

The conversation analytic studies examined so far, both of older and younger children's language and interaction, lend weight to findings in Kahila et al.'s (2021) content analysis of twelve- to fifteen-year-old children's reported metagame activities, which include game-enabling activities, strategizing activities, discussing activities, information seeking activities and creating and sharing activities. In the reviewed studies, children deploy helping and learning behaviours such as directives, repair work and expert-novice orientations (Liddicoat & Tudini, 2013). These behaviours are accomplished by co-located child pairs and groups of various ages, genders and levels of expertise while playing both single and multiplayer games collaboratively. The co-ordination of voice talk and game actions indicate that in a collaborative gameplay session, game actions and the technology in general are central to the promotion of social interaction and learning behaviours.

In-Game Language and Interaction

Astrid Ensslin's (2012) research on the language of gaming investigates mainly the in-game language of gaming softwares, with some attention to 'live conversations during gameplay ("oral")' (p. 12) between adult gamers. Ensslin (2012) confirms that it is difficult to pin down a general 'language of gaming', given the variety of types and contexts of games. Hence, she recommends that analysis focus on individual games with a variety of players, to take account of individual players' language and unique aspects of each game. Many of the CA studies described in previous sections in fact have a single child pair/one game focus, which provides an appropriate starting point for this type of research. Ensslin also identifies and analyses the specialized, rich and creative vocabulary of games involving young adults, which becomes an in-group code. This code, also known as gamer slang or 'ludolect', promotes belonging for expert gamers, but often excludes 'newbies'. This gaming vocabulary adds an additional dimension to gameplay which Ensslin (2012) sees as promoting both gamer identity and diverse vocabulary to be used within the game world. As far as grammatical and other aspects of game language are concerned, we can expect some variety according to the type of game, based on game designers' objectives and individual players' age or linguistic and gaming proficiencies. As in studies discussed in previous sections, Ensslin (2012) notes that these can vary from commands, requests and suggestions, to the game specific language or fictional avatar responses to players, where the use of a 'you' construction simulates interaction between the game system and gamers.

Online Voice Interaction and Gaming

While a reasonable body of research has been conducted on gaming interactions by co-located children, research on online voice interaction and gaming between geographically distanced children is sadly lacking, despite it being a common interactional configuration for gamers (see Lenhart et al., 2015). Chien's (2019) study of vocabulary development by young L2 learners of English during *Minecraft* gameplay in English is one exception, though the focus in this case is not on mediated language interaction but on vocabulary development. One component of the study involved vocabulary analysis of a ten-minute recording of a Discord voice conversation between two geographically distanced boys based in Taiwan and Brazil, aged ten and nine respectively, who were using their English as L2. While the focus of this study is not on learning behaviours, it suggests that the two children were engaged in 'building, creating, collaborating and problem-solving' (p. 10) during the building of a pig in *Minecraft*. Example 4.5 provides a sample of the online voice interactions described in this study, with the addition of turn numbers.

Example 4.5

1 M: Okay, we need something dark.
2 E: Are you sure this is how it looks like? Doesn't look very good. There we go!
3 M: Because you started building!
4 E: Okay, let's just go! Go! Go! Make some more things!
5 E: We're making the pig face up there.
6 M: duh, duh, duh . . . (singing)
7 E: That looks good!
8 M: Oh, no, I forgot.
9 E: That looks good! It needs one touch to it.
10 M: Yes, I noticed that we need something very important. We need coal block.
11 E: Mattie, Mattie, be fast!
12 M: We need three coal blocks.
13 E: I'm gonna get coal.
14 M: What are you doing?

15 E: You've already got coal?

16 M: Yes.

17 E: We're doing pretty good Mattie? Anybody like our pig? We're making the pig up there.

On examining the language of the transcripts provided, despite lack of CA conventions or game actions, the interactions reveal a variety of directives including imperatives (turns 4, 11), positive and negative assessments (turns 2, 7, 9, 17), questions (turns 2, 14, 15, 17) with some corresponding answers and other conversational actions which are promoted by the task and which need to be completed collaboratively within time limits. This investigation, however, concludes that the combination of *Minecraft* YouTube videos and gameplay provide a source of authentic language input which promotes advanced vocabulary learning, based on word frequency lists in the *Brown National Corpus*.

While Thorne et al.'s (2012) focus was not specifically on children's social interaction, their analysis of the linguistic complexity of the MMORG *World of Warcraft* (WOW) environments, including the quest texts within the game and external WOW-related websites, found these environments to be lexically sophisticated and diverse, with a significant proportion of structurally complex sentences. It is therefore important to consider that while online interaction is the focus of this book, children are not only likely to chat while gaming online, but also to engage with other resources related to their chosen games, especially YouTube videos produced by children (see Niemeyer & Gerber, 2015 on *Minecraft*).

On-Screen Text Chat Language and Interaction

Most of the text chat interaction between children occurs on MMORGs which feature social interaction through the chat software as the principal component of the game, rather than requiring interaction as a 'side activity' (Mondada, 2012). And as noted earlier, most of the online interaction on other types of games software nowadays occurs using voice chat. Chapter 5 is dedicated to analysis of a single episode where a popular young gamer interacts with his fans via text chat while playing *Minecraft*. This will provide additional insights into on-screen text chat language and interaction during video game play, in addition to the analysis of MMORG *Club Penguin* (Chapter 3).

Multilingual Gaming

Where children are studying foreign languages, gaming with children abroad who speak the target language may be useful and should be encouraged, within limits, to motivate children to pursue their multilingualism. Online gaming for children who are growing up bilingual or trilingual is an obvious opportunity for multilingual social interaction. Researchers found that Finnish children learn English by repeating the language used by the game characters themselves (Piirainen-Marsh & Tainio, 2009). Many video games also permit young multilingual gamers to select their preferred language; English is not the only language available. So, there are many significant developments still to come in this area, though for the safety of children, it is essential that the identity of unacquainted long-distance gamers be confirmed and checked by caregivers.

Implications: Is Gaming Interactionally Complex but Linguistically Poor?

The glimpses into gaming provided by research so far provides some insights into the kind of language which is used between gamers of various ages, mainly during oral interaction *off-screen* while gaming. Where game actions are the main goal of the interaction, not including additional out of game resources, conversations which occur on the side are linguistically quite simple and limited to specific conversational functions. They may resemble the kind of language occurring in a card game or perhaps sport activity, which occurs at a similarly fast pace, without the physical benefits. Nonetheless, gaming in company rather than alone is both socially valuable and preferred by children (Linderoth et al., 2002). Collaborative gaming is therefore worth supporting in the home as well as at school. Instructions, requests and other linguistic game actions contribute to consolidating relationships and friendships, given the emotional nature of the game experience. Gaming in company is also where ZPD (Vygotsky, 1978) is most likely to occur. According to Sacks (1992), children's social games such as 'Button-button', are 'altogether fundamental to becoming a full-fledged human' (p. 363) and this is true of all games that comprise a social element. Research findings reinforce American Academy of Pediatrics guidelines (Brown et al., 2015), which recommend that parents should play with their children and encourage their social participation when engaging in virtual environments. Even when a single player video game seems particularly well designed to promote creativity and problem-solving, children should be encouraged to play the game with other children to promote interaction and socially oriented learning. Most games these days allow children to engage in collaborative play with other gamers, either in co-present play in the same room or online in different locations, thanks to the availability of in-built text and voice chat. As revealed in Davidson's findings (Davidson, 2010; 2012a; 2012b), even games that are oriented principally towards achieving game goals have the potential to promote ZPD and social and learning activities, when played with others. The restricted nature of off-screen language and the purposely addictive tendency of most games however reinforce the need to ensure that video games use up only a small proportion of children's precious leisure time.

As far as *on-screen* text language is concerned, there is evidence that children have the opportunity to engage in linguistic creativity through specialized game languages (ludolects). However, research so far indicates that this tends to be the domain of older children and adults and further research is required on children's use of ludolects. Another consideration is that in-game language is unique and significantly different from the standard language that children are immersed in when carrying out role-plays, using the internet for research, reading for leisure or during collaborative out-of-game interaction. Out-of-game language, including vocabulary, tends to be similar across games, while in-game vocabulary tends to be specific to a game or group of users. Reading, on the other hand, exposes children to new vocabulary and linguistic structures (see Nippold et al., 2005), which are understandable by all members of a language community.

The reviewed research literature indicates that video game interaction promotes learning behaviours and is important for children's social and academic development when played in company, with time limits, across all ages. Video games should, however, not take too much time away from reading, so a balanced approach is needed. Our society needs to promote addiction to books, including ebooks (see Rohlfing & Müller-Brauers, 2021 on digital reading tools in the early years), rather than video games, given their commercial orientations.

In Summary

- Multiple combinations and configurations of gaming interaction are available to children, but most research studies are focused on co-located collaborative gaming.
- As long as they are played interactively (collaboratively), with caregivers or other children and within time limits, video games have the potential to promote well-being, social development and learning behaviours such as expert-novice orientations, conversational repair, problem-solving, teamwork, advice-giving and ZPD.
- Even single player video games may be played collaboratively and promote learning when children negotiate their gameplay.

- Conversational work during video game interaction is mainly a side activity while the game actions are central interactional elements; in MMORGs, however, text chat interaction is a central activity.
- Despite evidence of the potential benefits of video game interaction, including literacy development, books should take priority over video games in children's leisure time, whether these are in paper or electronic form.
- Further systematic research and guidance is still required on appropriate video games for children of different age groups, developmental stages and reading abilities.
- Language and learning behaviours during interaction are likely to vary according to the game context and expertise of players.
- Ludolects are a creative linguistic expression of in-game, in-group text chat interaction which require further research on younger children's use.
- Response cries and private talk are fundamental components of video game interaction which provide evidence of learning behaviours and enjoyment.
- Swearing may be necessary for older children to build rapport and save face during gaming interaction.
- Depending on the type of game, children's out-of-game language and interaction may have somewhat restricted interactional functions which include directives, advice-giving and positive and negative evaluations.
- Interaction is only one dimension of gaming. There is evidence that relevant online resources which are external to the game promote engagement with lexically sophisticated and structurally complex language.
- Further research attention is required on online voice interaction and gaming between geographically dispersed children.

5   *Minecraft* Interaction

Introduction

This chapter explores children's language and interaction during *Minecraft* play, based on principles developed in previous chapters, particularly Chapter 1 'What Is Talk and Why Do Children Need It?' and Chapter 4 'Video Game Talk'. While children may choose to play *Minecraft* alone, in this chapter we look at collaborative gameplay which involves multiple players, where one uses both voice and text chat and the others text chat only.

This particular game was chosen because it is generally considered to be one of the most collaborative and creative video games for children on the market. So much so, that *Minecraft Education Edition* has been integrated in school curricula (Karsenti, 2019, April 21). And importantly, it is considered socially interactive when played in company, as well as being a popular game with a reported active player base of 141 million by 2021 (Statista, 2022). Unlike games such as FIFA where point-scoring and winning the game are the main objectives, this game involves building digital environments, similar to LEGO. Additionally, survival and progression through levels are optional *Minecraft* objectives in most contexts. It is known as a sandbox game because players are free to create their own three-dimensional virtual environment using available building blocks, with the possibility of choosing between 'easy' and 'hard' mode and offline or online play. Niemeyer and Gerber (2015) note that this game resembles playing in the sand because players construct the game themselves by 'manipulating the world within it' (p. 2). While there are different levels to work through, there are no specific goals to achieve and players are able to explore, modify and interact with the game and other players. In addition to permitting interaction with other players via text or voice chat, this game typically involves construction of virtual buildings, landscapes, robots and animals, mining of ores, creation of avatars for the exploration of caves, defence from zombie and monster attack and other activities.

This chapter first reviews previous studies of *Minecraft* interaction between children and then briefly provides some background on YouTube gaming videos in general and Ethan Gamer YouTube videos specifically. This is followed by analysis of a single episode of public *Minecraft* gaming interaction between multiple players on YouTube and finally by a concluding and in summary section.

Previous Analyses of *Minecraft* Interaction and Related Resources

Wernholm and Vigmo's (2015) evaluation of a data collection tool during children's *Minecraft* gaming interaction on Skype considers the resources that children use when playing the game. Focusing on children's interactions with each other rather than with the game, the analysis draws on Vygotskian developmental theory (1986) and the concepts of object-, other- and self-regulation developed by Thorne (2012) in the context of L2 fan fiction writing. The investigation captures geographically dispersed Swedish children's 'knowledge making dialogues' while interacting on *Minecraft* and identifies three main categories of resources which the children draw upon to play the game, namely, crossing between languages (Swedish and English), previous knowledge and experiences and resources connected to *Minecraft*. For example, creative switching of languages often involves turning English game-related verbs into Swedish forms by using Swedish grammar. The authors also identify instances of ZPD (Vygotsky, 1986), where joint activity leads to gameplay assistance from a more knowledgeable child, which permits them to accomplish more than if they were on their own.

Niemeyer and Gerber's (2015) study instead considers YouTube *Minecraft* video recordings and other game-related resources produced by children and provides evidence that they promote collaboration, sharing, learning and participation in *Minecraft* user communities. Chien's (2019) study of English vocabulary, reviewed in Chapter 4, comes to a similar conclusion, that *Minecraft* activities promote collaboration and problem-solving, but also that combining YouTube *Minecraft* videos and gameplay contributes to the development of advanced vocabulary learning for learners of the English language by providing authentic language input with normal speech rate from native English speakers with different accents, British and American.

On the issue of participation, Donkin's (2017) study documents the adult researcher's first experiences as an avatar on a public *Minecraft* server and the bullying or 'griefing' she experienced at the hands of unknown participants, either children or adults. While the researcher was able to gain support from *Minecraft*-related resources and communities online, these disconcerting episodes suggest that to gain the social and learning benefits associated with *Minecraft* gaming, care needs to be taken in choosing family-friendly *Minecraft* servers or, alternatively, set up private servers for known participants[1].

Pellicone and Ahn's (2018) study examines a fourteen-year-old *Minecraft* player's game-related activities and finds that he interacts with at least three different technologies due to his gamer, YouTuber and server administrator

---

[1] See Taylor et al. (2019) for further details on the risks associated with children's interaction on public *Minecraft* and other game servers.

role. For example, when interacting with the game he would often record the gameplay for his YouTube channel. He also interacted with other game-related resources and used Skype to engage with other players, especially when designing and building servers. The authors identify Skype as the technology that binds all of the activities together as it permits the participant to chat socially and solve problems collaboratively with other players. The Skype conversations were often used as the commentary track of YouTube videos during recordings. The authors see these multiple digital activities as affinity spaces, as described by Gee and Hayes (2012), because they support a shared passion among the participants and promote equity.

In their book-length ethnographic study, Hjorth et al. (2021) document the intergenerational and creative nature of *Minecraft* gameplay from children's perspectives. They consider the intersection of formal and informal learning, given the purported educational affordances of this game. They conclude that use of digital games as pedagogical tools does not automatically render them educational but requires careful planning and consideration of how a specific game can add value in educational contexts, including formal recognition of game activity. The intergenerational nature of gameplay in general is also a finding in Aarsand and Aronsson (2009b), who document gaming between parents and children in public spaces of the home, such as the office or playroom, and the blurring of traditional age hierarchies in this context.

In a study by Danby et al. (2018a) where the focus is on gaming interaction between children, the authors also examine *Minecraft* specifically. The detailed conversation analysis finds that two siblings aged respectively four and seven years, playing on their own Ipad on the sofa, monitor each other's actions on their screens and jointly tackle a shared problem. In particular, the younger child's instructional work towards his sister provides guidance which is supported by his actions on screen. The authors conclude that both players use the strategies of collaboration and instruction to achieve the objective of the game, that is, destruction of intruders.

In summary, the *Minecraft* research reviewed suggests that interaction between children or across age groups in various settings may promote collaboration, linguistic creativity across languages, learning and ZPD, as well as creating affinity spaces. However, private *Minecraft* servers are to be preferred over public ones for social and safety reasons.

YouTube and Ethan Gamer Gaming Videos

As noted by Thorne et al. (2012), gamers do not just play video games, they also engage with game-related resources that are available on the internet, including watching other gamers' play. Reasons for video gamers' viewing of other YouTube stars' gaming vary but include entertainment, vicarious gameplay when viewers do not have their own game, finding out more about a game prior to purchase, and learning how to improve gameplay (McCormick, 2014, August 26). YouTube is not the only resource for this type of activity, as *Twitch TV* (www.twitch.tv/) is also popular with gamers for livestreaming and viewing video gameplay (Recktenwald, 2017). According to Gandolfi (2016), one of the reasons livestreams are attractive to gamers is the exhibition of player skill, combined with talk, as is the case with celebrity gamers playing *Minecraft* and other games. There are in fact some parallels between *Twitch TV* and YouTube gameplay, however, *Twitch TV*'s broadcasts are in real time whereas YouTube videos are recorded prior to broadcast and made available to public viewers.

Judging by the number of views of the gaming episode chosen for this chapter (EthanGamer, 2019, May 28), Ethan Gamer and his publicly available gaming activities are very popular with other *Minecraft* gamers, with 4,213,667 views (as at September 28, 2022). Furthermore, he has around three million subscribers at time of writing. Ethan Gamer is a pseudonym for a popular young British gamer, born in 2006, who set up a YouTube channel where he presents recordings of himself playing video games. His YouTube videos were recorded at different times of his life, from age seven onwards and are intended to attract viewers who are mainly of the age group for which *Minecraft* is officially rated, namely seven to thirteen years (Wikitubia Fandom, 2013, August 28).

The specific YouTube video analysed in this chapter (EthanGamer, 2019, May 28) commences with a brief segment of gameplay on Ethan Gamer's computer screen, where his avatar, a piece of chocolate, is being attacked by a polar bear. This segment is in fact repeated later in the video, as it is part of the longer video recording of gameplay which occurs after Ethan Gamer's presentation. By the tenth second, the camera's attention shifts briefly to Ethan Gamer himself at the computer with headphones, where he introduces and invites viewers into his new fan's world, to celebrate the ten-year anniversary of *Minecraft*. Game participants, led by Ethan Gamer, then proceed to complete building work on a pre-existing, software-generated *Minecraft* world, using available game resources. Building work occurs while encountering a variety of aggressive and unaggressive animals which are generated by the software. Collaboration between participants entails numerous game actions which include providing assistance with a variety of situations, objects and other resources which permit the game to proceed. This assistance is often requested or mentioned in the chat interaction if it is not self-evident from game actions. One of participants' first collective objectives is the building of a base, which is an important element of gamers' *Minecraft* world. Specifically, the base is a refuge for gamers' avatars and materials required to build the game world. Ethan Gamer also initiates the creation of a craft table, which is required for building to occur.

Analysis of a Single Episode of *Minecraft*

The primary data source for the analysis in this chapter is focused on one publicly available, thirty-one minute videorecorded episode of gaming between YouTube star Ethan Gamer and his fans (EthanGamer, 2019, May 28). The microanalysis of a single episode (see Schegloff, 1987) conducted in this chapter draws attention to the interactional complexities of multi-party gaming that are evident during a public YouTube video between chat participants and gaming celebrity Ethan Gamer. It allows readers to gain insights into how children may accomplish online language and interaction during gaming. In this episode Ethan Gamer uses mainly voice, with some text chat, while other participants use only text chat to communicate. Ethan Gamer himself appears only briefly, once at the start and again at the end of the video. Hence, only game participants' text chat and Ethan Gamer's voice turns are the focus of this chapter. While this analysis is not representative of a wide range of *Minecraft* gamers' linguistic and interactional work, it nonetheless provides a detailed microanalytical snapshot of how geographically dispersed children use text chat to pursue social and game objectives during *Minecraft* play. This requires attention to how participants talk, post by post using text chat and turn by turn using voice chat (Ethan Gamer only), with the interactional resources that are available within each medium. The examples discussed in this chapter were selected because they occur within a complete gaming session which presents both text and voice chat interaction, together with gaming actions.

The analysis seeks evidence of linguistic, interactional and learning behaviours which have previously been identified in reviewed research on gaming. The context is an unexplored online gaming environment involving geographically dispersed young participants interacting in text chat while gaming. Single case analysis respects a basic premise of conversation analysis that talk is context-shaped as well as context-renewing (Seedhouse, 2005, p. 166). As Schegloff (1987) notes, 'social action done through talk is organized and orderly not, or not only, as a matter of rule or as a statistical regularity, but on a case by case, action by action, basis' (p. 102). Analysis of this single episode in fact reveals that scaffolding and ZPD are recurrent features of the chat exchange as participants engage in gaming on *Minecraft*. This is possible despite the constrained environment, where gamers complete game actions and text chat under pressure. The content creator is under additional pressure as he juggles gaming, voice narration and text chat with gaming participants. Hence, the presence of such features of interaction and learning in this specific episode demonstrates potential for them to occur in other similar contexts, as well as confirming previous research on *Minecraft* interaction.

Audience of the Gaming Video and Interactions

The video game context examined in this chapter is quite different from contexts discussed in Chapter 4, where most research focuses on gameplay between co-located rather than geographically dispersed gamers. Additionally, participants in the selected game context become aware of the public nature of their gaming with Ethan Gamer; hence, there is an audience beyond the group of game participants. Another distinctive interactional element of this context is that participants rely predominantly on text chat to communicate with each other and Ethan Gamer, as they do not have access to Ethan Gamer's voice. Given the reliance on text chat, the analysis therefore pays attention mainly to conversational resources that might be deployed by chat participants to assist them in understanding interaction and promote the achievement of game objectives. Naming of intended addressees and conversational repair are two such resources which are available to participants in chat environments and are therefore considered in the analysis.

Evidence of ZPD and Collaborative Learning in Interaction

Where learning behaviours are concerned, this chapter seeks evidence that ZPD (Vygotsky, 1986) and collaborative learning are promoted in the chat interactions. Such evidence would include expert-novice orientations, conversational repair, problem-solving, teamwork, advice-giving, instructions and scaffolding related to the game. Extracts from the gaming session were therefore selected where such evidence is made relevant by participants in their talk. This will assist us in gaining an understanding of the collaborative learning potential of gaming sessions such as these for children. While the analysis is focused on a small group of participants, including at least one very capable young gamer and presenter, some insights should be visible in the text interactions with other *Minecraft* gamers.

Transcription and Perspective

Prior to the selection of examples for this chapter, voice and text chat of the analysed *Minecraft* gaming episode interactions were transcribed by a professional transcription service using the Jeffersonian transcription system.[2] The author then reviewed the transcription, checking accuracy and

---

[2] See details of the guide to the symbols used here: www.universitytranscriptions.co.uk/jefferson-transcription-system-a-guide-to-the-symbols/. On a few occasions chat did not come up on the screen, then it all came up at once when Ethan was typing; hence, timing of chat in these instances is approximate. Chat contributions are referred to as 'posts' and voice contributions as 'turns'. To protect participants' anonymity, time stamps are not reproduced in this chapter. Game screenshots are not available for the same reasons and for copyright reasons, given that in any case the

making any required adjustments prior to selection and reproduction of the examples in this chapter. All posts from the chat conversation were de-identified and copied verbatim, retaining any original linguistic errors and non-standard language. Text chat is presented in sequence in italics with Ethan Gamer's voice talk in normal script. During Ethan Gamer's co-ordination of voice and text chat, voice turns and chat posts may overlap during interaction, so the [] symbol indicates overlap when it occurs. The examples may also include the analyst's description of game actions and comments relevant to the ongoing chat and/or talk within double brackets ((. . .)). While time stamps have been recorded in the transcript to inform the analysis, they are publicly available and have therefore not been reproduced in this chapter to protect game participants' anonymity. The perspective of the gaming session is that of the YouTube audience. However, it should be noted that in real time, chat participants have only the perspective of the text chat interaction and the game on their console. Hence, from their perspective their chat posts would appear in sequence without access to Ethan Gamer's voice.

Game Participants' Interaction Modes

In the focus episode for this chapter, there are eight participants in total, including Ethan Gamer. There are an additional two participants who are not included in the count as they join the game late, in the twenty-ninth minute, though the total duration of the video is thirty-one minutes. Hence, only seven chat participants are actively playing *Minecraft* and chatting with Ethan Gamer throughout. Ethan Gamer uses voice talk to communicate with public viewers of the game on YouTube. However, he does not use voice chat with in-game participants, only text chat, though he frequently vocalizes the chat for public viewers of the game, as in Example 5.1.

> Example 5.1
>
> 1 Ethan: Er: sorry ah::: (1.2)
> 2 Ethan: *Sorry, i cant voice chat*
> 3 Ethan ((typing)) sorry <I:::m ca::n't voice chat,>
>   (0.5)

This apology is a negative reply (refusal) to a chat invitation for all participants to 'get into a party', which would allow multi-party voice or text chat through video game console or other softwares, including telephone. The apology 'sorry' is repeated three times, including in text chat (in italics). It also includes a justification for the refusal '*i cant voice chat*'. This justification may be for

full video recording is publicly available to readers on the YouTube website (EthanGamer, 2019, May 28).

technical or other reasons – Ethan Gamer does not specify – and the conversation returns to discussing participants' game actions, which is the main topic of interaction in the video.

Chat participants, who are also Ethan Gamer's gaming partners, cannot hear Ethan Gamer's voice during real time gameplay; hence, Ethan Gamer often needs to use chat to communicate with them. Game participants use the *Minecraft* chat tool in this context. The total number of text chat posts of chat participants in this episode is approximately 175, not including system posts or inaccessible chat posts. Ethan Gamer's voice turns instead number 636. Many of these voice turns, however, consist of Ethan Gamer voicing the text chat posts as he reads them. Of the 175 text chat posts, Ethan Gamer's total 46, with fans posting around 129 of them. The fact that Ethan Gamer's voice turns are more numerous than his fans' text chat posts, from the perspective of the videorecording audience, suggests that Ethan Gamer is in control both of game interaction and video content, which is unsurprising given his role as YouTube content creator. This role requires him to record the screen of his device to publicly display gameplay and chat interaction with fans while broadcasting his own voice narrative to the public. To some extent there are also technical considerations which explain the larger number of voice turns compared to chat posts, namely, the faster pace and ease of delivery of voice turns when compared with text chat posts, which are delayed due to the writing process required to construct a post. Thus, chat posts are delivered quasi-synchronously, whereas Ethan Gamer's voice turns are delivered in real time. Co-ordination of voice talk with text chat and game actions is interactionally complex and highlights the constraints of the context being examined. It is possible to summarize how interaction is structured in the specific YouTube gaming context examined in this chapter (see Table 5.1).

Game actions are a key component of the interactional structure, as interaction revolves principally around these. Ethan Gamer and chat participants have 'active' access and the YouTube viewing audience (including the analyst) have 'passive' access to game actions. Ethan Gamer juggles his voice narrative between the audience and chat participants, who are also present as avatars in the game. His text chat interaction is directed to chat participants only, though he would be aware that the public viewing audience will eventually be seeing most of this as well, once the recording is published on YouTube. Chat participants too become aware of the 'vid' recording of the game for public view, as will be discussed in greater detail below.

Social Talk

In this section we identify social talk between Ethan Gamer and chat participants. Social talk is defined here as talk between participants which is not

Table 5.1 *Public video game talk-in-interaction modes, configurations, and combinations*

	Spoken interactions	Written interactions	Game actions
Communication mode	Virtual long-distance voice via out-of-game recording software	Virtual written long-distance text chat	Hands/keyboard/gaming software
Participants	Ethan Gamer	Multiple geographically dispersed players, including Ethan Gamer, in real time	Ethan Gamer and chat participants as avatars
Audience	1 Public YouTube audience 2 Chat participants viewing YouTube video asynchronously 3 Game avatars through Ethan Gamer's role-play talk	1 Game/chat participants in real time 2 Public YouTube audience asynchronously.	1 Gamers access chat and game 2 Public audience accesses video of game, Ethan Gamer's voice narrative (no active game access but may choose to actively participate in YouTube comments)

specifically related to game actions under way. As indicated in Chapter 4, previous research on talk between participants who are playing a video game in the same location indicates that interaction during a video game is mainly a side activity while the game actions are central interactional elements (Mondada, 2012). We examine the 'side activities' occurring mainly in text chat, however, within these activities, the analysis differentiates between social talk and talk which specifically facilitates gameplay relating to the game-in-progress. Specifically, the main forms of social talk identified in text chat entail greetings, positive evaluations and requests for information which are not directly relevant to the gameplay under way. Response cries, defined by Aarsand and Aronsson (2009a) as public displays of emotion such as 'self-talk, imprecations and audible surprise' (p. 1557), also feature in participants' language and interaction in both social and game-related talk, as will become evident in the analysis. Furthermore, they are more frequent in Ethan Gamer's voice talk than in chat, probably because they are more spontaneous and less time-consuming to articulate using voice rather than writing. Expressions of emotion such as response cries are also likely to be considered entertaining by viewers.

Greetings

The main protagonist of the *Minecraft* game analysed in this chapter is of course the content creator Ethan Gamer. He deploys prosocial conversational actions such as greetings, often combined with smiley emoticons. In Example 5.2 Ethan Gamer responds to User E's greeting both by text chat and voice. In both Examples 5.2 and 5.3, in fact, Ethan appears to welcome the arrival of User E with a greeting when he joins the game.

> Example 5.2[3]
>
> [User E joined the game]
> [Software instructions: Press T, RETURN or controller-D Pad right to open chat]
>   (2.0)
> 1 Ethan: *HEY! :D*
> 2 Ethan: ↑Hi:::_

In Example 2, User E is one of the first users to join the game and the software provides instructions on how to access text chat. Ethan greets him with a text greeting combined with a big smiley emoticon and then a voice greeting. The latter is audible only to himself and viewers. User E responds to Ethan shortly after and greets him using text chat, as shown in Example 5.3.

> Example 5.3
>
> 1 User E: *hi ethan!*
> 2 Ethan: *Hey! :D*
> 3 Ethan: Hey (double) hey?

User E's greeting specifically names Ethan and receives a greeting 'Hey!' from Ethan, combined with a smiley emoticon ':D'. His repetition of the same greeting by voice, for the video audience, signals his awareness that the greeting is being completed twice as suggested when he qualifies his greeting as a 'double hey' with rising intonation, which suggests initiation of repair, for the video audience only.

In Example 5.4, the affiliative greeting sequence between User C and Ethan consists almost entirely of emoticons.

> Example 5.4
>
> 1 User C: *big xd*
> 2 Ethan: *xD*

---

[3] Where game participants' nicknames indicate a gender as a component of the name, relevant gendered pronouns are used in the analysis for clarity. Only three participants' names comprise a male component, namely, Users C, F and G. It was therefore necessary to rely on participants' own use of pronouns to adopt the correct ones. While a decision was made to adopt feminine pronouns where gender was unclear, it became clear from the interactions that all participants were male. An attempt was made to adopt the neutral 'they', as this is more inclusive, however it was discarded because it was found to impede understanding of the analysis.

User C proffers the '*xd*' emoticon to represent laughter with squinting eyes. Ethan responds with the same emoticon; however, it features a capital rather than small D, which does not alter the meaning, based on responses of interlocutors. This exchange shows from the start that Ethan uses chat to engage with other gamers despite being occupied with the game and a public audience. This engagement with gamers through affiliative chat and game actions promotes a prosocial gaming environment for participants.

There is also evidence of virtual in-game greetings, as in Example 5.5, when Ethan Gamer's chocolate avatar approaches User E's avatar.

Example 5.5

((User E's avatar is in close proximity and facing Ethan's chocolate avatar))
1 Ethan: Hi:.
　　↑↑huh huh↑↑
(0.5)
2 Ethan: Do::n't judge me h .hh just cus I'm a piece of chocolate_

In this case Ethan's voice greeting is for the audience rather than User E, who cannot hear him in real time. However, he is voicing the greeting as part of his in-game virtual approach to User E. Hence, his actions in proximity to User E's avatar are playful and a type of in-game greeting, similar to children roleplaying with dolls. The playfulness is reinforced by his accompanying laughter tokens and continues in post 2, where he suggests that User E is judging him for his 'chocolate' appearance.

Positive Evaluations

Ethan Gamer frequently voices positive evaluations of the game and other gamers as part of his narrative both to himself and viewers. Regular positive evaluations by gamers through text chat are also present and contribute to a prosocial environment. One of the first positive evaluations is deployed by User E.

Example 5.6

1 User E: *all hail the king Ethan!*
2 Ethan: He::y.
(0.5)
3 Ethan: ↓↓Who's up for ay- all-all hai::l the £ki:ngy£-
　　　　　(0.2)
4: User C: *YAS*

In post 1 User E implies that Ethan is a 'king' as '*all hail the king*' was once used to greet and acclaim English kings. In this case it consists of an indirect positive evaluation in the form of a request that other gamers pay homage to Ethan. It thus expresses a positive assessment of Ethan with 'king' as a metaphor, which implies that he is a superior gamer. User C expresses agreement in post 4 '*YAS*' which is a colloquial, emphatic modification of 'Yes'.

Similarly, in Example 5.7 User C provides a positive evaluation of Ethan's gaming.

Example 5.7
1 User C: *he a pro player*
2 User F: *Creepper got me*

User C omits the verb in this evaluation of Ethan as a good player, which is a grammatical feature of African American dialect (Washington, 2023). This could be accidental, due to the need to type quickly while playing the game at the same time. However, popular music has influenced young people's use of African American dialect and this is possibly reflected in the language of User C in this instance. The use of '*pro*' is a commonly used, informal truncated version of 'professional'. There is no response to this evaluation as users subsequently prioritise chat regarding the game-in-progress in post 2 ('*Creepper got me*').

The 'king' metaphor is picked up on another occasion, in the form of a command.

Example 5.8
1 User D: *MAKE ETHAN A THRONE NOW!!!!!*
        (0.2)
2 Ethan: "Make Ethan a thro::ne NO:W."
        (1.0)
[User A has changed from James skin to Minecrat Squid skin]
3 User A: *ok*
4 Ethan: Guys you don't need to make me a throne you know °it's-it's fine.°

In Example 8, post 1, user D emphatically requests that other users make Ethan a throne, with the final '*NOW!!!*' in 'shouted' capitals and exclamations, which suggests urgency and possibly excitement. This comment is again a metaphorical reference to Ethan Gamer's gaming ability in response to his gameplay under way, as thrones are associated with royalty. User A agrees to User D's request in post 3 '*ok*'. In the meantime, Ethan vocalizes the chat request for viewers and politely discourages participants from making a throne, though they are unable to hear him in real time. There are many examples, not repro-duced in full due to lack of space, of chat participants' use of terms related to aristocracy or even religious figures, to positively evaluate Ethan, such as 'Ethan equals savior' and 'ALL HAIL LORD ETHAN' which are not necessarily noted by Ethan in either chat or voice interaction. Game participants also regularly evaluate Ethan using superlatives, for example, 'You're the best Ethan' and similar statements, to which they often receive affiliative replies, including smiley emoticons (not reproduced here). The implications of sequences regarding Ethan's 'superior' gaming ability are that participants' talk positions him as an expert and themselves as novices in comparison. These evaluations imply that gaming with Ethan provides opportunities for game-related learning.

Evaluations may also be deployed by Ethan when users request that he evaluate other celebrity gamers during the game. However, in Example 5.9, Ethan only provides a voice rather than chat evaluation.

Example 5.9

→1 User A: *Ethan do you still think DanTDM Is the best yter?*
2 User E: *i'm so exited*
3 Ethan: Wait (0.5) "Ethan do you <u>still</u> think Dan>TDM< is the best YT ever."
.hhh
4 Ethan: Best You choob ever.
(0.2)
5 Ethan: I mean <u>I</u>: like <u>lots</u> of You choobers so:: it's hard to choo::se?
(0.5)
6 Ethan: But Da:n is (0.5) no he's great he's awesome.
(0.5)
→7 Ethan: But it <u>is</u> pretty hard to choose (0.5) so:: (1.0) er::m >oright<
let's see::.

Ethan expresses his difficulty in choosing one particular YouTuber, however, his evaluation of the named celebrity is positive and abounds in superlatives 'Best You choob ever', 'he's great he's awesome'. In the final segment of post 7 he transitions to closing the social talk sequence about the celebrity gamer to return to talk about the game. He achieves this by implicating closure using words such as 'so', 'oright' and 'let's see'. According to Liddicoat (2021), turns such as these work to close down a topic, in this case evaluation of the celebrity gamer, and prepare the way for another action. However, this conversational work is for viewers' ears only, as no response has been provided to User A and other chatters using text chat. Therefore, later in the conversation, the same user (A) repeats the request twice, thus initiating repair of the first request. This is necessary because Ethan's response is by voice; hence, chat participants do not receive the response. The full sequence is visible in Example 5.10.

Example 5.10

→1 User A: *Opinion on DanTDM?*
2 Ethan: >I need to< pick that.
→ 3 Ethan: .h ((reads post from User A)) "Opinion on
Dan>TDM<."
→ 4 Ethan: <u>Cool</u> per:son.
(1.0)

→ 5 Ethan: Nuff said.
             (0.5)
→ 6 Ethan: He's coo:l (.) he's a good <u>You</u>>Chuber<.
             (0.5)
7 Ethan: No::w the:n ((singsong voice)) I don't know
             how I'm gonna get out of her:::e,
             (2.2)
8 Ethan: Hi_
9 Ethan: Oh wow.
10 Ethan: .hh O:kay now we have <<u>six</u> st:one,>
             (0.5)
→11 User A:*??*
12 Ethan: (↑Please ↓sir.)
             (0.7)
→13 Ethan: Cool_
14 Ethan: Wait-
             (3.0)
→15 Ethan: *He's a cool guy*
             [User D hit the ground too hard]
→16 User A:*You met him a few times*
→17 Ethan: >He's a cool< guy.
             (1.2)
→ 18 Ethan: >↑↑That's ↓enough that really needs to be
             said<=he's cool.

Example 5.10 shows an interspersing of social and game talk, as most of Ethan's positive evaluations of the celebrity gamer are deployed using voice while he is gaming. User A posts his evaluation requests on the celebrity gamer in post 1 '*Opinion on DanTDM?*' and post 11 '*??*'. While these are separate posts, they are adjacent in chat, which is the only conversation that chat participants have access to in real time. Post 11 does, however, appear to be posted quite a while later, after eighteen seconds according to the time stamp (not reproduced). This is a significant amount of time later and indicates that users are engaged in gaming between posts and that post 11 is a repair initiation of post 1. This repair occurs because Ethan does not provide a chat response. Ethan's chat response to User A is finally provided at post 15, which resolves the repair.

Within his voice narrative, in Example 5.10, Ethan very capably deploys conversational actions at turns 5 and 18 which imply that no further talk is required on the matter of the celebrity gamer, who is evaluated as 'cool'. He uses the adjective 'cool' on six occasions (4, 6, 13, 15, 17, 18), including once in text chat at post 15. Turns 5 'Nuff said' and 18 '>↑↑That's ↓enough that really needs to be said<=he's cool' have two functions, firstly, as components of Ethan's positive evaluation of the celebrity gamer, and secondly, as an interactional device which attempts to close the conversation on this topic.

The faster tempo and higher pitch with which turn 18 is delivered also suggests that the celebrity's 'coolness' is indisputable. This voice narrative is accessible to viewers but not to chat participants, unless they view the YouTube video recording online. It illustrates the importance placed by successful YouTube celebrities on positive evaluations in this context. One likely effect is that they model prosocial affiliative behaviours between gamers, gaming celebrities and the viewing public. Furthermore, the repair episode within this evaluation sequence indicates that repair is a key interactional resource for game users in a context where juggling game actions, voice chat and text chat disrupt and constrain interaction, which in this case is social. In particular, Ethan's talk addresses two main groups of interlocutors, the public (invisible) YouTube audience, whom he addresses using voice, and gamers who are addressed using chat. In-game actions are also an integral component of this interaction, which are visible to both the YouTube audience and other gamers. For this reason, repair is an important interactional resource for gamers to achieve understanding and pursue social and game actions, to be discussed further in the section entitled 'Promoting Understanding'.

The prevalence of prosocial behaviours is clear when Ethan evaluates his gaming partners' in-game actions. Example 5.11 is one instance among many.

> Example 5.11
>
> ((User F's avatar hovers above Ethan's avatar))
> 1 Ethan: There we go::- .h oh you s::ca::red me.
>   User A *bows*
> 2 Ethan: .hhh hih hih °↑↑That's so coo::l.°
>   (1.0)
> →3 Ethan: *That's so cool!*
> 4 Ethan: I actually thought there was a ↓(wiber) there.
>   (1.5)
> 5 Ethan: h h Make a base that spells out Ethan.
>   (0.2)
> 6 Sma::rt person.
> ↑↑h huh huh↑↑
> 7 That's a brilliant idea.
> (.)
> 8 User D: *EVERYONE FOLLOW ME TO BASE LOCATION*
>   (0.5)
> 9 Ethan: ((mock tour guide voice)) Everyone follow me::: to base location.
> →10 User F: *Ty*

As with the celebrity gamer episodes discussed previously, Ethan uses the adjective 'cool' to evaluate a surprising in-game action by User F (post 3). On this occasion he ensures the evaluation reaches his gaming partners by using chat, as well as voice, to communicate. User F expresses his appreciation '*Ty*' meaning 'thank you' to Ethan (post 10). While this post appears in chat two posts after the positive evaluation, it appears on the YouTube video screen thirteen seconds later, based on the time stamp, after an intervening voice and gaming sequence, including one chat post (post 8). This delay in chat posts from a temporal perspective may be due to the need for chat participants to attend to two tasks at the same time, that is, gaming and chatting, which both require use of hands and keyboard.

Ethan also provides positive evaluations and expressions of appreciation of game participants when they provide assistance in the game, as in Example 5.12.

> Example 5.12
> →1 Ethan: ((typing)) <"You guys are (1.2) legends.">
> →2 Ethan: *You guys are legends :D*
> →3 Ethan: >You guys are< legends_
>   (0.7)
> 4 User C: *there you go ethan*
> 5 Ethan: .hh There you go Ethan_
> 6 Ethan: ↓Oright <let's no::t ↓di::e.>
>   (4.2)
> →7 User C: *np! Anything for ya ethan*
> →8 User A: *Ty*
> 9 User D: *Lets a wide mine so we all can*

After chat participants create a mine for Ethan, he deploys a positive evaluation ('*you guys are legends*') in text chat (post 2), suggesting that they are heroic ('legends'), to express his appreciation of participants' game actions. This evaluation is vocalized twice, once while typing the chat post (post 1) and repeated once it is posted, as if to reinforce his point (turn 3). User C's chat response (post 7) '*np! Anything for ya ethan*', where 'np' is an acronym for 'no problem', acknowledges Ethan's positive evaluation. This post is an appropriate response, an acceptance of the compliment (Pomerantz, 1978). User A instead expresses appreciation for his positive evaluation in post 8 '*Ty*', which is also a common response that denotes acceptance of positive evaluations (Pomerantz, 1978). User D's post 9 then returns the chat to talk about the game.

There is only one instance of a negative evaluation by game participant User E, regarding his own gaming skills, in Example 5.13.

> Example 5.13
> →1 User E: *i'm just gonna say that I am bad at Minecraft*
> →2 User A: *Lol*
> 3 Ethan: mm mm mm mm hah hah hah hah hah hah hah hah .hhhh ↑↑↑oh my gosh↑↑↑
> 4 Ethan: this is brill_
> 5 Ethan: This is incredible ↓oh:::.
>   (1.0)

6 User B: *Iv got 2*
→7 User C: *nah its all good yo*

User E's self-deprecating comment that he is '*bad at Minecraft*' receives a first response from User A '*Lol*' which expresses laughter in post 2. Ethan's subsequent three voice turns (3–5) ignore the chat interaction as they express enthusiasm for game actions under way. Then in post 7 User C expresses disagreement ('*nah*') with User E's negative self-evaluation, which is the preferred response to self-deprecation according to Pomerantz (1978). This is followed by '*it's all good yo*' in post 7, which suggests that everything is fine. This component of post 7 is also an appropriate response to User E's negative self-evaluation in post 1, as it expresses reassurance that the situation (his gaming) is not as bad as he thinks. On examination of game actions prior to User E's post, there is no evidence of any error on his part, only that he was unable to provide birch when Ethan Gamer calls for assistance in chat. It is therefore possible that User E thus produced the negative self-evaluation due to his inability to provide assistance. As in other instances, User C's use of 'yo', the final element of post 7, from African American English, indicates that this language is common among young gamers. In this instance, 'yo' is most likely an interjection which seeks to gain the other user's attention. Furthermore, it might provide added emphasis to the encouraging remark in post 7. User C's supportive response towards User E is a further contribution to the prosocial environment created by gamers in this context.

To summarize, greetings and evaluations occur frequently both in Ethan's voice talk and in participants' text chat. While game participants deploy mainly positive evaluations towards Ethan and his in-game actions, Ethan reciprocates by providing positive evaluations of game participants and their in-game actions. When prompted, Ethan may also deploy positive evaluations of third-party celebrities who are not participating in the game. These interactional behaviours are affiliative and prosocial. They thus contribute to a supportive gaming environment for both real time participants and asynchronous YouTube video audiences. Participant evaluations of Ethan's gaming ability using metaphors related to royalty position him as expert and them as novices, as they suggest his superior ability. This in turn suggests that, according to participants, this relationship provides potential for learning about the game, though Ethan frequently reciprocates with positive evaluations of other gamers' abilities.

Information Requests

Most requests for information in the social category are in the form of a question. These are different from requests in the form of directives discussed by Mondada (2012) and which relate to game actions. Example 5.14 presents one of the gamers' first information requests regarding whether the game is being recorded. This appears to be important information to gamers, as others repeat the same question later in the chat.

Example 5.14

1 User F: *Yeah and hey ethan*
→2 User D: *Is this a vid*
3 User G: *hello*
→4 Ethan: Le::t's go- is this a vi:d.
        (0.5)
→5 Ethan: ↓↓Ma:::ybe?
        (0.5)
6 Ethan: ↑Hi I did-
→7 Ethan: *Maaaaaybe*
→8 Ethan: *xD*
        (3.0)
→9 User E: *omg*

User D's question in post 2 occurs between other users' greetings, at the start of the gaming session. Possibly for the benefit of YouTube audiences, Ethan voices User D's question in post 4, after a directive 'Le::t's go' designed to encourage commencement of play. He then responds to the question ambiguously rather than affirmatively ('↓↓Ma:::ybe?'), with rising intonation, using voice (turn 5). He posts the same response in chat (post 7), followed by a squinting eyes smile emoticon in post 8, which adds an element of playfulness to the ambiguous response. Both these responses suggest that video recording, which implies a public airing, is highly likely. User E's subsequent interjection '*omg*' (post 9) suggests excitement at the prospect of being recorded and going public. In this case the interjection is more likely to be socially rather than game-oriented as it is part of the conversation regarding the video.

In Example 5.15, User B later also requests information on whether the game is being recorded.

Example 5.15

→1 User B: *Is this a vid*
→2 Ethan: *xD*
3 User C: *Hello Ethan!*
4 User A: *Eyy*

Requesting information about the status of the game, that is, whether it is being recorded, appears to be part of the gaming session's opening chat sequence. Ethan's chat response to User B's question (post 2) consists only of an ambiguous squinting eyes big smile emoticon and is thus playful, as in

Example 5.14. User A shortly after also seeks confirmation that the session is being recorded.

> Example 5.16
> →1 User A: *Ethan ru actually Recordin?*
> 2 Ethan: >I need my stuff.<
> 3 Ethan: I don't care about the sapling_
> 4 User C: *OOF*

User A receives no response to his question regarding video recording of the gaming session because at this point talk is focused mainly on in-game actions. These actions also comprise a game-related response cry '*OOF*'.

Further requests for information in the question format relate to Ethan's public activities on open *Minecraft* servers.

> Example 5.17
> →1 User A: *Ethan will you be doing open lobbys often?*
>   (4.0)
> →2 Ethan: er:::r Ethan >will you< be doing open
>   lobbies often.
>   (0.5)
> 3 Ethan: .h YES HOPEfully (0.7) I will.
> 4 Ethan: I would love like- litchrully ha- since I've
>   gotten back into Mine↑craft (0.5) ↓I've
>   absolutely loved it.
> 5 Ethan: It's been amazing.
> →6 User A: *??*

User A's question at post 1 is vocalized by Ethan at post 2 and then an appropriate response provided in posts 3 to 6, which includes positive evaluations of *Minecraft*. However, he does not provide a response in chat and User A does not have access to the voice response in real time. So he initiates repair at post 6 ('*??*'). This repair is unresolved, as gaming talk resumes.

To summarize, social requests for information are consistently deployed by game participants to Ethan in a question format. The topics are variable and may relate to video recording of the game or Ethan's activities outside the game in progress. These requests provide Ethan with the opportunity for playful chat interaction using emoticons and other linguistic devices or to engage in positive evaluations of *Minecraft* for his YouTube audiences.

Getting Acquainted

As might be expected, there is minimal social talk which allows game participants to get acquainted, as would occur in a predominantly social chat setting (cf. Strambi & Tudini, 2020; Tudini & Strambi, 2017). However, it is worth discussing why this might be the case from an interactional perspective. If we start with the only example of 'getting acquainted' talk identified in the data (Example 5.18), we can see that this exchange occurs towards the end of the session.

> Example 5.18
>
> 1 User A: *Where's everyone from?*
> 2 Ethan: ((Reads User A's post)) "Where's everyone <u>fro:m</u>."
>   (1.7)
> 3 Ethan: <u>Ing</u>land ((typing)),
> 4 Ethan: England
>   (1.2)
> 5 Ethan::*D*
> 6 User A: *Same*
> 7 User E: *Brazil*
> 8 User A: *Manchester*
> 9 Ethan: Look I'm >making< a chew on the feet.

User A initiates this exchange in post 1, addressing 'everyone' rather than a specific participant. The question about other participants' background confirms that game participants are most likely unacquainted. Ethan responds to the question a few posts later in chat (post 4), after voicing the question (post 2) and his response (post 3), possibly for the audience's benefit. His response is followed by a big smile emoticon in post 5, which reinforces his willingness to engage in social talk which is unrelated to the game. User A responds in post 6 by revealing that he too is from England ('*Same*'). User E also replies to User A's question by revealing that he is from Brazil (post 7). User A subsequently provides additional details about the city he is from (Manchester) in post 8. Ethan's voice talk (post 9) returns the conversation to game-related interaction.

This interlude from gaming talk, where participants engage in 'getting to know you' behaviours is only brief and occurs late in the video. While additional gaming sessions would need to be examined, this sequence does, however, confirm that even brief, unacquainted children's gaming sessions may lead to attempts at social connectivity between participants where interactional constraints permit. Thanks to the availability of text chat, game participants may attempt to get to know one another after spending time engaged in gameplay, but this is also achievable at other moments in the session. The fact that there is minimal interpersonal talk until this point confirms that the priority for participants is gaming, as in Mondada's (2012) research, where a significant proportion of interactions revolve around game actions. The concluding interpersonal interactions are most likely promoted by the supportive prosocial nature of interaction between game participants, especially Ethan, in this specific context.

Promoting Understanding

As noted earlier, repair is one conversational resource which is deployed by game participants to ensure that text chat participants, including Ethan, understand each other. Repair is especially necessary in this context, where interaction is constrained by a variety of factors. These include the constraint of engaging in fast moving gameplay while simultaneously posting text chat messages. In the case of the content creator, Ethan, there is the additional constraint of simultaneously narrating out loud for the video audience's benefit, which, however, is facilitated by the use of voice rather than hands.

Selected repair sequences presented here display both social and game-in-progress orientations. Repair episodes occur mainly where Ethan responds to questions using voice rather than text chat, as participants do not have access to his voice. Two such episodes discussed above are initiated by the same game participant (User A). They occur within evaluation and information request sequences (Examples 5.5, 5.10 and 5.17 above) and are resolved by Ethan in chat. The same game participant, User A, again initiates repair as part of a request for information. This time the request concerns another Ethan Gamer YouTube video on a different game.

> Example 5.19
>
> →1 User A: *ethan will you bring back gang beasts.exe?xD*
> 2 User E: *ethan I wnna be ur friend on roblox*
> 3 User F: *Anyone have foid?* [food intended]
> →4 Ethan: ((Reads User A's post)) Er "Ethan will you bring back GANG Beasts."
> →5 Ethan: .hhhh I:: would like >to do some more movies and Bang Beasts_<
>   (0.2)
> →6 Ethan: But with fre::nds would be great.
>   (0.2)
> →7 Ethan: Or >we could< just do it on my own.
> →8 Ethan: Or with ↑fa::ns.
>   (0.7)
> →9 Ethan: Da- >da- well da will< da won't wor::k=I don't no.
>   (0.5)
> →10 Ethan: >Either way< it's good to try things out_
>   (0.2)
> 11 Ethan: Er so we need one piece of iyurn.
>   (0.7)

In post 1 User A poses an information seeking question, naming Ethan specifically, regarding previous YouTube videos where Ethan plays *Gang Beasts* gaming software (post 1). Ethan acknowledges and replies to the question but again only through voice rather than text chat (turns 4–10). He then returns to game-related talk in turn 11. He does not respond to User E's friendship request in post 2, but nineteen seconds later, he does return to User F's game-in-progress related request for help *'Anyone have foid?'* (post 3). Example 5.20 below continues interaction from Example 5.19.

> Example 5.20 Anyone have food.
> 12 Ethan: ((reading User F's post)) "Anyone have foid." [food intended]
> 13 Ethan: h h .hhh Bro (.) you're not alone_
>   (0.2)
> 14 Ethan: Er:: I mean I could eat rotten flesh bert °ergh it's gross°.
>   (0.2)
> 15 Ethan: So::: (0.5) ((makes noises under his breath))
>   (0.7)
> →16 User A: *Ethan*
> 17 Ethan: ↑I ↓would like to see:: quickly what's going on ↑up °her::::e°,
>   (0.2)
> 18 Ethan: Wo:::::.
>   (0.7)
> 19 Ethan: They're making like ↑battlements.
>   (2.2)
> 20 Ethan: That's cra:::zy cool.
> 21 Ethan: Okay (0.2) I'm gonna change my skin_
>   (0.2)
> →22 User A: *Will u bring gang beast back?*
> 23 Ethan: Once mor::e (0.2) I'm the peetza bra.

Ethan's response to User F's request for food (posts 12–14), an item which is essential to survival in *Minecraft*, is sympathetic but integrated into his game-related voice narrative to the audience. User A initiates repair on his original request for information on *Gang Beast*, by repeating it in post 22. This is posted by User A after attempting to gain Ethan's attention by naming him in post 16. However, no response is forthcoming as Ethan and other players pursue game-in-progress related talk both in voice and text chat. Similar instances where User A requests information unrelated to the game in progress are also visible elsewhere in the chat, with repair initiated using a double question mark '*??*' (see also Example 5.17). This text chat interactional resource and naming are functional ways to achieve a text chat response where a specific interlocutor, in this case Ethan, is being addressed and is not responding. It is in fact common for chat participants to rely on conventions of writing, such as punctuation symbols, to communicate in written conversation (Tudini, 2015).

The final repair to be discussed, is also deployed by User A and appears to be related to the game in progress. It is unclear whether it relates to a specific game action or a text chat sequence which is unavailable to viewers. It is derived from a long chat interaction sequence which appears suddenly and briefly on screen towards the end of the gaming session.

Example 5.21

→1 User A: *Nooo User F*
[User G had changed from Party Pig skin to Party Pig skin]
→2 User A: *Its oak*
[User G had changed from Party Pig skin to Hotdog skin]
→3 User A: *Not birch*
→4 User F: *Oops*
5 User E: *ineed coal!*
→6 User A: *My dads a* [name of profession] *trust me*

User A alerts User F specifically to an error in his choice of building material by posting the negative '*Nooo*' in post 1. In post 2 User A then corrects User F by providing the correct alternate material in post 2 '*Its oak*', followed by User F's apparently incorrect material in post 3 '*Not birch*'. User F seems to accept his error by interjecting '*Oops*', which is normally used in interaction after a mistake occurring either in talk or in action. User A follows up this other repair (correction), which is content rather than linguistically oriented, with a justification for a usually dispreferred action (post 6). This justification suggests User A's knowledgeability of building materials thanks to his father's profession.

In summary, based on this analysis, repair may be used as an interactional resource in the text chat context during gaming. It may be either social or directly related to the game in progress. Naming of addressees is also a component of these multi-party interactions to promote conversational coherence and understanding. Social repair sequences usually revolve around activities outside the game and highlight the constraints of this environment, as gaining Ethan's response to questions requires additional conversational work, whereby questions need to be asked twice and, hence, repair initiated, usually with the double question mark '??'. Hence repair is required to obtain a response from Ethan, who is juggling multiple interactional tasks. Unsurprisingly, there is no evidence of linguistic repair between chat participants, however, Example 5.21 is a content-related correction of a participant's choice of building material. Lack of access to the chat relating to the original repaired item does not permit a complete understanding of this episode but judging from the context, and participants' regular requests for assistance in gaining specific materials, it is possible that the item was a chat request for assistance in obtaining birch, similar to User E's request for coal in post 5 (Example 5.21). While this repair would usually be considered socially dispreferred, it appears to support User F's gaming by providing instructions on the correct required material. It should also be noted that only User A initiates repair in these episodes; hence, these repair types may be dependent on the personalities of gamers, who need to be sufficiently confident to enact them in this constrained interactional environment.

Collaborative Learning Behaviours

Collaborative learning behaviours related to the game in progress are prevalent in text chat interaction between *Minecraft* game participants in the YouTube video recording being examined (EthanGamer, 2019, May 28). Problem-solving and teamwork are evident when participants enact various types of requests and offers of assistance with the game under way. Instructions and other forms of scaffolding which promote ZPD (Vygotsky, 1986) regarding the game in progress are also evident. Wernholm and Vigmo (2015) identify similar instances of ZPD where joint activity leads to gameplay assistance from a more knowledgeable child, which permits them to accomplish more than if they were on their own. In the case under examination, *Minecraft* gamers stay connected by both game actions and text chat, despite being geographically dispersed.

In Example 5.22, various collaborative learning behaviours related to the game in progress are evident as part of participants' text chat interaction. These include requests for advice and a mock request for assistance.

Example 5.22
1 Ethan: ↑We need to make a ↓blast furnace.
2 Ethan: Isn't that like- (0.5) or is it smoo:th cobble.
            (0.5)
→3 Ethan: Er how do you make s:moo:::th ((typing)) (1.2) smoo::th (0.5) cobble.
            (0.5)
→4 Ethan: Er::m not smooth cobble,
5 User F: *Should i extend base?*
            (0.5)
6 User C: *yeah sure*
7 User G: *Help i am lost XD*
→8 Ethan: ((typing)) <Ho::w do you get smoo::th sto::ne,>
→9 Ethan: How do you get smooth stone?
            (0.7)
→10 Ethan: >How you get smooth sto::ne,<
            (0.2)
11 Ethan: Help and welp- welp and help.
            hh
12 Ethan: I'm lost.
            (0.5)
13 User A: *Can i take the oak to build?*
14 Ethan: Er:: can I take the oak to the build.
            (0.2)
            [User G has changed from Hotdog skin to Ol' Diggy skin]
15 Ethan Er::m what?
→16 User C: *you gotta furnance cobblestone*
            (0.7)

17 Ethan: ((reads User C's post)) "You gat a furnace cobblestone."
18 Ethan: Oh::.
             (0.5)
19 Ethan: Oh ↑that's- (0.2) ↓easy?
→20 Ethan: *Thanks :D*
             (0.5)
21 Ethan: I can make< a ↑<u>blast</u> furnace then.
             huh huh ha::y
(. . .)
24 User C: *np!*

Ethan's first request for assistance in this sequence is posted in chat (post 9). This occurs after he verbally expresses doubts regarding the material he actually needs in post 2. After vocalizing his typing aloud in turn 3, however, he subsequently initiates self-repair aloud in regard to what he is about to post. Specifically, his repair regards the building material he requires 'Er::m not smooth cobble' (post 4). After some intervening chat posts, by the time he posts the request to other participants in chat, it is modified to 'How do you get smooth stone?' in post 9. His self-repair is related to uncertainty about the materials he requires for building. The thinking aloud process he goes through on this topic for the audience, and probably for himself, leads to identification of what he considers the correct material he needs prior to posting on chat.

In post 16, User C solves the problem and provides relevant advice, specifically, that Ethan needs to '*furnance cobblestone*', intending 'furnace', which suggests that the cobblestone needs to be placed in a furnace to gain a smooth stone. Hence, Ethan engages with other game participants to gain assistance with the game, whereby he takes on the role of novice and in this case User C the role of expert. These actions reflect the expertise of gamers other than Ethan. This is the opposite of what occurred when participants' provided positive evaluations of Ethan, as discussed above, where he is cast as the expert gamer. It indicates that game participants, including Ethan, may exchange their game expertise on a reciprocal basis. Ethan subsequently vocalizes an acknowledgement of the received advice and thanks User C in chat with a large smiley emoticon (post 20). This is followed in post 24 by a relevant second pair part which follows thanking '*np*' (no problem) by User C.

Prior to Ethan and User C's advice sequence, User F also requests advice in Example 5.22, when he asks, 'Should i extend base?' (post 5), to which User C provides an affirmative response in post 4. In this same extract, User G also seeks assistance as he appears to be lost (post 7). However, in this case the squinting eyes laughing emoticon 'XD' suggests playfulness rather than a serious need for assistance. Additionally, user A appears to ask permission to '*take the oak to build*' (post 13), which, however, does not receive a response. The various posts show participants' collaborative dispositions during the game, where they are comfortable asking each other for assistance in playing the game and providing support to enable other participants to complete the game successfully.

In Example 5.23, there is additional evidence of game participants supporting one another. In this case, User C appears to have acquired coal, which is required for survival in this game. Ethan had posted a request for this material twenty-six seconds earlier.

> Example 5.23
> →1 Ethan: *Anyone have any coal? :)*
>   (1.0)
> ((intervening voice sequence))
> 9 User D: *Ethan Cave! W/iron!*
> →10 User C: *I have aquired coal!*
> →11 Ethan: ((reads User C's post in a high-pitched old lady's voice))
>   "↑I have acquired coa::l."
>   (0.2)
> →12 Ethan:↑Who ↓has.
>   (0.2)
> →13 Ethan: ↓User C oh ya::y.
>   (0.5)
> 14 User F: *Could you set our spawnpoint to base?*
> →15 Ethan: >What did you-<
> ((User C places the coal into the furnace))
> →16 Ethan: ((gasps)) Oh::: thanks_
> →17 Ethan: *Thanks so much! :D*
> →18 Ethan:↓So (3.0) ↑thanks so much you:: ~a:::~bsolute legend.
> 19 Ethan: .h >Okay< le::t's (.) take this ou::t and then go::: ↑↑up_
>   (1.0)
> →20 User C: *np! Anything for yo ethan*

In Example 5.23, Ethan's request for coal in post 1 is followed by game activity and Ethan's voice narrative. This is then followed by a game-related post and User C's announcement that he has acquired coal (post 10). Ethan vocalizes User C's post for the audience (turn 11) thus acknowledging his post. He then queries who has posted it in turn 12 ('↑Who ↓has.') and utters a celebratory exclamation (response cry) in turn 13 when he identifies User C ('↓User C oh ya::y.'). Subsequently, after User F utters a request in chat (post 14) and Ethan articulates an unclearly defined question in post 15 ('>What did you-<'), User C places the coal in Ethan's furnace during the game-in-progress. This leads Ethan to gasp (turn 16) and express his strong appreciation, with a big smile emoticon in post 17 ('Thanks so much! :D'). This profuse thanking continues in turn 18, by voice, reinforced by a positive evaluation of User C ('you:: ~a::: ~bsolute legend'). Ethan then returns to his narrative about the game (turn 19), which is followed by User C's chat response to his thanking in post 20 ('*np!*

Anything for yo ethan'). In addition to providing a polite response to Ethan's thanking, User C's post indicates his availability to support Ethan.

Ethan is not the only game participant requesting assistance; it is common for other gamers to seek help too.

> Example 5.24
>
> 1 User A: *Give me any oak wood*
> 2 Ethan: ((reads User A's post)) "Give me any oak wood."
>   (0.2)
> 3 Ethan: I::: don't have any_

In Example 5.24, User A requests 'oak wood' on the chat, but on this occasion, no one is able to assist, not even Ethan. However, in Example 5.25 below User C requests instructions on making a blast furnace and smoker.

> Example 5.25
>
> 1 User B *Ethan how long is the vid*
> →2 User C: *how do you make a blast furnace and smoker*
> [new participant joined the game]
> 3 User B: *Because I have to go soon*
> →4 Ethan: *You can find it in the crafting menu*

Rather than providing User C with detailed instructions in response to his question, Ethan refers User C to the crafting menu. As is common in text chat interaction, Ethan's response is disrupted on screen by User B's explanation that his departure is imminent. The statement in post 3 '*Because I have to go soon*' indicates that participants have initiated closing of the session, as this episode occurs towards the end of the game. This may also explain why Ethan does not elaborate on instructions for User C and instead provides essential information to assist him in finding an answer independently.

Ethan may also 'rescue' game participants who call for help in chat due to in-game difficulties they are experiencing. In Example 5.26, User E shouts his request for help, in capital letters.

> Example 5.26
>
> →1 User E: *HELP I'M LOST*
> →2 Ethan: Help I'm <u>lost</u>.
> →3 Ethan: =Okay I'll go find him.
> 4 User D: *Im ethans bodyguard*
> →5 Ethan: <I'll come.>
>   (0.5)
> →6 Ethan: Fine I'll come ↑find yo::::u.
> →7 Ethan: *Ill come find you!*
>   (1.0)
> 8 Ethan: Er <u>wher::</u>e du du du de::r.

→9 Ethan: =What was it Us er Eee … ? [attempted vocalization of User E's nickname]
        (0.5)
→10 Ethan: Oh I think- (0.7) is that hi:::m_
        (0.5)
11 User G: *should I flatten out the land?*
→12 User E: *thx!*

Ethan vocalizes User E's call for help (post 2) and announces to viewers that he will search for him (turns 3, 5 and 6). He also advises User E of his search in post 7. The use of pronoun 'you' and contextual information suggest that Ethan's post is directed at User E rather than the entire group of game participants. The use of third person singular pronoun 'him' in turns 3 and 10 in his voice narrative suggests he is talking to the audience in think aloud mode. This think aloud mode is also evident as he vocalizes a word search for User E's nick, which he has difficulty recalling. This is required for success in identifying and rescuing him. The search is successful, as evidenced both in in-game actions and User E's expression of appreciation in post 12 (*'thx!'*). As this episode exhibits concern for other gamers and occurs in the early stages of the game, it is likely to promote an image of Ethan as helpful and inclusive, both for game participants and the audience. It also allows the game to proceed successfully without interruption.

Additional displays of game participants' supportiveness of others is evident in this same example (26) in post 4, when User D identifies himself as *'ethans bodyguard'*. This occurs on multiple occasions and by multiple game participants where there are perceived threats. These displays of supportiveness contribute to a constructive prosocial environment for gaming and interaction. They may in fact be essential for protection of game participants who need to eliminate threats and facilitate progress of the game, as discussed below.

Defending Others

In addition to declaring elimination of threats, game participants often announce the protection of avatars and collaborative protection of Ethan in text chat. One such post was evident in Example 5.26 above. The actions that accompany the declarations occur during the game in progress, as game participants are able to achieve many game goals without the support of chat. However, at times they find it necessary to declare certain game actions, especially where extra support is required. In fact, game participants regularly express their availability to support Ethan in chat.

Example 5.27 Protecting Ethan.
→1 User D: *Me and User A are bodyguards*
2 Ethan: >I have another one< okay.

3 Ethan: =That's fine_
           (4.0)
→4 User B: *Evryone protect Ethan*

In Example 5.27, User D announces that he and User A are bodyguards, which suggests that someone needs protection, most likely Ethan. User B in fact calls for all participants to be involved in protecting Ethan in post 4 '*Evryone protect Ethan*'. User C also declares that he is available to protect Ethan in Example 5.28.

Example 5.28

1 User C: *i gotchu ethan!*
2 Ethan: I GATCHU Ethan.
3 Ethan: °Oh yay° thank you?
           (3.2)

In Example 5.28, User C uses the colloquial expression '*i gotchu ethan!*' (I've got you Ethan) to advise Ethan that he will be protecting him. These text chat declarations are in fact interspersed in Ethan's voice narrative early in the gaming video session. In Example 5.29, three game participants announce their role as protectors of Ethan.

Example 5.29

→1 User D: *Ill be protecting etan*
2 Ethan: ((mock sad voice)) He was alway was a good chicken.
           (0.2)
→3 Ethan: I'll be protecting Ethan.
           (0.2)
→4 Ethan: ↓Thank you very much?
           (0.5)
5 Ethan: ↓A:::nd here we go >okay<.
→6 User D: *Ethan*
7 Ethan: So:: is this gonna be:: the earea?
           (1.0)
8 Ethan: Or is it her::e.
           (2.0)
→9 User A: *Same*
10 Ethan: Oh WO:::W creeper went ↑cray ↓cra::y.
           h huh huh .hh
11 Ethan: A::bsolutely insane.
→12 User C: *Same*

User D's declaration that he is a bodyguard in post 1 is followed by User A and User C's offer, in text chat, to do the same (posts 9 and 12). Based on chat participants' perspective, the text chat posts are likely to be adjacent to one another. Hence, they are relevant to the prior posts and express agreement with previous posts rather than Ethan's voice turns.

To conclude the analysis, we focus on three episodes which provide further insights on how collaboration is enacted in gaming contexts where participants are geographically dispersed and using only text chat to communicate. These episodes are considered significant as they indicate that even in constrained environments such as text chat, gamers are able to ensure that the game can proceed against the odds. In one of these (Example 5.30), it appears that a danger to Ethan's avatar is eliminated by a game participant for his protection. In the second episode (Example 5.31), the protection provided by game participants does not prevent Ethan from being killed. However, in Example 5.32 (third episode) the chat shows game participants' collaborative efforts at recovery from the incident.

In Example 5.30, User D announces that he has killed the polar bear.

Example 5.30

→1 User D: *I killed the polar bear ethan rip*
2 User G: *just like a my fortnite mpa XD*
3 User A: *Lol*
4 Ethan: Oh it's a pig.
                    (2.0)
5 Ethan: Hello.
(0.7)
hih hih hih hih
6 Ethan: I'm sorry.
                    huh ↑↑hah hah_
. . . .
→7 User D: *I killed the bear*
→8 Ethan: (1.0) oh oh no you killed the bear.
→9 Ethan: ↑↑↑Oh::::.
                    (0.5)
10 Ethan: (Hi did_)

Prior to these posts, the polar bear has been attacking Ethan despite his avatar's attempts at running away from it. User D's announcement that he has killed it, in post 1, is reinforced by '*rip*', an acronym for 'rest in peace', which is normally used on gravestones. However, it appears that Ethan has not initially noticed this announcement as he does not acknowledge it, either in the game or in chat. His voice narrative, from turns 4 to 6 and others not reproduced here, indicates that he is occupied with the game, in particular with pig avatars. User D thus repeats (repairs) his announcement in post 7 and receives at least a voice response from Ethan, who subsequently proceeds with the game from post 10. Hence, this is just one instance of game participants collaborating in defence of Ethan when he does not do it himself, by eliminating possible threats to the game.

Example 5.31 presents Ethan's voice narrative when he is killed by a skeleton.

Example 5.31

1 Ethan: ↑↑↑OH GEE::Z!↑↑↑
2 huh huh
3 Go win- >go go go go go go go go go.<
            (.)
4 Destroy it,
(6.0)
5 Ge-get ou::t.
6 Get- (0.5) huh huh huh huh huh
→ [ETH4N6AMER was sht by Arrow]
→7 NO:::::::::! I di::ed.
            (0.5)
→8 >I need my stuff back_<

The voice narrative in Example 5.31 is characterized by response cries and
other indicators of emotion which are a response to the appearance of skeletons.
Skeletons are considered monsters, and they use bows and arrows in *Minecraft*.
After 'dying', in turn 8 Ethan focuses on recovery of his 'stuff' which he needs
to proceed with the game. He subsequently engages in a frustrating search over
ten turns (and two unrelated chat posts), where he only expresses himself in the
voice narrative. He finally requests assistance of other game participants in
chat, as presented in Example 5.32.

Example 5.32

→1 Ethan: *Wheres my stuff*
→2 User D: *I got ur stuff*
→3 User E: *here ethan if you need it*
→4 Ethan: Who- who's got my stuff?
            (0.2)
→5 Ethan: >You have< my stuff?
            (0.2)
→6 Ethan: Oh my gosh tha::nk you.
7 Ethan: °(hhhh)aw you are such a legur:::nd_°
            (0.5)
8 Ethan: Er >here are you thing< if you need it.
            (0.5)
9 Ethan: Er::: s- oh my gosh yeah I've messed up.
10 Ethan: Yo::u are- (1.0) ↑what >did he< just give me.
            (2.0)
[User D has changed from Steve skin to James skin]
→11 Ethan: Tha::nks so mu:::ch!
→12 Ethan: *Thanks so much! :D*

Ethan can only receive assistance from other game participants by posting his
request in text chat (post 1). He receives supportive responses from User D and
User E. User D, in particular, appears to have his 'stuff' according to turn 5,

which indicates that Ethan has noticed the chat posts. His profuse thanking and positive evaluations are expressed by voice and finally he expresses his appreciation in text chat (post 12), reinforced by a big smile emoticon. This expression of appreciation receives an appropriate polite second pair part response from User E a little later in the chat, accompanied by other gamers' offer of assistance (not reproduced here). This exchange indicates that text chat is an important communication mode to promote collaborative learning and gaming support between geographically dispersed gamers where voice chat is unavailable.

Conclusion

This chapter analysed chat interactions between geographically dispersed, mostly unacquainted, young participants in a publicly available YouTube video recording of *Minecraft* play presented by Ethan Gamer. Insights from interactional analysis of this previously unexplored context indicate that chat is an essential communication tool to ensure that the game proceeds collaboratively and successfully. The analysis distinguished interactions which were social from those which were related specifically to the game in progress. Social interactions entailed mostly affiliative chat interactions and voice narrative such as greetings and reciprocal positive evaluations between Ethan Gamer and game participants. These behaviours promote a reassuring and prosocial environment where participants can engage comfortably in the game with other game participants. They also model appropriate behaviours for the YouTube audience, of whom chat participants become aware during interaction through information-seeking questions. Small talk has a similar role in institutional talk, whereby participants may move between personal and professional identities to achieve their institutional goals (Dooly & Tudini, 2016). In the gaming context participants adopt the role of both gamers and social beings. Social talk builds mutual trust which enables participants to scaffold one another, solve problems and engage in teamwork to progress the game.

Game participants' positive evaluations suggest Ethan's supremacy in gameplay and position him as expert and themselves as novices. However, game-in-progress interactions indicate that requests for assistance and collaboration are reciprocal rather than a one-way process during this gaming session. Interactional resources such as repair and naming of addressees are, however, sometimes required to promote understanding in a context which is constrained by the content creator's movement between voice narrative, which attends to the audience, and chat interaction, which attends to game participants. Game-in-progress related chat interaction, on the other hand, promotes collaborative learning and ZPD in key moments of the game when joint game actions and reciprocal support are required. Thinking and typing aloud processes by Ethan also appear to lead to improved knowledge of game requirements prior to posting or acting on requests for assistance in chat. They are therefore likely to benefit the YouTube audience as well. Response cries are also evident in both chat interaction and Ethan's voice narrative.

The analysis confirms previous research on children's interaction in video gaming contexts. While Danby's et al (2018a) research focuses on voice interaction between children playing *Minecraft* side by side, similar strategies of collaboration and instruction to achieve game objectives were evident in the chat exchange between geographically dispersed gamers in the YouTube video under examination. The presence of instructions, requests and advice-giving are common research findings in the gaming interaction context. For example, directives and advice-giving were identified as a component of gaming language by Mondada (2011; 2012). These strategies were enacted online by game participants through text chat despite the interactionally constrained fast-paced environment and additional time required to write and submit posts, when compared to expressing them by voice. Furthermore, the content creator's think-aloud processes during his voice narrative are likely to promote learning about the game, for himself and his YouTube audience.

While all chat interaction activities between video game participants analysed in this chapter might be considered side activities and game actions central interactional elements (Mondada, 2012), a focus on the 'side activity' of chat interaction in this analysis yielded further insights on gaming interaction. Specifically, further distinctions appear relevant in a context where gamers are unacquainted and geographically dispersed, with social elements of the chat comprising an essential component of the interaction to promote constructive gameplay. Collaborative elements of the interaction which are directly related to the game in progress are thus likely to proceed more smoothly thanks to the supportive social behaviours of participants in chat, including Ethan Gamer himself as organizer of the gaming session.

In Summary

- Ethan's text chat greeting exchanges and other affiliative social talk are important elements of the initial gameplay to promote a prosocial and reassuring gaming environment for chat participants.
- African American English is commonly used by game participants in this context, as are colloquial positive evaluations such as 'cool'.
- Positive evaluations after a helpful game action may be interpreted by game participants as expressions of appreciation.
- Chat participants' positive evaluations position Ethan Gamer as an expert and themselves as novices. These also imply perceived learning possibilities due to Ethan Gamer's alleged superior gaming expertise.

- Reciprocal greetings, positive evaluations and smiley emoticons deployed by game participants promote a supportive gaming environment while also modelling prosocial affiliative gaming behaviours for viewers.
- Other-repair and naming of addressees are used as resources by game participants in text chat to pursue social and game actions in a constrained interactional environment where Ethan alternates voice and text chat, and game participants have access only to text chat and the gaming software in real time.
- Enactment of other repair may be dependent on the confidence of individual gamers.
- Game participants may deploy social requests for information, not directly related to the game in progress, on a variety of topics in question format.
- Participants may take the opportunity to engage in 'getting to know you' behaviours where gaming participants are unacquainted.
- Teamwork and problem-solving behaviours which scaffold game participants in their gameplay are enacted frequently and reciprocally in text chat. These consist mainly of requests or offers of assistance and advice-giving related to the game in progress. While participants are able to pursue gaming objectives without these, text chat is an essential resource to deploy questions and instructions for successful gameplay.
- Some thinking and typing aloud processes by Ethan lead to improved knowledge of game requirements prior to posting or acting on requests for assistance in chat. These processes, which include self-repair and word search, promote the progress of the game and may benefit the YouTube audience.
- Game participants often announce elimination or protection from a perceived threat to Ethan's avatar in chat. Such defensive actions occur in-game and do not need to be announced. However, text chat is used when defensive actions require collaborative teamwork to progress the game. These public chat announcements promote a supportive prosocial environment which can be shared with all participants, including YouTube video viewers.

6   Children's YouTube Comments on Ethan Gamer

Introduction: YouTube Comments Interaction

One form of participation in the gaming experience is the posting of public text comments on gaming celebrities' YouTube video sites. YouTube comments afford fans the opportunity to participate publicly in content creators' gaming activity as commenters, not just viewers. While the level of participation is not equivalent to that which occurs by actually gaming with Ethan Gamer, as in the *Minecraft* interaction presented in Chapter 5 (EthanGamer, 2019, May 28), it is more interactive than merely 'viewing' the game. Specifically, fans who are located remotely, in a variety of locations, have the opportunity to respond to the YouTube video activity through written conversation. This should in theory also foster interaction with other viewers, which may lead to learning benefits. Yet for this to occur, users need to choose the correct interactional resources, to gain the attention of other commenters and Ethan Gamer himself. On the surface, this is vastly different from television broadcasts, where interaction is a one-way non-interactive process, unless integrated social media resources are made available by broadcasters for this purpose. An example of a more participatory type of interaction experience is current affairs programs such as the Australian Broadcasting Commission's (ABC) *Q+A* program, which permits and includes selected Twitter (now X) comments of remote viewers as a component of the broadcast (Q+A, 2008). However, this is only a one way process from an interactional viewpoint, with viewing television audiences and panel members unable to respond to broadcasted tweets unless they are logged. This chapter considers the different levels of participation and interactivity afforded by YouTube comments for children, based on analysis of user comments on two Ethan Gamer videos (EthanGamer, 2015, February 20; EthanGamer, 2020, February 17). This will allow us to understand the capacity for the comments tool to promote collaboration and learning in an additional type of children's online language and interaction related to gaming.

How Data Was Collected

For the purpose of interactional analysis in the current chapter, substrand comments are the main data source as they allow users to engage in more coherent conversations than the main strand comments (see section below on 'How YouTube Comments Interaction and Sequencing Work'). These comments include the first post which initiated the substrand, from the main strand sequence. Both main strand and substrand comments were originally collected from Ethan Gamer's Baby Cow Processor video, (EthanGamer, 2015, February 20), which focuses on *Minecraft* play. However, only a single substrand was collected from the I Have a Big Belly video (EthanGamer, 2020, February 17). The latter substrand relates to a video which showcases *Roblox* gaming (see Appendix for details on data collected for this study). It was chosen for its extended nature (104 posts), compared to other substrand sequences, to understand whether length of sequences is likely to be associated with users' sustained interactive and collaborative activity.

At the commencement of data collection, use of Snipping Tool ensured precise reproduction of comments interaction with full original data, including profile pictures and names. All identifying material was subsequently removed and substituted with pseudonyms for this publication. Examples of comments included in the analysis reproduce de-identified text contributions verbatim and without images, as posted on the specified YouTube comments section of the relevant Ethan Gamer YouTube page. Any comments which are potentially copyrightable have been excluded from the analysis, in keeping with international copyright laws.

Challenges in Creating Pseudonyms for YouTube Comments Users

YouTube permits users to create both a profile picture and a profile name, for which a single pseudonym has been created to preserve participant anonymity in this research. Hence, these components of the comments are not included in the analysis presented for this chapter. However, they may reveal general information which assists us in understanding the online conversations. Specifically, some profile pictures and names reveal whether the user is apparently a child or whether commenters are using adults' accounts, often of parents, to post comments. As far as profile pictures are concerned, many participants use photographs, apparently of themselves and sometimes of family members. Many, however, do not use photographs at all and use the initial of their first name as a profile picture. These profile pictures appear in larger font than the profile names, within a circle, in a prominent position to the left of each profile name and comment, as in Figure 6.1 (EthanGamer, 2020, February 17).

4 years ago

Chake your inventory frist

REPLY

Figure 6.1 Initials as profile names in YouTube.

Profile names may consist of apparently real names, including first and family names. Many users instead choose nonsensical and humorous names, some of which are inspired by cartoon or gaming characters and a range of popular culture figures. As occurs with nicknames used in other social media and gaming platforms, users choose these profile pictures and names because they reveal an aspect of their identity. It is thus likely that users identify with the chosen characters who become part of users' persona online. As pointed out by Crystal (2006), online nicknames may say 'something about who they are, and act(s) as an invitation to others to talk to them' (p. 166). Nicknames also provide anonymity for users, which is important for safety, but they may also allow some users to express themselves more freely and even inappropriately, under cover of a fictional identity, sometimes to the detriment of other users.

Where there are real rather than fictional profile names, there is evidence that most users are of English-speaking background. There is also a strong presence of Hispanic and other cultural background names which would ideally be reflected in creation of pseudonyms for this research. There is, however, such a range of user backgrounds and fictional names that it was not possible to reflect such diversity in the pseudonyms. This is also the case where adults' accounts appear to be used, as gender or cultural background of the actual commenters are unclear. However, in keeping with Conversation Analysis (CA) methodology, such identities are discussed if they are made relevant by commenters in their online talk, as occurs when age is a topic of conversation (see 'Participants' Age in Interaction' section). Findings in this chapter remain relevant regardless of the L1 of participants, nonetheless.

Pseudonyms in this chapter are based simply on the alphabet, for example, 'User A' in the analysis and 'A' in the extracts. At times, participants address specific other users in the substrand interactions; hence, in such cases the relevant pseudonym (e.g. User C) is used in place of the original name. Letter use for posts in the extracts is alphabetical-chronological, based on the sequence of user posts. Hence, 'A' is usually the first poster to whom other users respond in the substrand. The longer substrand with 104 posts (e.g. EthanGamer, 2020, February 17) is, however, distinguished from the other multiple shorter substrands with an asterisk as part of the pseudonym. For example, the first main strand poster is 'A*' for the 2020 substrand. Where a specific user posts more than once, a number is added to the letter to signal this for readers, as this assists both analyst and reader in recognizing more active commenters and in understanding the conversation. For example, User A1* is the first commenter who initiates the extended substrand (EthanGamer, 2020, February 17) and responds to other commenters later in the strand. Hence, she is recognizable to readers as a repeat commenter through use of the same pseudonym (User A1*).

How the Analytical Sections Are Organized

The following analytical sections firstly consider how YouTube comments interaction works, as there are a three main options for users. Understanding how these options work assists us in contextualizing and understanding substrand interaction, which is the main focus of this chapter. The focus then shifts to how comments regarding the age of participants assist us in confirming that commenters in the data are in fact children, for whom age appears to be a relevant concern in interaction. Additionally, analysis considers intended recipients of posts and how commenters design their posts accordingly, including techniques for addressing recipients other than the first poster. How commenters design their posts impacts on conversational sequencing and coherence; hence, sequence organization is also discussed briefly. Another consideration in the analysis regards whether the non-standard language used by commenters might be recognizable as that of children, rather than the language of online text interaction in general. This is important also to understand whether age is a recurrent user orientation in these interactions. Other factors include linguistic and interactional features of first posts that prompt substrand discussion, including instances leading to repair and collaborative work, which have potential to promote learning.

How YouTube Comments Interaction and Sequencing Work

The default display of YouTube main comments is 'Top' comments rather than 'Newest' first. While the system displays many recent comments, they are rarely sequential and appear to be random. The position in the sequence depends on various criteria and is based partly on content creators' or YouTube moderators' intervention. For example, content creators may have set up comments as reviewable by themselves, or certain words have been prohibited and hence unacceptable comments deleted (YouTube, n.d.). Users post their comments at various stages of viewing the video; however, there is no detailed time stamp and other commenters only have access to approximate information on when comments have been posted. For example, they can see how many days, weeks, months or years ago they are posted. They would need to select 'Newest first' by clicking the 'sort by' function, to be able to view the most recent contributions of other participants. Compared with 'top' comments the 'newest' contributions are in fact reverse chronological with the most recent posts presented first and earliest comments displayed at the bottom. Nonetheless, even these comments appear to be somewhat randomly sequenced.

Users are acutely aware of the non-sequential nature of main strand 'Top' comments, as evidenced in Example 6.1, a main strand comment:

> Example 6.1
>
> User A: I also made a semi automatic wheat farm on my old iPad inspired by you when you made it, and I made it the exact same way and it worked the exact same way I hope I don't get lost in the comments 🌱💜

User A in Example 6.1 composes and posts a rather lengthy contribution to the comments thread, addressed to Ethan Gamer, about her own work on *Minecraft*. This post is almost entirely without punctuation, apart from a comma, and concludes with a statement which expresses concern about possibly getting lost in the comments ('I hope I don't get lost in the comments'). No substrand is prompted by this comment; however, this and similar comments indicate commenters' awareness of interactional difficulties of the main strand comments. Only the more private substrand comments provide a sequential ordering of comments to promote user interaction. One aspect which is common to main and substrand comments is that they both occur asynchronously rather than in real time.

To post a comment in the main strand, users are required to sign in before they can use the public comment box which is beneath the video and above the first visible comment (top or newest), as shown in Figure 6.2 (EthanGamer, 2015, February 20).

The newly created post in the main strand appears above the latest top comment. This is quite different from the substrand interaction, which does not require participants to post after the top comment in the list. The 'reply' option is in fact available independently of the first post in the main strand, which promotes a chronological sequencing. The first post in these substrands is, however, always a main strand comment to which other users and sometimes the content creator may reply.

Commenters also have the option of 'liking' using the thumbs up icon, to positively assess a main strand comment. Likes are frequently elicited in the

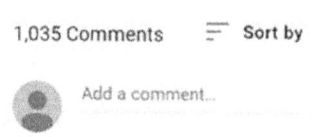

Figure 6.2 YouTube public comment box.

9 months ago

Dang, it's been a long time since I watched this channel.

👍 148   👎   REPLY

▲ Hide 103 replies

Figure 6.3 Display of thumbs up and number of replies at start of substrand.

comments and are a regular component of interaction in these conversations. In addition to the substrand comments, they too constitute an additional figurative type of second pair part of an adjacency pair which relates to the main strand first pair part comment being 'liked'. There is in fact a correspondence between number of 'thumbs up' deployed by participants and length of substrands, with the longest substrands more likely than short substrands to receive numerous 'thumbs up' responses. This suggests that main strand comments with the most expressions of approval through the thumbs up icon are more likely to receive multiple substrand responses than those with smaller numbers of 'thumbs up' approvals, with some exceptions (see Example 6.9 below). Participants may in fact prefer to use the comments option to articulate their approvals (or dis-approvals) of the YouTube video verbally while at the same time using the anonymous thumbs up or down icons. While there are multiple examples of this pattern in the data, the I Have a Big Belly substrand of 103 replies received 148 thumbs up, as presented in Figure 6.3.

This entire substrand conversation is affiliative and abounds in colloquial expressions of agreement, in particular 'Same', in relation to participants' long-standing participation in this gamer's videos. The first post in fact frames the entire substrand conversation, which is dedicated to establishing a common interest in Ethan Gamer's YouTube gaming videos and nostalgia for Ethan Gamer's and their own younger days. The affiliative nature of this 'conversation' is reinforced by the predominant use of 'likes' and absence of 'thumbs down'.

Participants' Age in Interaction

While the chosen YouTube videos and games are intended for children, we cannot be sure of the ages of the commenters, who are posting their comments publicly. Furthermore, user profiles are not reliable because children often use adults' accounts. This is evidenced by the profile pictures and names of adults, which contrast with users' stated young age or name, which is different to that in the profile name. For example, profile names occasionally include titles such as Dr, which indicate that the account is that of a well-educated adult rather than a child. Profile pictures which show photographs of adults cannot be exhibited here to protect users' identity. However, they include group photographs, probably of family, single women or men, or single adults with one or more children.

Despite lack of clarity on commenters' identities, it is appropriate to assume that participants commenting on the videos are approximately of the age group for which *Minecraft* is officially rated, namely seven to thirteen years, depending on the version of the game (Webwise.ie, n.d). *Roblox*, on the other hand, suggests an age limit of eight to eighteen (E-SafetyCommissioner, n.d.), which is relevant to the EthanGamer (2020, February 17) rather than EthanGamer (2015, February 20) video. However, the fact that age is a regular orientation in participants' public interactions on YouTube requires further analytical attention, to better understand children's online language and interaction.

YouTube commenters often reveal their age in the public conversations, with age and date of birth frequently a topic. There are in fact many posts, both in the main and substrands, where children appear eager to reveal their age. In Example 6.2, user A reveals their birth date and other identifying information, which in this case leads to a strong rebuke by another user.

Example 6.2

1 A: Ethan when's your birthday mine Jane [June intended] 12 2010 India home USLR) got hacked on March 2017 25 my roblox account got stolen or hacked
2 B: User A mlooolooo
3 B: postw
4 B: Lel [LOL intended]
5 C: USER A DON'T TELL YOUR BIRTHDAY ON YT LIKE THIS IDIOT NOW DRINK ME

The date of birth revealed by User A at post 1, in the public main strand, indicates that he lives in India and is approximately ten years old. This can be assumed because the YouTube video and comment were created in 2020 and his declared birth date is apparently 2010 (post 1). User B's responses are nonsensical or suggest laughter ('Lel'). User C's post 5 instead is a request in the form of a negative imperative, without any form of hedging to soften the request, which includes verbal abuse ('IDIOT'). It is 'shouted', as denoted by capital letters, which reinforces the offensiveness of this message, despite the otherwise appropriate advice on revealing identifying information on YouTube.

In Example 6.3, a few users respond to User A's question on Ethan Gamer's age.

Example 6.3

1 A: how old are you
2 B1: He is 8
3 C: User A
4 D: Me old is 7
5 E: He is actually 10 now

In post 2, User B1, a repeat contributor, replies that Ethan is eight years old to User A's question to Ethan Gamer requesting his age. User D (post 4) instead replies to User A as if the question to Ethan Gamer were intended for her and states her age as seven in 'Me old is 7'. This comment is in non-standard English language despite the profile name denoting English-speaking background and may be due to the developing literacy of the child, who is apparently seven years old. Rather than producing the standard 'I'm 7', this user's post mirrors the syntactical structure of the original question 'how old are you' in response. It is ignored by other users in this strand, who do not repair the language used by User D. However, an episode of repair related to content rather than language ensues in regard to post 2. In post 5, User E corrects User B1, who is posting approximately one year later, as the platform permits, and states that Ethan Gamer is now ten, not eight. Given that a response from Ethan Gamer is unlikely in this setting, Users B1 and E's repairs are collaborative towards User A as they answer his question.

User A1, who prompted the extended 104 post substrand (EthanGamer, 2020, February 17), submits another post in the same substrand when a user expresses agreement and reveals her age.

> Example 6.4
>
> 1 A: Me too im 9 ive stped watching when i was 7
> 2 A1*: User A I stopped 4 years ago lmao [laugh my arse off]
> 3 B: Same
> 4 C: Same
> 5 D: Same

User A's post is a substrand reply to User A1*'s original main strand comment 'Dang, it's been a long time …'. In post 2, User A1* names User A to indicate that she is being addressed. Naming specific users is a commonly used linguistic and interactional strategy in multi-party chat to promote understanding by signalling the intended recipient. In this substrand conversation, fans reminisce over their past viewings of Ethan Gamer's YouTube channel, when they were younger. Hence, age is a relevant topic of conversation when they compare their current age with that at past viewings. In this entire substrand conversation (EthanGamer, 2020, February 17) participants clearly seek commonality by deploying colloquial expressions of agreement, in particular 'Same', in relation to participants' long-standing participation in this gamer's videos. Age is one element which is made relevant by participants as a component of interaction to establish commonality and promote affiliation, with 'naming' a commonly used interactional device to promote understanding.

Example 6.5 provides further evidence of how young users promote affiliation by recounting past experiences with Ethan Gamer's channels in EthanGamer (2020, February 17), the extended substrand, which may lead to talk about age and the passing of time.

Example 6.5

1 A1*: 'Dang, it's been a long time since I watched this channel'
2 B: User A1* agreed. I remember one time when I snuck my iPad in my bedroom in America, watched his videos and got in trouble by my parents. Still love this channel, but miss his young voice :(
3 C: Same
4 D: Same
5 E: I think I last watched him like 4 years ago.

User B's rather long post in Example 6.5, comprises a 'telling' or story about a past event, which contributes to the nostalgic tone of this substrand. This telling conforms to Schegloff's (2007) definition of an announcement which is considered 'a telling packaged in a single, grammatically simple, turn-constructional unit' (p. 42). Tellings have also been identified in Facebook (Farina, 2015) and can lead to a second telling in response. The reminiscing which occurs in this substrand leads to users sometimes talking about their age. After User B's telling on an occasion where he got into trouble for watching Ethan Gamer, he provides a positive assessment of the channel ('still love this channel'), though he appears to prefer the previous young voice of the star ('but miss his young voice :()', a comment which is reinforced by the sad emoticon. Users C and D's comments ('Same') in posts 3 and 4 express agreement with one or more components of User B's post while User E responds with another brief second telling regarding his last past viewing of Ethan Gamer's videos. No profile pictures are available in Examples 6.2 to 6.5 to indicate age or gender of participants, as users choose initials in these cases.

As noted in the analysis so far, time and age is frequently made relevant by users in both the I Have a Big Belly (EthanGamer, 2020, February 17) and Baby Cow Processor (EthanGamer, 2015, February 20) main strands and substrands. Related to these concerns, it is common for users to introduce a nostalgic element. They frequently do this by announcing their return to Ethan Gamer YouTube videos after a break or by recounting their past positive experiences, as we observed in the first posts in Examples 6.4 and 6.5.

In summary, the fact that participants appear to be using adults' accounts is evident when children reveal their young age in YouTube substrand talk, which contrasts with profile names and pictures. Talk about age is especially evident in participants' comparisons of one anothers' age to establish commonality and in tellings, where they share previous experiences related to viewing of Ethan Gamer gaming videos at various ages. This contributes to the nostalgic element of the conversations, including EthanGamer (2020, February 17). This extended substrand is mostly dedicated to connecting and agreeing with other users regarding their return to Ethan Gamer TV after a break, though brief tellings from the past are also a feature of this environment within longer posts.

Achieving Understanding Where Recipiency Is Disrupted

This section focuses on the Baby Cow Processor comments initially (EthanGamer, 2015, February 20) and then considers the extended substrand (EthanGamer, 2020, February 17) for comparison. In EthanGamer (2015, February 20), there are a total of sixty-five substrands, elicited by single main strand comments. Of these, sixteen were self-posts or posts that main strand commenters posted to themselves. This leaves a total of forty-nine collaborative substrands where main strand posts prompted responses from other users.

First Post Questions: Gaming Hardware

Of the forty-nine collaborative substrands in the 2015 data, eleven were initiated by questions, which suggests that this is one linguistic format which is likely to prompt substrand responses, given the ability of questions to project answers in conversation (see also Examples 6.2 and 6.3).

Many first post questions which prompt substrand responses regard what appear to be simple technical matters related to gaming hardware. Information about Ethan Gamer's gaming console is in fact important to understand the gaming video participants are watching, since buttons and controls may be different according to the device. In Example 6.6, users do not always agree on which gaming console Ethan Gamer is using when they reply to the first poster's question; hence, this seems to be an important concern.

> Example 6.6
>
> 1 A: X-BOX OR PS4?
> 2 B: User A [other name] my user name is [other name]
> 3 C: Do u have xbox 360 if u do my gamer tage is [User C's other name]
> 4 D: Ps4
> 5 D: User B oh
> 6 E: User A ps4
> 7 F: User A [other name] it is PS4
> 8 F: Sry it is PS3
> 9 G: He's using PS2
> 10 H: Look at the bottom left corner those are PS4 controls
> 11 H: There's R2 and L2
>
> (EthanGamer, 2015, February 20),

The final two comments (10 and 11) indicate that users may sometimes use the YouTube video they are viewing as a resource to achieve understanding in their comments interaction. In the repair sequence triggered by post 9 'He's using PS2', User H requests other users to look at the console on screen for proof that Ethan Gamer's console is a PS4 (posts 10–11). This is a repair of fact rather than language and expresses disagreement with posts 8 and 9 regarding PS3 and PS2, while at the same time answering User A's question. User H completes this repair by justifying his comment in a 'teacherly' way (Liddicoat & Tudini, 2013), which is usually an attendant activity to exposed correction (Jefferson, 1987). There is also evidence here and elsewhere in the data that users are known to each other by other names. In Example 6.7 the first poster most likely has another name, possibly a gamer tag, as posts 2, 6 and 7 address User A with a different nickname from the visible YouTube one while clearly responding to post 1. Familiarity with commenters' other nicks or gamer tags confirm the social affordances of YouTube substrands, as users do not just connect with unknown users but also reconnect with gamers they already know. Learning affordances are also evident from the question and repair sequence, as it contributes to users' understanding of the YouTube video on gaming; hence, the learning is related to *Minecraft* play. This talk therefore provides users with a form of scaffolding of the gameplay which promotes ZPD. Knowledge of the hardware is a concern for users because this knowledge promotes understanding of the YouTube video and users' own *Minecraft* gaming, one of the reasons gamers watch other gamers. As far as technical affordances of the YouTube platform are concerned, substrand posts reply mainly to the first post; however, this extract also indicates that responses may address a group of users in general or a specific user, other than the first poster. This is especially clear when specific users are named, as in post 5 (User D) which addresses User B (post 2). This example confirms that naming is therefore an additional interactional resource which users deploy to ensure understanding of YouTube comments interaction in a multiple user context. This is likely to promote understanding of the video, thus allowing users the possibility of learning through peer scaffolding.

The substrand in Example 6.7 is prompted by another question, again regarding gaming hardware, which is directed at 'u' (you), either Ethan Gamer or another user. There is in fact confusion among two substrand participants as to the intended recipient of this first post.

Example 6.7

1 A: do u have Xbox 360?
2 B: ldk
3 C: i do
4 D: No he plays on a ps [repair]
5 E: he plays on place staihion 3
6 F: I have PS3 and PS4
7 F: Because it was just released
8 B: Cool. Same
9 F: I have Xbox ONE
10 G: +User F cool I have Xbox 360
11 H: I do
12 I: User A yes
13 I: I have apsp

Posts 3, 6, 8, 9, 11, 12 and 13 respond using the first person singular pronoun 'I' as if the first poster were addressing them. Only one post (10) names a preceding poster (User F) as recipient by using the + sign to signify 'at', while participants use the third person singular pronoun 'he' in posts 4 and 5, as if the first post were addressed to Ethan Gamer, who is not participating in the substrand. The first poster does not provide further comments in this substrand; however, their first post question seems to provide the opportunity for other users to share information about their gaming hardware, seek commonality with other users, and assist User A. Similar to Example 6.6, it also appears to permit users to connect with other users who have consoles other than PlayStation, such as Xbox 360 (posts 9–10). Post 10 includes the interjection 'cool', which indicates excitement at finding another Xbox 360 user, who is in fact named to avoid any confusion (User F). This example therefore suggests that naming is an important device to address substrand users other than User A, the first poster. It also suggests the possibility of further engagement with users who have similar gaming hardware outside the YouTube context. Users' orientations to talk about consoles also scaffold each other's understanding of the game, as knowledge of Ethan Gamer's game console is likely to promote understanding of his gameplay.

Example 6.8 is similar to examples discussed thus far, both in terms of topic and how recipiency is managed in YouTube comments involving children.

> Example 6.8
>
> 1 A: Do you have xobx 360
> 2 B: I do
> 3 C: no
> 4 D: HE HAS A PS3
> 5 E: lol
> 6 F: [Other username]
> 7 F: I also have xobx 360 to
> 8 G: I do!

In this substrand interaction, most participants interpret the first post question as being directed at them rather than Ethan Gamer, where they use the singular pronoun 'I'. Only one user (post 4) interprets the question as being directed at Ethan Gamer, as indicated by use of the pronoun 'he'. Post 6 is an instance of naming another user in the strand by another known name, possibly a gamer tag. Posts 7 and 8 indicate that one of the YouTube substrand's affordances is the possibility for users to connect with other users who have hardware in common ('I also have xobx 360 to'), which suggests the possibility for gaming interaction outside the YouTube context, as was noted also in regard to Example 6.7.

In summary, where the third person singular 'he' is used, as in Examples 6.6, 6.7 and 6.8 described earlier, users may be responding to the main strand post (post 1) on Ethan Gamer's behalf. However, it seems that main strand questions about gaming hardware are likely to provoke more private substrand discussions than other types of questions. These allow young fans to briefly establish contact with each other and discuss similar interests in an otherwise chaotic interactional context. Naming is an important linguistic and interactional device to promote understanding of the substrand interaction and establish contact with specific users. Gaming hardware questions and responses may also assist users in understanding the public gameplay and apply new knowledge in their own context, which may vary according to users' hardware. Hence, these examples indicate that substrand interaction may have both learning and social affordances for young users.

First Post Questions: Users as Time Travellers

Some main strand comments questions are specifically designed to reach out to users other than Ethan Gamer and they are likely to prompt substrand responses. In particular, the following first post questions in Examples 6.9 to 6.11 indicate users' awareness of YouTube comments' asynchronousness across long spans of time, as they seek users who may be posting in the same year.

> Example 6.9
>
> →1 A: Who's watching this in 2018 leave a like if you are
> [10 likes]
> 2 B: VIOG ALL day 9000 i [VLOG or video blog intended]
> 3 C: GOOD LUCK ON PART 7
> 4 D: You're the best Ethan gamer TV

In Example 6.9, the first post in the substrand includes two components, a question and a request. The question is in present continuous form 'Who's watching this in 2018' with no question mark. The use of present continuous verb suggests a real time action, simultaneous with the posting of this contribution. The deictic marker 'this' also indicates the immediate YouTube interactional context. The post is concluded with a request to users to leave a like if they are viewing the video at the same time as User A. This post achieves its goal of receiving ten likes; however, the comments do not appear to respond to the first poster specifically but rather address all users in general (posts 2 and 3) and Ethan Gamer (post 4).

Time is also made relevant by participants in a question which elicits a small substrand with only two responses in Example 6.10.

> Example 6.10
>
> →1 A: who's waching in 2020
> 2 B: Came back for nostalgia
> 3 C: Meeee

Similar to Example 6.9, using a present continuous verb, User A's question in Example 6.10 refers to the year she is posting, 2020, to connect with other users who are present online at around the same time. She receives two affiliative affirmative responses, one of which represents in writing the lengthening of the vowel in 'me' and is hence emphatic ('Meeee'). It shows enthusiasm for making a social connection in the YouTube environment thanks to temporal copresence or presence at a common time. It is notable that User B (post 2) names 'nostalgia' specifically here as a relevant motivation for engagement with Ethan Gamer.

As in Examples 6.9 and 6.10, the first post in Example 6.11 asks a question to connect to users engaging in the same year.

Example 6.11

→1 User A: Anyone here in 2020 I loved this series u helped me when I was younger u where my childhood i know you won't respond but I want to tell u that you are amazing amd u have grew up a lot 😢
2 Ethan Gamer: Ty for the support! 🌑
3 User C: Just like me.
4 User D: Ethan!!!!!!!

User A's post includes a series of conversational actions without punctuation, which conclude with a crying face emoji. These actions address fans in general at the start but then address Ethan Gamer specifically, as indicated by use of pronoun 'you/u' (post 1). Specifically, she first reaches out to fans viewing the video in 2020 using a question and deictic marker ('here'), indicating the immediate YouTube context ('Anyone here in 2020'). She then expresses a positive assessment of the series ('I loved this series'), the important role of Ethan Gamer in their childhood ('u helped me when I was younger u where my childhood'), the unlikeliness of a response ('i know you won't respond'), further positive assessments ('I want to tell u that you are amazing'), sadness at Ethan Gamer's growing up, indicated by the crying emoji. Contrary to User A's expectations, Ethan Gamer does in fact respond with an expression of appreciation in post 2, which prompts User D's exclamatory 'Ethan!!!!!!!' in post 4.

To summarize the discussion of first post questions in Examples 6.9, 6.10 and 6.11, it is notable that they prompt only brief exchanges in the substrands compared with questions on gaming hardware. However, they show fans' awareness of the temporal constraints of the asynchronous YouTube comments environment and how these might be overcome linguistically and interactionally to connect with other users and the star himself. Users' desire to connect with people viewing the YouTube video in the same time period is also evident. This is different from the connections made between users through common gaming hardware (Examples 6.6 to 6.8). It reveals, however, that naming the current year is another interactional resource used by participants in this environment, similar to naming users, to connect with other gamers based on a common time of participation.

Temporal Orientations and Affiliation in an Extended Substrand

If we consider the extended I Have a Big Belly substrand (EthanGamer, 2020, February 17), it too is prompted by users' navigation between past and present after User A*'s announcement 'Dang, it's been a long time since I watched this channel'. Example 6.12 comprises a sample of the first ten posts of this substrand's responses:

> Example 6.12
>
> 1 A1*: 'Dang, it's been a long time since I watched this channel'
> 2 B: I agree
> 3 C: Same
> 4 D: Same
> 5 E: your awesome I like your vidios
> 6 F: Flick_YEAH
> 7 G: Same
> 8 H: Same lmao
> 9 I:
> 10 J: Same
> 11 K: 😵 😵 😵

This substrand is not elicited by a question; however, it generates 104 responses. The first post consists of two components, an interjection and a statement. The first component 'Dang' is a polite euphemism for expletive 'damn', followed by a comma. The second component is a statement about passing of time between A1*'s engagement with Ethan Gamer YouTube channels. This elicits mainly very brief expressions of agreement from multiple users. The most frequently used expression of agreement in this example is the colloquial 'same', used by sixty users (60 posts), rather than 'I agree' and 'agreed' (n=7), or 'me too' and 'me to' (n=12) and other variants. These responses suggest that the main recipient is User A1*, the first poster. However, other users in the chat are potential recipients in this extended substrand too because all the contributions which express agreement are equally appropriate responses to previous similar comments. In any case the first post constitutes the initial first pair part that projects second pair part responses, which in turn may be considered valid responses to the actions of 'agreeing' by other users in the strand. This reinforces YouTube's unique sequence organization compared with interaction in 'rapid fade' conversation. Clearly, the visual saliency of all the posts allows commenters to read, review and address mainly the first substrand post while at the same time addressing other users in this public forum. In many instances, as in examples discussed previously, when a specific commenter other than the first poster is addressed, those commenters are specifically named to promote understanding, given the multi-party nature of this conversation. In Example 6.12, there are also instances where the comment is directed at the content creator Ethan Gamer. In post 5, the user expresses a positive assessment of both Ethan Gamer and his videos.

Analysis of the extended substrand (EthanGamer, 2020, February 17) indicates that users respond mainly to the first post which elicited the substrand though the responses are equally relevant to other users' comments, given that 'agreeing' is a valid second pair part response to previous posts which express agreement. This is a unique aspect of YouTube comments interaction which relies on reading rather than listening to conversation.

Linguistic Evidence of Children's Developing Literacy

Developing literacy is evident in the non-standard language commenters use. While even adult chat language is generally non-standard and informal in written online conversation, with plenty of spelling errors and other irregularities due to the need for speedy typing of posts, commenters in the data regularly display language which typifies children's developing literacy. Specifically, it is common for chat participants, adult or child, to misspell words and use non-standard language in online interaction on social media, in part because this is a unique form of informal written conversation. This requires participants to adapt their 'talk' to a written environment when posting their contributions. Where online written interaction occurs in real time, they often need to write and post their contributions under time pressures. In any case, unconventional spelling and vocabulary is generally considered acceptable in this context.

Given the likely prevalence of child participants in YouTube comments interaction examined in this text, their language tends to reflect their developing written language and literacy. For example, as the reader may have noticed in some examples presented thus far, they tend to write as they speak and may at times confuse the spelling of words (homophones) that sound the same but have a different meaning, such as 'their', 'they're' and 'there' or 'two', 'too' and 'to'. This is because they are still becoming accustomed to rules related to correspondence between phonemes, the smallest units of speech, and graphemes, the smallest units of writing (letters or groups of letters). This is also the case where grammatical irregularities are evident. There are multiple instances of non-standard spelling and grammar in the data and sometimes 'invented' spelling (Gleason Berko & Ratner Bernstein, 2009, p. 418), which is common to children. The following examples provide evidence of a variety of non-standard items which might be considered typical of the developing language of children, though some may be typographical errors. They may also be present in adult writing.

In Example 6.13, also reproduced in Example 6.11 above, User A uses 'grew' instead of 'grown' in a positive but nostalgic assessment of Ethan Gamer.

> Example 6.13
>
> A: I want to tell u that you are amazing amd u have grew up a lot 😊 .

While 'u' is an accepted abbreviation of 'you' in social media interaction, the use of past tense verb 'grew' instead of past participle 'grown' with 'have' indicates developing knowledge of English verb use which is less likely to occur in adult language.

The misspelling of 'processor' in 'cow proseser' in Example 6.14 is another example of young users' developing language and literacy which is visible in the data.

> Example 6.14
>
> →1 A: I think he was copping the cow proseser from the internet
> 2 B: [User A] He was
>
> (EthanGamer, 2015, February 20)

Despite the fact that the YouTube video being referred to is entitled Baby Cow Processor, with the title visible on the landing site, this user does not reproduce 'Processor' exactly and contributes his own version by mapping the sound to the written word.

A similar solution to writing the sound corresponding to 'videos' occurs in Example 6.15.

> Example 6.15
>
> Videos.
> →1 A: I love your Minecraft fidiows
> User A [signs with real name]
> 2 A: I want to visit you
> User A [signs with real name]

In the main strand comment (post 1), the user posts his own invented version of 'videos', that is, 'fidiows' which is nonetheless likely to be comprehended by other users. In this example, it is relevant that User A appears to sign using his real name, which is masculine, beneath the main post. This allows him to distinguish himself from the profile name, which is feminine. This also suggests that User A may be a child rather than an adult.

In Example 6.16, the star's name is spelt as 'Ethen' rather than Ethan.

Example 6.16

1 A: did you miss the guys
→2 A: Ethen you havent died
3 B: Arleene Gray

While this could be a typographical rather than spelling issue, as with other spellings noted thus far, this rendition of 'Ethan', with an 'e' in place of 'a', may occur because writers do not distinguish how certain sounds in English are realized in written form if they sound the same, as in this case. We saw a similar case in the 'Who's waching' sequence (Example 6.10), where the 't' in 'watching' is dropped by a user without any social consequences in the comments.

Homophones such as 'to', 'too' and 'two' sound the same and children (and often adults) confuse them in their written form, as in Example 6.17.

Example 6.17

1 A: I love you Ethan I love you so much
2 B: Lop 8th St Louis Vuitton Monogram
→3 C: me to

In this case User C's 'me to' rather than 'me too' in post 3 is an affiliative response to User A's emotional expression of endearment towards Ethan Gamer. This post expresses agreement and suggests she feels the same way about Ethan Gamer as User A.

In Example 6.18, User A receives a response to his main comment from Ethan Gamer in the more private substrand.

Example 6.18

1 A: I've been watching you since 2016 and your videos are amazing! You are the only YouTuber that is epic! (main strand)
2 Ethan: Tysm! 😄 💬 (substrand)
→3 A: Your welcome :)
4 A: Keep on making amazing videos

Ethan Gamer's 'TYSM' (thank you so much), an expression of appreciation, responds to User A's positive assessment in post 1. User A then responds with an appropriate second pair part to complete the 'thank you' routine with 'your welcome' where she does not appear to distinguish the pronoun 'your' from the verb phrase 'you're'.

To summarize, there is evidence that children use non-standard spellings in their language to express themselves on YouTube comments, as is likely to occur in written interaction on other social media or in traditional offline writing where English is used. These spellings may be due to their developing ability to match spoken with written renditions of English words, so they may write words that sound the same but are written differently. Hence, their spelling reflects how these words are spoken phonetically. What is interesting about the various linguistic irregularities which abound in the data is that there is little evidence of other users repairing this language in the more private substrands where this would be less face-threatening. This is most likely due to the general tolerance towards the unique language of chat and non-standard versions of written language. Any instances of other-repair are in fact more likely to relate to errors of fact than language. For example, we earlier discussed examples where users correct one another in relation to gaming hardware used by Ethan Gamer (Examples 6.6 to 6.8), which are worth considering in the next section on other-repair.

Other-Repair Sequences

This section explores how children deploy conversational repair in the constrained YouTube comments context. Evidence so far in fact suggests that other-repair or correction is more likely to concern errors of fact related to technical issues rather than of linguistic expression (see Examples 6.3, 6.6 and 6.7). This section also considers whether repair as an interactional resource is likely to lead to learning in the substrands, given its potential role as a scaffold.

Example 6.19 is an extract from previously discussed Example 6.7, where repair was not considered. In this case, the repair is related to gaming hardware used by Ethan.

Example 6.19

1 A: do u have Xbox 360?
2 B: ldk
3 C: i do
→4 D: No he plays on a ps
5 E: he plays on place staihion 3

User D interprets User A's question 'do u have Xbox 360' as being directed to Ethan Gamer, because he uses the pronoun 'he' rather than 'I' in his response to User A. His negative response 'No' in post 4 initiates a repair and indicates there is a problem with User A's suggestion. In the same post he also corrects (other repairs) the suggestion that Ethan Gamer is using an Xbox 360, by providing information on what he considers the correct alternate, that is, the correct gaming hardware, a PlayStation ('ps'). So there are two components, a negative response and justification for that response (attendant activity), which constitute the repair post.

In Example 6.20, there is a similar repair of fact related to gaming hardware.

Example 6.20

1 A: What x box do u have I love u Ethan 👾 👾 👾 👾 👾 👾 👾 👾 👾
2 B1: He have a PS3 and not a xbox

In Example 6.20, User A assumes that Ethan Gamer is using an Xbox in her main strand question and seeks clarification on which particular version he is using. She addresses Ethan Gamer directly and in the same post she expresses strong endearment towards him both verbally and by deploying nine couple emojis with a heart, which suggests a relationship. User B1, a regular contributor to this substrand intervenes with a correction (other-repair) since Ethan Gamer apparently uses a PS3 rather than an Xbox. No further interaction occurs between these participants in the substrand; however, it seems that User B1 in this instance has used the substrand, a more private environment than the main strand, to complete his correction and assist User A in understanding the gameplay.

Other instances of other repair may relate to language though these are uncommon in the data. In Example 6.21, one user, a regular contributor, plays with language and produces a pun in the repair format.

> Example 6.21
> 1 A1: Ethan in Mincraft can u make a elephant plz?
> 2 A1: #BuildThisComment
> 3 B: You mean a . . . Ethanphant? :D PUN INTENDED

User A1 uses a question format to request that Ethan Gamer make an elephant in *Minecraft*, assuming that he will respond and that his gameplay is occurring in real time, which is not necessarily the case. He receives a response from User B, who begins his contribution as a correction 'You mean' and concludes with a mock linguistic correction of 'elephant', suggesting 'Ethanphant' instead, playing on the word 'elephant' to include Ethan Gamer's first name. User B signals the playful nature of the repair by including a big smile emoticon ': D' followed by verbal clarification that her statement is in jest 'PUN INTENDED' in capital letters for emphasis. Hence, this is not a true repair despite its being in repair format linguistically and suggests that users may occasionally engage in linguistic play in this environment.

Linguistic play also occurs in Example 6.22, which includes an other-repair related to language of the *Minecraft* game.

> Example 6.22
> 1 A: he said cow it's mushroom
> 2 B: +User A
> it's mooshroom
> 3 C: it's a type of cow . . . . . .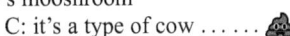

Example 6.22 includes two repairs. One may in a sense be considered an indirect repair of Ethan Gamer's language in post 1 because it addresses other users while referring to the star's talk using a third person pronoun ('he said'). The subsequent repair by User B ('+ User A it's mooshroom') in post 2 on the other hand is a direct repair of the main strand post by User A, who uses 'mushroom' in place of the correct *Minecraft* descriptor 'mooshroom'. This term denotes a mushroom-covered variant of a cow. Hence, User B's repair consists of an explanation 'it's' followed by the correct alternate 'mooshroom'. User A is in fact named specifically with the + symbol. This correction post is reinforced with an additional explanation by User C, that a mooshroom is 'a type of cow'. A humorous element is introduced as part of this comment, with the inclusion of a pile of dung emoji, which might be associated with a cow. Hence, this repair is linguistic but relates to the language of *Minecraft* which only *Minecraft* users would understand. User C collaborates with User B in completing the repair with a further explanation and the support of a humorous emoji to lighten up what might otherwise be perceived as a face-threatening act.

While in Example 6.22 we see participants' efforts to use the correct language of *Minecraft*, Example 6.23 shows a rather anomalous repair, where an accepted term in text chat 'u' is corrected.

> Example 6.23
>
> 1 A: Ethan i love your vids Keep up the best work i think you're the Best in the world nearly have a halve a million
> 2 B: YOU NO SQIDDY [Squiddy intended]
> 3 C: J
> 4 D: no Dan tdm [DanTDM intended]
> →5 E: +User D, U So mean I Love DanTDM. I Don't Like U.
> 6 E: +User D, Or I May Of Made A Mistake Of The Text.
> 7 F: he has 2 million
> 8 G: [Other user name] that makes no sence
> →9 G: User E I don't like u
> 10 H: On my sword I got knoockback unbreaking fire aspect and sharpness
> →11 I: You

In Example 6.23, users compare Ethan Gamer with other YouTube gaming celebrities, Squiddy and DanTDM, but do not always agree. User E in fact disagrees with previous assessments that 'sqiddy' and 'Dan tdm' are not as good as Ethan Gamer, as suggested by User B and D, who agree with the positive assessments by User A in the first post. User E takes issue with User D in particular by using the + sign to name him ('+User D'). He then expresses his strong appreciation of DanTDM, who User D appears to consider inferior to Ethan Gamer. He follows this with an expression of dislike of User D (post 5). In post 8, User G also takes issue with a prior post, addressing a user (unknown user), who is known to him with another pseudonym but which is unavailable in the comments. He then takes aim specifically at User E, for whom he expresses dislike in post 9 'I don't like u'. User I follows this post with a linguistic correction, specifically of the widely accepted abbreviation of 'you' which is widely adopted in online communication as 'u'. This is somewhat unusual according to previous research, as gamers and social media users tend to promote the use of language which is appropriate to online contexts. There is in fact no further conversation in the substrand after this correction, though this may be due to reasons other than the repair.

In summary, despite the existence of examples of linguistic other-repair discussed above, it is clear that linguistic repair is less frequent than errors of fact in the data, despite the fact that substrands would permit this to occur in a more private context than the main strand comments. While it is possible to engage in repair thanks to the affordances of YouTube substrand comments, in the context under examination, young YouTube commenters appear to be more preoccupied with other matters, such as understanding the video they are watching, comparing Ethan Gamer with other celebrities and connecting with other gamers with similar interests. Therefore, linguistic repair in YouTube comments is unlikely to be used as a learning tool, but rather, the preference is for repair of errors of fact to promote understanding and learning related to the video and *Minecraft* gameplay, in collaboration with other users. While learning is not evident in the online conversations, it is clear from participants' efforts to scaffold other users through conversational repair, that watching the gaming video provides gamers with possibilities for learning, as stated by User A in the main strand comments.

Example 6.24

User A: 'I consider dis a tutorial'

While there is no apparent response to this statement, the use of the term 'tutorial' indicates that the video has a pedagogical role in relation to *Minecraft* gaming.

Other Forms of Collaborative Interactions

Repair is not the only interactional resource used by YouTube commenters to assist and scaffold each other. Other interactional resources which are available to users in this context, for example, questions, have been presented above. Another important resource is advice-giving, though such collaborative interactions are mostly directed at Ethan Gamer. The main strand interactions abound in such advice, as in Example 6.23, where advice posts follow each other, though they may not have been posted sequentially deliberately.

Example 6.25

1 A: Ethan you should do peaceful you don't get hungry a lot in peaceful
2 B: You should have said MOO-ve sheep XD

As often occurs in main strand contributions, these posts provide advice to Ethan Gamer in different ways. At the same time they fulfil other conversational actions apart from advising. Post 1 recommends that Ethan Gamer use a different mode from the one he is currently in ('you should do peaceful') and provides a justification for this recommendation. This may also be interpreted as a polite request, as 'you should' hedges this statement rather than a more peremptory command in the imperative. Post 2 instead provides an attempted pun on the verb 'move' with a version which includes the sound made by cows 'MOO' except this is in reference to sheep. The intended humour in this comment is reinforced by the big smile emoticon at the end and appears to be an attempted, mock linguistic repair of an utterance produced by Ethan Gamer in the video. Hence, the target audience of these posts is Ethan Gamer whose video is, however, not a livestream; it is prerecorded. Hence, while linguistically the target audience is Ethan Gamer, users may be aware of 'overhearing' audiences who are participating in the comments interaction without posting comments or perhaps limiting their responses to 'likes'.

Example 6.26 also consists of advice-giving except that it is followed by likes and agreement in a substrand.

Example 6.26

→1 A Ethan should Milk them to.
You get leather and meat and milk of them. With the wheat farm Just add more animals With a chicken for farm you Can have a cake Business [5 likes]
2 B: Yup

This gaming advice is not clearly directed at anyone in particular. The first comment 'Ethan should Milk them to' is in the third person and is therefore about Ethan so it is a form of indirect advice and attempt to engage with YouTube comments audiences. However, the pronoun 'you' is subsequently used and may either be impersonal or directed at Ethan Gamer. Hence, it is another case of unclear recipiency which is common in this environment, especially main strand comments. It does, however, provide advice in a rather lengthy post, with a series of suggestions related to the game which is available to all commenters. User B's substrand response ('Yup') agrees with these suggestions but the post also receives five likes which denote approval and other commenters as recipients of the post.

An additional use of YouTube comments is for participants to seek assistance from other commenters, which promotes understanding of both Ethan's and users' own video gameplay. This is evident, for example, in our previous discussions on the use of questions and repair regarding gaming software. These are likely to contribute to participants' understanding of the gaming video, thus promoting ZPD. There are, however, instances where participants may directly request assistance of other participants on a technical issue, as in Example 2.27.

Example 2.27

1 A I Nedd help getting on line
2 B1: Yes I have Internet but I'm can't make a PlayStation network
account. :-/

In Example 2.27, User B1, who is a regular contributor in this context, responds to User A's call for help in the substrand, but appears unable to assist. User A appears to be online on YouTube or she would not be able to post comments. However, her issue is probably related to accessing her gaming console, which suggests that participants engage in their own gaming activity concurrently with Ethan Gamer's asynchronous gameplay as they are connected. Hence, her post is a clear request for technical assistance to which User B1 responds with a troubles telling about his own access woes. The complaining is reinforced by the concluding emoji which appears to express annoyance or frustration.

Conclusion

Based on available data from selected Ethan Gamer YouTube comments, the analysis indicates that YouTube comments interaction is a unique form of interaction with numerous affordances, which may provide children with social and learning advantages related to gaming, despite its constraints. While in Chapter 2 on emojis we observed the prevalence of positive evaluations directed at Ethan Gamer in YouTube main strand comments, in this chapter we have identified a wider range of conversational actions, with substrands used as a resource by young participants to connect with other gamers, whether known or unknown to them, and to improve their understanding both of Ethan Gamer's videos and their own gameplay. These actions may include questions, repair, advice-giving, expressing agreement and tellings. Responses to questions, repair and advice-giving may potentially scaffold users' understanding of Ethan Gamer's gameplay and promote ZPD in relation to gaming. It should also be noted that the variety of conversational and linguistic functions in YouTube comments depends on the video as the YouTube video provides a framework for comments according to Boyd (2014). For example, a political video is likely to provoke political commentary while gaming language and commentary related to gaming are visible in the data examined in this context.

As noted in Chapter 5, Gee and Hayes (2012) see the multiple digital activities related to gameplay as affinity spaces because they support a shared passion among the participants. This is especially obvious from the extended substrand where a post elicited 104 comments and 148 likes. These comments were predominantly dedicated to expressing agreement with other users on their previous and current participation in the Ethan Gamer YouTube video, using various colloquial synonyms of 'I agree' (EthanGamer, 2020, February 17). The mostly affiliative actions by individual participants in the data examined allow them to establish a presence and promote participation in this public online gaming community.

The video viewing and related comments have the potential to facilitate improvements in gameplay through use of interactional resources which scaffold users on the YouTube comments platform. This is especially the case for the substrands, where the platform permits sequential conversations and creation of relevant first and second pair parts thanks to clearer interactional access to recipients compared to the main strand comments. Access to recipients is constrained in the main strand comments, which are interactionally disrupted due to content creators' and the platform's subsequent editing and reorganization of the comments based on various criteria. Specifically, interactional disruption is mainly due to disrupted recipiency in the main strand comments; however, it is reconstituted by users who engage in substrand comments. While some disruptions are generated by the software, content creators and YouTube moderators may also play a role in altering the appropriate presentation of adjacency pairs especially of the main strand.

All comments may address either Ethan Gamer, other users or an invisible audience constituted by reader-viewer recipients. According to Chau (2011), many users are on the periphery as non-interactional viewers, who do not use either likes, dislikes or comments. Hence, while linguistically the target audience is Ethan Gamer and other interactional users, participants who post comments are possibly aware of 'overhearing' audiences who engage non-interactionally in the comments interaction and may benefit from their advice, humour and general online conversation.

Analysis indicates that age is a recurrent topic in YouTube comments as participants often connect to YouTube comments using adults' accounts. Use of an adult's account may have the advantage of promoting safety, as adults are able to monitor their children's online activities for safety reasons if they wish. However, this requires children to complete additional conversational work to reveal their real age and name, often using gamer tags, to other users for the purpose of interaction and gaming. This is necessary for children to participate in a support network and informal community of practice related to gaming on *Minecraft* and other gaming platforms. Their interactional efforts are therefore both social and learning related. They are dedicated to connecting and reconnecting with other gamers for the purpose of asking questions and seeking technical assistance in understanding the games played by content creators and possibly applying new learnings from the video to their own play.

Repair, especially other repair or correction, is an important activity afforded by the YouTube substrand environment; however, it regards mainly errors of fact, especially related to gaming hardware used by Ethan Gamer. Users are generally tolerant of non-standard linguistic features which may be due either to children's developing literacy, accepted conventions of chat language and typographical errors. This tolerance may be due to users' polite avoidance of face-threatening actions or their predominant interest in gaming rather than language. Gaming platforms are in fact often made relevant by users in these interactions, where differences and commonalities are established between users. Playful repairs and direct requests for help are also present, which highlight other affordances of YouTube comments for participation in social activities and gaming.

Interactions by individual users are usually brief and mostly limited to one post each in the same substrand, though some may intervene again with additional posts at various points in conversations. While there is potential for learning, this environment's affordances are therefore limited to promotion rather than enactment of learning. Its affordances for social connectivity are however clear, though participants need to use various interactional resources, such as naming addressed participants and use of the substrands to overcome constraints related to recipiency and sequence organization, which impact on understanding of the conversations. As far as the extended substrand is concerned (EthanGamer, 2020, February 17), the interaction was predominantly social as it was dedicated to affiliative conversational work between users. It features likes and repetitive expressions of agreement, with the first post based on users' common experience of returning to an Ethan Gamer channel after a break. It was, therefore, less varied linguistically than the briefer substrands of EthanGamer (2015, February 20).

In Summary

- Age is a relevant concern for participants in interaction due to the need to reveal their true age when using adults' accounts, to facilitate connection with other young gamers.
- An age-related tendency by participants is to recount past experiences (tellings) on their previous engagement with Ethan Gamer YouTube videos, as part of a search for commonality with other participants.
- YouTube comments users may sometimes use a question format to seek out participants from the current year, to connect with other gamers based on a common time of participation (temporal copresence).
- All YouTube comments interaction is asynchronous, sometimes with significant differences in time of contribution.
- Substrand posts can only be elicited by a mainstrand post, which constitutes an initial first pair part to which substrand posts mostly respond, as second pair parts of adjacency pairs. Additional first and second pair parts may however sometimes be created when new conversational sequences are created between substrand participants other than the first poster.

- Main strand comments interaction is not usually sequential, even when the 'newest first' option is selected; hence, only the more private substrand comments are likely to permit coherent interaction.
- Likes or 'thumbs up' may be seen as a form of second pair part which is posted in response to a main strand comment, to form an adjacency pair.
- Recipients of substrand and main strand comments are not always clear unless they are named by users. This may cause interactional confusion and disrupted adjacency pairs and recipiency, though most posts are intended for either Ethan Gamer, users in general or specific users if named. Naming is thus an important interactional device which promotes understanding in YouTube comments multi-party interaction.
- While linguistically the target audience is Ethan Gamer and other interactional users, active users are probably aware of 'overhearing' non-interactional reader-viewer recipients.
- There is often a correspondence between number of likes and length of substrands elicited by a main strand comment.
- Questions quite often elicit substrand responses, which suggests this is a linguistic format that projects answers even in the YouTube comments environment.
- YouTube commenters use this forum to connect with both unknown and familiar users.
- YouTube users engage in technical talk, to better understand Ethan Gamer's gameplay and to apply new knowledge derived from the video to their own gaming efforts. This talk also allows them to connect with users with similar hardware for possible gaming outside the YouTube space.
- Children's non-standard spellings in their language on YouTube comments may in some cases be due to their developing ability to match spoken with written renditions of words. Repair of such language rarely occurs, given social media users' general tolerance towards non-standard renditions of written language and the unique language of chat.
- The rare instances of other-repair which occur in YouTube substrand interaction are more likely to relate to errors of fact than language; they are sometimes completed collaboratively and accompanied by emojis or emoticons that mitigate the possibly face-threatening nature of repair.
- While other-repair is clearly an affordance of YouTube comments substrand interaction, it is not commonly used. The data indicates that users are more preoccupied with understanding the video and game they are watching, comparing Ethan Gamer with other celebrities and connecting with other gamers with similar interests and gaming platforms.
- Linguistic play, especially puns, is one creative feature of YouTube substrand interaction which is usually related to the gaming context, in this case *Minecraft* gaming.

7   Online Grooming Talk

Introduction: The Problem

There has been a rapid rise in the use of online social networks by children, especially during the recent pandemic. Paedophiles use such networks to exploit children. When children interact online, they are therefore likely to come into contact with paedophiles, who use social media and games sites to access children for illicit sexual activities. The constrained text chat environment is ideal for paedophiles, as it hides their identities and facilitates deception (Chiang & Grant, 2019). Hence, children may easily be fooled into thinking they are chatting with other children or benevolent adults, thanks to the manner in which paedophiles design their language and interactional resources for the sexual exploitation of children.

This chapter uses conversation analysis techniques to shed light on online grooming, as it is unfortunately an unavoidable element of many children's online interactions. For example, online safety unexpectedly became a relevant aspect of *Club Penguin* interactions (Chapter 3). This chapter instead focuses specifically on children's online safety, exploring how paedophiles design online language and interactional resources for child recipients to gain their trust, and how children respond. It builds on knowledge about the online grooming process, where grooming 'does not necessarily involve any sexual activity or even discussion of sexual activity' (Victoria's Crimes Amendment (Grooming) Act 2014). Thus, online exchanges where sexual topics and abuse are evident from the start, as described in Powell et al. (2021), are not considered. Online-facilitated abuse of children by adults who are known to them has also received research attention (e.g. Mitchell et al., 2010; Wolak & Finklehor, 2013; Wolak et al., 2018). However, there is a paucity of research on how text chat between unacquainted adults and children is used successfully to groom and exploit children, from a linguistic and interactional perspective. Specifically, given the scale and impacts of child sexual abuse, systematic analysis of online perpetrators' and children's language is needed to understand how they establish relationships despite being unacquainted at the initial stages of non-sexual online grooming exchanges.

While anonymity facilitates deception, participant invisibility in written interaction is also a concern because internet and gaming sites remove any visual cues that children might use to identify the age, gender and general trustworthiness of an interlocutor. For example, the use of avatars in gaming sites facilitates the process of hiding paedophiles' true identities, so other means are required to identify them. Thanks to experts and educational programs in child protection, families are aware of some of the most obvious signs of danger. Some of these include requests to move into a private chat room, requests for a meeting, photos, phone numbers, addresses and school of the child. The Australian Federal Police (AFP, 2022, January 30) have revealed common offender tactics to gain children's trust, including 'preying on insecurities, feigning common interests, in-game chats and bribes, flattery and fake modelling offers'. Nonetheless, despite awareness of these signals and educational efforts, many children may often have difficulty suspecting the 'nice guy', girl or child they have met online, who says what they want to hear. This is because grooming strategies which previous research has pointed out (e.g. Chiang & Grant, 2017) may initially appear like a form of rapport building which children are unable to recognize as potentially dangerous. For example, they may not consider their interlocutor's conversational efforts to establish physical distance as an attempt to assess their accessibility. This may include requesting information on the child's general location, immediate surroundings and family schedules of both parents and the child.

Increasing numbers of unsuspecting children continue to be snared by online paedophiles, despite the best efforts of police, online grooming experts, parents and schools (Dorasamy et al., 2021). In particular, the reported volume of child sexual abuse imagery has been rising exponentially (Gale, 2017; Internet Watch Foundation, 2015; WeProtect Global Alliance, 2018). This growth is reflected in the increased number of domains hosting child exploitation material. Coronavirus lockdown has apparently led to a doubling of child abuse images and videos (7.4 million) circulating in the Australian state of Victoria alone (Vedelago, 2020, June 19). A recent independent inquiry in the United Kingdom highlighted the global crisis in this area, due in part to the ease with which millions of child sexual abuse images, including images of young children and babies, can be accessed within just three 'clicks', (Independent Inquiry Child Sexual Abuse, 2022). The nature and scale of the abuse of children online and the impact on children's mental and physical health demands that this area receives urgent attention. In regard to perpetrator behaviours specifically, the report found that they commonly posed as friends in online activity with children, with the ultimate intention of securing indecent images of the child or meeting the child for the purpose of committing sexual abuse in person.

Surveys of Australian children and young people have found that being contacted by strangers on the internet is extremely common. Approximately 50 per cent of teenagers aged thirteen to seventeen and 27 per cent of children aged eight to twelve communicated with a stranger online (e-Safety Commissioner, 2017). According to the Pew Research Center in 2015, girls are more likely to meet new friends via social media (78% vs 52% of boys), while boys are substantially more likely to meet new friends while playing games online (57% vs 13% of girls). Hence, paedophiles targeting boys are more likely to be found on game sites and those targeting girls tend to use social media. Their goal may be either to groom a child for virtual sex and more immediate gratification or to engage in virtual and real sex and other forms of exploitation in the longer term.

It is clear that interaction with human beings, not just with the game system, is at the heart of play within many popular video games and social media generally. As we have seen so far in this book, interaction with others contributes to collaborative learning and the development of colloquial language and interpersonal skills. Online interaction unfortunately also makes children vulnerable to online paedophiles, especially where games provide unrestricted access to unacquainted players. Online paedophiles are known to be very skilful at setting up relationships with unacquainted children so it is important to understand how they design their online language and interaction for child recipients and how children are likely to respond. This would facilitate education of children and their carers on how to avoid or manage such conversations.

While legislation is in place to facilitate the apprehension of perpetrators engaging in real time online-facilitated sexual exploitation of children, it is not always equivalent to laws on face-to-face abuse. In the state of South Australia, legal history was made when a paedophile admitted his abuse of a teenager, via social media, was as heinous as face-to-face sexual assault and deserving of a maximum life sentence (Fewster, 2022, September 17). By confessing to having maintained an unlawful sexual relationship with a child, this individual was able to be charged as if the online abuse had occurred in person. Otherwise, a lesser sentence would have been applied. This episode indicates the limitations of existing legislation in this area, most likely not just in Australia.

This chapter addresses the online-facilitated child exploitation issue by analysing grooming language and interaction where text chat is the medium of communication. It first discusses the role of conversation analysis methodology in this area, followed by a summary of previous research efforts, findings and gaps in the online grooming language research area, before proceeding with single case analysis of a real life episode of online grooming involving a paedophile and a child during a text chat session. The chapter concludes with an in-summary section.

Applying Conversation Analysis to Online Grooming Interaction

Conversation analysis is an untapped tool for understanding how adults co-construct interaction to establish relationships with unacquainted children online. It requires naturalistic data consisting of genuine paedophile-child interactions. The application of these analytical techniques has the potential to reveal new insights about the online grooming process for police use and public dissemination. Additionally, new knowledge which reveals unsuspecting child recipient responses within online grooming exchanges provides all children with the opportunity for reflection on their own online interactions with strangers through educative efforts. While numerous resources have been developed and key typologies of paedophiles identified, research so far has not attended to the more subtle language and machinery of interaction that is deployed by paedophiles when attempting to gain children's trust during online interaction such as text chat. Specifically, there has been little attention paid to the trajectory of language and interaction to establish an online relationship with children. Such a trajectory is achieved through a conversation which is co-constructed by both paedophile and unsuspecting child.

Various online interactional contexts have been fruitfully investigated which are not grooming-related but focused on institutional and social interaction (Dooly & Tudini, 2016; Giles et al., 2015; Meredith, 2017; Tudini, 2010, 2015; Tudini & Liddicoat, 2017; Tudini & Strambi, 2017). This line of research also has the potential to provide significant new knowledge about the online grooming process, especially where the focus is on small talk. Additionally, it has the capacity to facilitate protection of children by identifying typical and recurrent patterns of paedophile-child pairs' language and interactional behaviors, prior to commencement of abuse proper. This chapter therefore aims to provide an initial contribution to the prevention of online exploitation of children, based on analysis of one past real life episode, where the perpetrator was subsequently apprehended by police (Crystal, 2011). This will assist us to begin to understand which conversational resources are most commonly used by paedophiles and accepted by children. One of the benefits of such research is to raise awareness among children, parents, carers, teachers and police on which apparently innocuous but interactionally effective conversational actions to look out for, where these are currently unknown. As most research so far is based on interaction between paedophiles and child decoys only (e.g. Black et al., 2015; Lorenzo-Dus & Kinzel, 2019; Williams et al., 2013), future research attention needs to focus on online interaction between paedophiles and genuine children.

The single case analysed in this chapter provides important insights. It is, however, only the beginning, as systematic analysis of additional cases involving genuine children is required to gain a complete picture of how these exchanges are co-constructed, for the protection of children in the longer term. Identification of the most commonly used online conversational resources, especially those which unsuspecting children find credible, has the potential to prevent abuse through education. This analysis focuses on an online exchange between a fifteen-year-old girl[1] and a male perpetrator, to gain insights into how online grooming language and interaction is co-constructed between adults and young participants. As it is only a small sample, only limited conclusions can be drawn from the analysis as it requires replication on additional similar chat data.

What We Already Know

There are various types of sexual exploitation in online contexts. For example, while many paedophiles declare their illicit intentions to children immediately or so on after approaching them (e.g. Powell et al., 2021), others do not. Additionally, online abuse is often perpetrated by adults who are already known to children (Mitchell et al., 2010; Wolak & Finklehor, 2013; Wolak et al., 2018). This chapter is focused on online grooming where participants have only met online rather than in a face-to-face context. Hence, online grooming interactions are known to prepare children for abuse by developing a relationship of trust, secrecy and compliance. This may lead to abuse either online or in person.

Thanks to the anonymity and invisibility afforded by internet communication, paedophiles are able to take on one or more identities to establish an online relationship with children (Chiang & Grant, 2019) prior to commencing abuse. In the early stages of an online relationship, it is generally known that many paedophiles aim to gain the trust of the child and then to introduce sexual themes into the conversation, prior to moving onto either virtual or real sex. Strategies used by paedophiles at the initial stages of online grooming relationships, prior to commencing sexually oriented interactions, have been described as 'indirect' by Kloess et al. (2019). These strategies are often successful in achieving their objectives due to the power differential between adult and child, of which the latter may be unaware if the perpetrator enacts the role of a child.

Previous research indicates that some children are more vulnerable than others and more likely to be targeted by paedophiles (e.g. Whittle et al., 2013; Davidson et al., 2016; Webster et al., 2012). Children who are in

---

[1] Due to difficulties in gaining access to data in this area and uncertainty about its provenance (personal communication by author of Crystal, 2011), it is possible that the fifteen-year-old target is in fact a child decoy, where an undercover agent is impersonating the child. If this were the case, it would alter the analysis somewhat and at the same time illustrate the detective's interactional expertise at assuming the role of a fifteen-year-old girl, due to the credibility of the conversation. However, this analysis is based on the assumption that this is in fact a victim in an actual criminal case, as reported in Crystal (2011).

a dysfunctional family, or have difficulty with friendships, may seek to fill these emotional voids through online interaction. In fact, they may find it easier to make friends online than in face-to-face real life contexts. Paedophiles are apparently most successful with children who are naive, low in self-esteem, lacking in self-confidence or curious about sex (Whittle et al., 2013). Children are most vulnerable when their interactions are less likely to be monitored by protective adults and where perpetrators are freer to engage in manipulation, threats and extortion culminating in exploitation of children (Quayle et al., 2014; Wolak et al., 2018). The form of this exploitation can vary depending on the vulnerability of the child (Davidson et al., 2016), characteristics and preferences of paedophiles (Gottschalk, 2011; Martellozzo, 2015; Quayle et al., 2014) and opportunities they are able to facilitate through grooming (Finklehor et al., 2016).

Traits of 'vulnerable' children tend to apply to a large percentage of children; hence, parents' and carers' roles are crucial in keeping communication channels open with their children. Children may also seek alternative parent figures online, if their relationships with the real parents are unsatisfactory. Additionally, we need to consider that teenagers generally tend to take more risks than younger children or adults, regardless of whether they belong to the most 'vulnerable' category of young people. It is therefore important to understand how individual paedophiles operate online, especially in instances where they successfully gain children's trust, and whether there are linguistic and interactional patterns which are common to all chat exchanges between perpetrator-target pairs.

Research has shown that paedophiles use various tactics in online interaction to exploit children. According to Quayle et al. (2014), they may consult other paedophiles and their written guides to develop new tactics and expertise in grooming. Tactics may involve elaborate multiple false identities (Chiang & Grant, 2019; Independent Inquiry Child Sexual Abuse, 2022). However, Wolak et al. (2010) and Powell et al. (2021) suggest that deception and trickery is infrequent and more typically, in many online contexts, adults groom children online without hiding their identities.

The initial stages of grooming are, however, a critical point for preventing abuse because many paedophiles will seek reciprocal relationships with children rather than engaging in sexual exploitation from the start, according to Tener et al. (2015). We therefore need to develop deeper understandings of the conversational actions deployed by paedophiles to gain children's trust and which of those are most likely to be accepted by children and then used as a foundation for exploitation and abuse. In one of the few online grooming studies which apply a linguistic analysis, Black et al. (2015), analysed forty-four transcripts of perpetrators' online interactions with adult decoys to identify strategies used across each distinct stage of online grooming. This study was based on computerized (Linguistic Inquiry Word Count) analysis, with content analysis also applied through manual coding of chat transcripts. It shed some light on the online grooming process, where strategies were found to be similar to those used in face-to-face contexts. For example, flattery, assessing parents' work schedules and discussions of sexuality in past relationships were present; however, the manner and timing of these strategies were likely to differ in online environments, compared with face-to-face encounters. This suggests while there are similarities between face-to-face and online grooming interactions, the latter require specific research attention if progress is to be made in research and education in this area.

Previous research has proposed typical stages of paedophile-target relationships in online contexts. For example, Wager et al. (2018) identified key initial grooming stages such as friendship formation, relationship formation and securing the target's trust. Williams et al. (2013) describe three primary themes in their content analysis, which was drawn from analysing grooming tactics observed by 'undercover adults'. Firstly, the adult establishes rapport by demonstrating warmth, friendliness and empathy to the target. This may be easier with more socially isolated children without a protective parent. Perpetrators may even be communicating with multiple children concurrently and will select those who are likely to be most receptive to abuse (Webster et al. 2012). Secondly, when a comfortable environment is established, the perpetrator will introduce sexual content into the conversation, often incidentally at first, and attempt to make it central to the ongoing conversation. Finally, perpetrators will make an assessment of the target (child) and their environment, as to the level of trust and the target's interest in sexual topics, in determining whether they proceed to abuse. Stages which have been reported in the research are summarized in Table 7.1.

It should be noted that Stage 4 may occur prior to Stage 3, depending on the perpetrator's chosen strategy. Unlike grooming stages based on research presented in Table 7.1, this chapter focuses on exchanges where paedophiles approach unacquainted children to gain their trust and friendship, prior to introducing the idea of sex into the conversation. It is especially important to

Table 7.1 *Grooming stages summary reported in previous research*

1. Approach target/s online	2. Develop relationship to gain child's trust, in some cases after identifying one of multiple possible targets	3. Introduce idea of sex as normal to make target comfortable with notion of sexual activity	4. Assess target before taking next step to engage in virtual and/or real sex

understand the more subtle advances which succeed in gaining children's trust based on children's responses, at Stage 2, prior to introducing the idea of sex (Table 7.1). Specifically, analysis in the following section identifies some of the conversational resources successfully deployed by one individual chatting with a fifteen-year-old at Stage 2, though further chat interactions involving paedophiles and children need to be systematically analysed to ascertain which of these behaviours are recurrent across most online grooming contexts where participants are unacquainted.

Gaining Children's Trust: An Analysis

This section provides evidence that gaining control of the conversation may be a precursor to emotional control of children, which may lead to extortion. Conversation Analysis techniques are applied to an episode of grooming previously investigated by David Crystal (2011), derived from the early stages of an online paedophile-target relationship in a chat room. Crystal (2011) observes the turn-taking asymmetry of the conversation, where the child seems to post two thirds of the posts. Interactional analysis goes into detail on how this turn-taking imbalance is enacted. We shall see that even though the child does most of the 'chatting', she is not the one who is in control of the conversation. The analysis will show how this paedophile uses text chat to successfully enact controlling actions in interaction with his target, a fifteen-year-old girl.

Example 7.1 is derived from early in the paedophile-target interaction which was held over several weeks. As Crystal notes, at this stage the paedophile (46-year-old male) is attempting to gain a young girl's sympathy and establish a relationship. It is an authentic example of how paedophiles might attempt to gain older children's trust, though further cases are required to confirm findings. On reading the online exchange (Examples 7.1 to 7.4 below), we can immediately see that it is one-sided, with the child posting most of the posts, as noted by Crystal. This impression is reinforced by counting the actual number of posts comprising this small extract of conversation, where of the fifty-three total posts, fourteen (36%) are by the paedophile and thirty-nine (74%) are by the child. Through microanalysis we can discover why this is the case and how it is likely to be due to a deliberate interactional strategy enacted by the paedophile to encourage the target to 'talk' about herself and disclose personal information.

Apologies, Delays and Personal Announcement

In Example 7.1, at the start of the chat conversation, the paedophile explains why he was delayed in responding to the child's email, which suggests a separate email or other type of conversation was established in addition to the chat under examination.

Example 7.1

1 P: got your mail, sorry I haven't replied, rather busy at present (death of mother)
2 T: oh Im so sorry
3 T: I woried in case I was being too forward
4 T: my gran died a couple of years ago and I remember how much that hurt
5 T: It must feel pretty awful
6 P: very sudden, but not in pain, still these things happen to us all at sometime or other, must not dwell on it, plenty to do and sort out

We can see a couple of important conversational resources deployed by the paedophile at the start of the exchange (post 1). Firstly, he apologizes for not replying to the child's email, in a separate unavailable exchange. This suggests that there has not been contact for a while (exact length of time unknown) and that this online conversation is the first interaction since the child sent her last email. Normally, after an apology for a 'dispreferred' action, in this instance, not responding to a separate email in a timely manner, it is customary for people to explain or justify why this action occurred. In this case the paedophile announces a significant personal event, the death of his mother, as the reason for his delay. Given the subsequent outcome of this conversation, this may be a lie which is used to gain the girl's sympathy and emotional engagement. She in fact responds appropriately to his announcement by producing a strong expression of sympathy ('Im so sorry').

The target follows her expression of sympathy with an additional three posts, with her responses to the paedophile's announcement amounting to a total of four subsequent posts, with no response from the paedophile until post 6. The target's response indicates her emotional engagement with the paedophile's announcement. However, the paedophile also appears to be delaying his response. Unfortunately, no time stamps have been provided with the transcript, to assist us in understanding whether the target produced the additional three posts due to the paedophile's lack of response, or if she is simply faster than the paedophile at typing and posting her comments. Lack of timing information prevents us from establishing whether this is in fact a delayed response on his part. This is important, as it would mirror the delay in responding to her prior emails and suggest that delaying tactics are part of the paedophile's way of operating by playing 'hard to get' and displaying a (false) lack of eagerness in the initial stages of the relationship. Delays in responding may be reassuring to a potential child target, who could become suspicious of an overly eager conversational partner, especially if this person is a stranger she met online. Delayed responses may also encourage the child to keep posting contributions. This contrasts with his behaviour further into the conversation, where he does not hesitate to ask probing and vague intimate questions to his target.

Personal Announcement, Emotional Closeness, Lowering Target's Guard

There is also another related effect of the paedophile's delay in responding to her email, which is evident in the child's post 3 ('I woried in case I was being too forward'). Bearing in mind we are dealing with a fifteen-year-old female, this statement suggests that she was concerned ('woried') about her email, sent prior to the chat exchange under examination. It is unclear whether this statement refers to the fact of sending it or the content of it being overly familiar behaviour in the early stages of their 'relationship'. Hence, her post 3 suggests she is relieved at the paedophile's revelation about his mother's death as a justification for his delayed response, as she was initially concerned about being too forward. There is still no apparent response from the paedophile to her posts at this stage of the exchange and at post 4 the child contributes a personal story (telling) related to the death of her grandmother, to express her understanding of the paedophile's loss and pain ('I remember how much that hurt'), further reinforcing her empathy and display of understanding and closeness towards the paedophile. In post 5 ('It must feel pretty awful') she adds a further affiliative expression of empathy and understanding for the paedophile's feelings at the loss of his mother. So it is clear that the paedophile's personal announcement promotes preferred affiliative conversational behaviours on the part of the child, with her expressions of understanding bringing her closer to him in the relationship. Such an announcement is an especially effective tool to gain a child's trust because she lowers her guard. When the paedophile finally responds to her posts at post 6, he adds to the 'story' about his mother's death, providing details about how she died and his stance on the situation, with a suggestion that he 'must not dwell on it', and sort out practical aspects of the death. His attempt at gaining her sympathy, delayed responses and apparent lack of interest are likely to be deliberate tactics prior to moving onto Stage 3, when sex is introduced as an acceptable conversation topic, or Stage 4, which leads to virtual or face-to-face sex (see Table 7.1).

Taking Control of the Conversation with Requests and Questions

It will become evident from analysis of Example 7.2 that announcing his mother's death is an effective strategy to gain the child's sympathy, thus ensuring that she trusts and opens up to the paedophile. This sets up the exchange for more probing questions.

Example 7.2

7 T: yeh i bet
8 T: theres not much wrong in dwelling on it though
9 T: thats an Ok thing to do

10 P: lets change to subject
11 T: OK
12 T: no prob
13 P: lets change the subject
14 T: k
15 T: any sugestions?
16 P: Tell me about you, why submissive
17 T: um
18 T: do you know, I dont realy know
19 T: it started as a laugh and then . . .

The child posts three comments (posts 7–9) on the perpetrator's mother's death. Post 7 expresses agreement ('yeh I bet') and then ratifies the death as a valid topic in conversation ('theres not much wrong in dwelling on it though'; thats an Ok thing to do'). These posts signal a supportive stance on the part of the child, in response to a rather lengthy post 6 by the perpetrator ('very sudden, but not in pain, still these things happen to us all at sometime or other, must not dwell on it, plenty to do and sort out').

Rather than following the child's suggestion to continue talk about his mother's death, however, the paedophile suddenly requests a change of topic. He posts the same request twice due to a typing error in post 10 which he repairs in post 13. The child agrees to change topic twice, first in posts 11 and 12 and then again in post 14. She then follows up by suggesting that the paedophile choose the next topic (post 15: 'any suggestions?'). The paedophile then launches into a series of questions which shift the discussion from serious personal topics about himself to personal topics related to the child's personal life. He begins by requesting that the target talk about herself, probing her use of the term 'submissive' (post 16). The text does not indicate where this term is previously used. It would either be associated with the child's online nickname, or could have been used in a previous chat session or email. The paedophile's post 16 is quite forceful from an interactional and emotional point of view. He uses a command ('Tell me about you'), followed by a question ('why submissive') without any form of hedging to soften these two requests for the child to talk about herself and explain why she refers to herself as submissive. While it may seem innocuous to change topic by showing interest in the child's own life, we are dealing with a known paedophile, so this knowledge justifies our suspecting that this stage of the conversation is part of the initial grooming process.

The paedophile's topic shift from his own life to the child's ('Tell me about you, why submissive') appears to catch her by surprise, as she expresses hesitation in post 17 ('um') and an inability to answer the question in post 18 ('do you know, I don't realy know'). She then explains her use of 'submissive' as being initially for laughs; hence, not to be taken seriously. This statement is followed by dots which denote further pausing or hesitation at the end of the post (post 19).

Overall, the child's response by post 19 might suggest discomfort with the question, as clearly the conversation has moved from an interpersonal exchange regarding the paedophile's mother's death and related issues, to an exchange which focuses on her personal thoughts and feelings, sparked by her previous use of the descriptor 'submissive', probably in reference to herself. This term is subject to multiple interpretations which the paedophile has asked her to explain. So, while she initially downplays the significance of her choice of term, she then begins to open up and express her opinions and feelings.

Opening Up to the Paedophile

The child continues to open up in response to the paedophile's questions in Example 7.3.

> Example 7.3
>
> 20   : its just such a high
> 21 T: trouble is I dont think too many people understand
> 22 T: theres too many kids out there i gues
> 23 P: why did it start as a laugh
> 24 T: just from messing on the net
> 25 P: in what way?
> 26 T: um
> 27 T: (thinks)
> 28 T: you want the whole thing?
> 29 P: I want to know what makes you tick
> 30 T: ok
> 31 T: thats easy
> 32 T: giveing control away is what makes me fly
> 33 T: like its my choice too, but you kinda get yourself to the point whare its a point of pride to stick with it
> 34 T: BUT
> 35 T: it needs someone whos got some life experience to take that control
> 36 T: and people like that are hard to find
> 37 P: thats true
> 38 T: you ever got involved like this before?
> 39 P: So I take it that you have had no real time experience
> 40 T: yeh I have
> 41 P: yes
> 42 T: it was another world
> 43 T: anything I do, I do for real
> 44 T: not head stuff

The young girl's response to the paedophile's request/question 'Tell me about you, why submissive' continues to post 22 (Example 7.3), where she speaks of her emotions 'it's just such a high' to justify her choice of 'submissive' (post 20). She then complains more generally of people's lack of understanding (post 21), for which she proposes a reason, related to the presence of 'kids out there'. She does not explain this statement further.

This is where the paedophile follows up on her initial statement regarding the use of 'submissive' for a laugh, at post 23 ('Why did it start as a laugh'). This is another question rather than a comment, which shows the rather one-sided nature of the conversation, where the paedophile is the one asking questions and the target providing answers and most of the contributions in the online conversation. Her response to this question 'just from messing on the net' is followed immediately with a further question by the paedophile 'in what way?', which requires the child to elaborate further on her previous statement. Questions are known in conversation analysis to be one of the most effective ways of projecting a response from other people. The paedophile is clearly 'fishing' for personal information. The target again responds to the latest question with a display of hesitation over three posts (26–28): firstly, the hesitation marker 'um', then an indication that she's pausing to think ('thinks') and finally a question which seeks clarification on what exactly the paedophile wants to know, in particular whether he wants to know everything: 'you want the whole thing?'

The paedophile explains further that he wants to know what makes his interlocutor tick (post 29), which is understood as an affirmative answer to her question and that the paedophile does want her to explain how she thinks without holding back in any way. This is where the paedophile believes he has achieved his goal of consolidating this relationship to the point where the target opens up on personal matters, which include talk about the kind of relationship she prefers, including the fact that she needs 'someone whos got some life experience' (post 35) and the difficulty of finding such a person (post 36), to which the paedophile expresses agreement (post 37). The paedophile also suggests that the child is unlikely to have had 'real time experience' (post 39) and she reveals that she is in fact experienced, with the remainder of the conversation extract (posts 40–44) indicating that she is opening up about her previous relationships, without going into specifics.

When the Paedophile Goes Too Far

After declaring that she has 'real' experience in relationships 'not head stuff' (Example 7.3, post 44), in Example 7.4, which continues the same conversation, the paedophile requests details about those experiences. This request causes the target to question his motives.

> Example 7.4
> 45 P: what did you experience? how did you enjoy it?
> 46 T: wow
> 47 T: this sounds like an interview!

48 T: lol
49 P: in a way yes, I need to know, if what we have in common
50 T: bit reluctant to get into big personal stuff with someone I dont realy
   know . . . . . . yet
51 T: but if that someone is right
52 T: diffrent matter
53 P: fair enough . . .

The paedophile's double questions 'what did you experience? how did you enjoy it' (post 45) are cast as inappropriate by the target, who expresses surprise ('wow!') and suggests that they sound like an interview (post 47). Her 'lol' post which occurs immediately after her response to the questions has the effect of softening her dispreferred actions, which delay her answer and require the paedophile to engage in additional conversational work. The paedophile is therefore forced to justify his questions as necessary to find common ground between them (post 49). The girl justifies and explains her refusal to answer by expressing reluctance about 'getting into big personal stuff with someone I don't realy know . . . . . . yet' (post 50). The dot points followed by 'yet' suggest she is still open to a relationship with the paedophile, as she follows this up with a post beginning with 'but', 'but if that someone is right', which suggests that she still considers the paedophile a possible partner, which leads to the paedophile's acceptance of her refusal 'fair enough . . .' (post 53). At this point the target's conversational actions suggest that she is open to continuing the exchange, which is important to the paedophile, to continue the online conversation.

Grooming Preliminaries: A Summary

Overall, we see the following phases in this episode of online grooming. At the initial stages of the interaction, there is evidence of delay of responses to the target's emails and initial posts. We cannot be sure that this is done intentionally, because there may be a legitimate reason for the delays. Further data analysis would be required to confirm this as a recurrent conversational action in online grooming contexts. Additionally, we do not see the chat time stamp which tells us how long the target is waiting after each post. Additional cases with timing details would need to be analysed to consolidate the possibility that paedophiles play 'hard to get' to avoid looking too eager, in a game of cat and mouse with their targets.

The second strategy is the announcement of a significant personal event which appears to succeed in gaining the child's sympathy, as an expression of sympathy is a preferred response to such an announcement. While the mother's death may actually be real, there is a strong chance that it is not, given what we know about how this relationship ends. We need to look at a larger number of such cases, to understand whether this is a typical deliberate ploy by more than one individual. This announcement and delays in responding to the girl's posts do provoke affiliative conversational actions, including expressions of sympathy, support and empathy, which are typical responses to talk about trouble, including death. This response includes sharing similar personal stories (ie. the death of her grandmother), which has also previously been identified as a typical response to troubles tellings in conversation. For example, Pudlinski (2005) found that sharing a comparable experience of similar feelings is a common response to people's stories about trouble, as in the case of the paedophile's mother's death. His conversational actions are therefore effective in promoting emotional bonding with the target, who has no apparent reason to suspect a falsehood. This sequence sets up the conversation for an interactionally appropriate transition to the paedophile's probing of personal matters.

Once the child appears to have, in a sense, 'softened up' in her attitude towards the paedophile, the paedophile moves quite quickly to change topic, where he orchestrates a focus on the term 'submissive' which is possibly used by the target as a form of online identification, most likely as a nickname or profile name. We observed that once he is on this topic, the paedophile pushes the child to open up about her 'real life' experiences, to the point where she eventually notices his persistent questions and resists providing further details about her previous relationships. She does this tactfully, by suggesting that the paedophile may nonetheless be the right person for a future 'experience'. The paedophile is also very tactful in accepting the child's refusal, possibly for a later attempt, which we understand occurs successfully in a later exchange (Crystal, 2011).

So, in summary the paedophile's and child's conversational actions show the following interactional features and trajectory in the examined chat exchange:
1. Paedophile's delays in responding to posts
2. Paedophile's announcement of major personal trouble/event (mother's death)
3. Child's sympathetic responses and sharing of a similar story
4. Paedophile's change of topic to focus on child's personal life, especially relationships (in this case her use of 'submissive' outside the chat interaction context provides him with an opening)
5. Child's opening up about personal feelings
6. Paedophile's questions which probe how the child thinks about relationships, especially past ones
7. Child's delay/refusal in responding to his persistent questions, expression of suspicion and retreat when she finds him too inquisitive
8. Child's mitigation of refusal to respond.

While the analysis above provides some insights, further interactional research on typical paedophile-child pair behaviours is needed to establish guidelines based on typical interactional trajectories. This research should be focused on genuine paedophile-child pairs rather than decoys to understand how children of different ages are likely to interpret and respond to paedophiles' deceptive interactional behaviours. The analysis above also reinforces what we already know about avoiding nicknames or language which are likely to draw attention from paedophiles. The child's choice of 'submissive' with its sexual overtones may have attracted the paedophile and provided him with an excuse to approach her and probe personal aspects of her life. However, further data analysis would be required to confirm this.

Pursuing Intimacy through Self-Disclosure

The exchange we have just examined is characterised by acts of self-disclosure, prompted principally by the paedophile. When we first meet someone, whether face-to-face or online, we engage in small talk and 'getting to know you' conversation, which may also involve humour (Tudini & Strambi, 2016). Depending on the context, type and stage of the relationship, we begin to disclose personal information about ourselves, including our personalities. This disclosure of personal information is known as self-disclosure, which is known to promote closeness and liking of conversational partners both in face-to-face and online interaction (Kito, 2005; Kashian et al., 2017). In certain cases, this may lead to more intimate talk about our feelings, or even sexuality. This is perfectly normal in close friendships and other relationships. It is also a likely element of the conversational trajectory in relationships established through online dating sites.

Paedophiles such as the one we have just considered and other types of criminals may use the technique of disclosing personal aspects of their lives and feelings, to promote a degree of comfort and intimacy in the relationship and possibly gain mutual disclosures on the part of their target. The ultimate self-disclosure, which may become a tool to control their targets and engage in extortion is of course the sexually explicit photograph, especially in dating sites such as *Tinder*. Criminals have managed to extort money and other favours by creating this trajectory in their conversations. So a typical conversational trajectory of self-disclosure may proceed as depicted in Table 7.2, not

Table 7.2 *Trajectory of online self-disclosure*

1 Express facts about one's life and background (small talk)
2 Announce major changes in one's personal life (deaths, engagements, graduation, etc)
3 Express feelings
4 Talk about personal relationships
5 Discuss sexual interests
6 Exchange photographs (from photo of face/clothed body to explicit)

necessarily in that order, and sometimes in combination. This trajectory may of course move from the online to the real world at any stage, from Stage 3 onwards, depending on participants' locations and degree of aversion to risk-taking behaviours.

As we saw in early stages of the chat between a paedophile and a fifteen-year-old young girl, a similar trajectory as that outlined in Table 7.2 was under way. First came the possibly fictitious 'bombshell' about the paedo-phile's mother's death, which created a suitably compassionate emotional reaction in the target. Then the paedophile began to probe quite insistently to gain self-disclosures from the target about her feelings regarding rela-tionships. He mainly uses questions. The conversation remains vague, but the child does reveal her feelings, until she suggests that her conversational partner is asking too many questions.

Due to sensitivity of the data and difficulty in accessing private chat exchanges, we know very little about how this trajectory proceeds with chil-dren of different age groups, especially younger children who are likely to be more vulnerable in unequal power relationships with adults. Further research on a range of online child-paedophile pairs involving children of various ages is needed for the community and police to gain as complete a picture as possible of typical, deceptive conversational actions deployed by paedophiles for sexual exploitation of children. It is, however, clear that written interaction provides significant advantages for paedophiles to achieve their objectives without revealing their identities. Children are disadvantaged and often powerless in these contexts. Adult guidance is essential and adequate safety restrictions need to be imposed on children's access to social media and game interaction environments. This analysis does however provide us with some behaviours to look out for when monitoring their online activity. This line of investigation can be replicated in other cases to facilitate children's and protective adults' recognition of suspicious online advances that might on the surface appear to be perfectly normal online conversation. The development of children's aware-ness of their own vulnerabilities in similar circumstances would also be an important element in their education.

By analysing various types of naturalistic data, as required by conversation analysis theory, researchers are able to draw conclusions which relate to real world interactions. This chapter nonetheless reveals a previously unknown picture of conversational actions deployed by one paedophile to easily gain control of an online conversation with a teenager. While self-disclosure might easily convince teenagers, we know little about how this is likely to affect less socially skilled younger children. Education of children and protective adults in foiling paedophile advances is crucial, as police intervention and techno-logical solutions can only go so far in detecting perpetrators of online child abuse.

In Summary

- Children are likely to come into contact with paedophiles on social media and games sites.
- The constrained text chat environment in social media and avatars in games are ideal for paedophiles, as they hide their appearance and age and facilitate deception.
- Given the scale and impacts of child sexual abuse, systematic analysis of online perpetrators' language is needed to understand how they establish relationships with unacquainted children at the initial stages of non-sexual online grooming.
- Feigning common interests, flattery and attempting to gain information are some of the signs that children are dealing with a paedophile. These conversational actions may initially appear like a form of rapport building.
- The global crisis in online sexual exploitation of children has been precipitated by the ease with which millions of child sexual abuse images can be accessed.
- Research has identified key typologies of paedophiles but has not attended to the subtle language and machinery of interaction deployed by paedophiles when attempting to gain children's trust during online interaction such as text chat; conversation analysis would be able to identify interactional trajectories which lead to online (and in-person) abuse.
- Single case analyses need to be followed up by analysis of multiple paedophile-child pairs, in a range of age groups, to ascertain interactional patterns which are typical across online grooming interactions between unacquainted participants. This will contribute to improved education of children for their protection in online environments.
- Based on previous research and the single case analysis conducted in this chapter, initial grooming trajectories which are co-constructed by both paedophile and child may include (1) getting acquainted behaviours and small talk, (2) troubles announcements and self-disclosures involving personal life, (3) expression of feelings, (4) requests for information about personal relationships, (5) discussion of sexual interests and (6) exchange of photographs (innocuous or sexually explicit).
- The child's response to the paedophile's personal self-disclosure about the death of his mother, whether fictitious or not, shows an expected typical response to 'troubles talk'. Her expressions of sympathy and sharing of similar stories of loss indicate she is concerned about her interlocutor. This sequence promotes an interactionally appropriate transition to the paedophile's probing of personal matters.
- The role of troubles announcements and self-disclosures in non-sexual online conversations between paedophiles and children requires further research investigation.

8   Summary of Findings, Implications, and Guidelines

Introduction

This chapter summarizes findings and considers implications of previous chapters, based on guiding questions introduced in Chapter 1. These questions provided a focus for both the review of previous research (mainly Chapters 1 and 4) and the analytical chapters (Chapters 2, 3, 5, 6, 7). The analytical chapters specifically examined the language and interactional details of how children talk, in selected online text chat contexts. When combined with a review of relevant research, analysis provided an initial snapshot of how children interact online.

Additionally, this chapter proposes guidelines on how to fit gaming and written online interaction into children's lives in a balanced, principled way. These guidelines summarize and elaborate on previously discussed criteria for selecting and setting up appropriate video game and social media interaction to guide readers in maximizing social and learning benefits to children. Suggestions for conducting further research in this area are also discussed.

Summary of Findings and Implications

Guiding question 1: Given the significant amount of time many children spend online, how are learning behaviours such as conversational repair deployed, and scaffolding and ZPD achieved during online interaction, which occurs mainly between peers, without the support of non-verbal interactional resources or guidance from adults?

The first guiding question of this investigation of online children's language and interaction relates to learning behaviours. Specifically, based on previous literature and analysis of text chat interaction in various contexts, this book considered how children enacted conversational repair, scaffolding and ZPD between peers during online interaction. This is an important area of research investigation given the popularity of social media and video games and the importance of play and face-to-face interaction for children's development, as outlined in Chapter 1. In social media interaction, in particular, text chat is the dominant mode of interaction though it is a unique hybrid form of social written interaction. This question was considered mainly in Chapters 2 to 6.

Chapter 2 specifically identified social functions of emojis and emoticons. Among other features, these devices signal children's awareness of preferred and dispreferred conversational actions and their understanding of polite online social interaction. The visibility of emoticons and emojis, in a range of interactional contexts and for various purposes, discussed throughout the book, point to children's confidence in deploying these devices. This is likely to benefit their social and interactional competence. Additionally, the visual saliency (Pellettieri, 2000) of emoticons is an affordance for learning through practice and modelling of other users' polite behaviours thanks to interaction in the written medium.

In Chapter 3 the analysis focused on multi-party and small group *Club Penguin* interaction and found that users do not always take the opportunity to support others. In particular, one user's request for technical help and opportunity for ZPD was ignored by peers engaged in a fictitious ball game. This request occurred in small group chat and resulted in her exclusion from the game. While further examples are required, this instance suggests that gaming interaction may take priority over collaboration and support for others in environments such as *Club Penguin*. This, however, is not dissimilar to what might occur at times in face-to-face contexts. This contrasts with another small group episode, where socially oriented other repair of a participant's hurtful negative evaluation of a child's hair leads to a new user being accepted into the group. Hence, repair has an important social function to promote inclusivity in this instance. The analysis conducted in Chapter 3 also suggests that small group interaction is more likely to support learning behaviours and collaborative interaction than multi-party interaction in *Club Penguin*. This is due in part to difficulty in accessing interactionally coherent conversations which, due to turn-taking constraints, are not presented sequentially with appropriate adjacency pairs but as separate speech bubbles above avatars, wherever these are positioned on screen. Evanescence of speech bubble posts was also identified as an interactional constraint which is likely to impact on children's understanding of the conversation. The unique sequence organization of *Club Penguin* chat impacts on conversational coherence, which is exacerbated by posts from multiple participants in large groups. The presence of multiple participants makes it challenging to identify recipients compared to small groups, which in turn is likely to impact comprehension of chat, especially for younger participants. Thus, while children adapt to the chat medium and reconstruct conversations as readers and writers, understanding and meaningful interaction can potentially be impacted in large group multi-party interaction. Nonetheless, while only static screen images are available for analysis, participants in these interactions would have the advantage of monitoring timing of posts in real time, which is likely to impact positively on understand-ing. Despite its constraints, *Club Penguin* was a popular children's MMORG for many years due to the social connectivity and opportunities for online play that it promoted.

Chapter 4 reviewed prior research on video game language and interaction and found that when played interactively and within time limits, with known adults or other children, video games have the potential to promote well-being, social competence and learning behaviours such as conversational repair, problem-solving, teamwork, advice-giving and ZPD. Expert-novice orienta-tions in video game interaction are also likely to promote learning thanks to potential support from the 'expert'. Language and learning behaviours during interaction are, however, likely to vary according to the game context and expertise of players. Learning potential is also likely to be fostered by single player games if children play in company and are able to negotiate their gaming with other children or adults. This review of previous research on video game language and interaction also found that gamers may not only engage in game actions and social interaction but also with online game-related resources. These resources have the benefit of promoting engagement with lexically sophisticated and structurally complex language, which is likely to impact positively on children's development and literacy.

Chapter 5 examined language and interaction in a public YouTube video game session on *Minecraft*, produced by Ethan Gamer (EthanGamer, 2019, May 28), and found that various social and learning behaviours were evident in text chat. However, repair was not a regular feature of the chat interactions, probably because the game in progress took priority. Repair was, however, deployed when chat participants were unable to gain a response from Ethan Gamer in the chat context, by initiating self-repair of a previous request or question, using conventions of writing (e.g. question marks). Other repair instead was infrequent and most likely depended on the confidence of individ-ual gamers. The predominant tendency of participants to engage in affiliative rather than dispreferred conversational actions in this specific context may also have been a factor influencing the use of other repair. The analysis differenti-ated conversational actions that were socially oriented from those that were related to the game in progress. There was evidence of regular teamwork and problem-solving behaviours, such as requests or offers of assistance, which scaffolded participants' gaming. Socially oriented conversational actions such as reciprocal positive evaluations by Ethan Gamer and game participants, however, fostered a supportive prosocial environment for gamers and YouTube viewers. The text chat medium was therefore a necessary tool to connect unacquainted geographically dispersed gamers and support their gam-ing both emotionally and technically. Ethan Gamer also deployed thinking and typing aloud processes such as self-repair and word search prior to posting his requests in chat, to promote other gamers' understanding and stay in touch with the YouTube audience.

Chapter 6 focused on YouTube comments interaction and found that the default YouTube comments presentation mode is 'top' comments main strand interaction unless 'newest first' is specifically chosen by users. However, not even the 'newest first' main strand option presents comments sequentially in a consistent way. This is due to YouTube moderation and other criteria which commenters have no control over. Hence, only the more private substrand comments are likely to permit sequentially appropriate posts between participants in YouTube comments. Appropriateness of sequence organization will vary according to number of participants and use of interactional resources, such as naming, to ensure addressees are clearly indicated. Specifically, addressees of substrand and main strand comments are not always clear, unless they are named by users to avoid interactional confusion and disrupted recipiency. In fact, sometimes even substrand first posts are intended for either Ethan Gamer, users in general or specific users. These interactional features make it difficult for users to engage in extended sequentially appropriate interaction, unless substrand comments are used. This explains why other-repair is not commonly used, though it is clearly an affordance of YouTube comments interaction in the more coherent substrand comments.

Analysis indicates that main interactional concerns expressed in users' posts are (1) understanding the YouTube video and game they are watching, (2) comparing Ethan Gamer with other celebrities and (3) connecting with other gamers who have similar interests and gaming platforms. YouTube users do, however, engage in technical talk at times, particularly in the substrands, to better understand Ethan Gamer's gameplay and apply new knowledge derived from the video to their own gaming efforts. The rare instances of other repair which occur in YouTube substrand interaction are more likely to relate to errors of fact than language and may sometimes be completed collaboratively with other users.

Guiding question 2: What is the language of children's online interaction like, lexically, syntactically and pragmatically?

Findings related to the nature of children's online language and interaction obviously vary according to context, with Chapters 2, 3, 5 and 6 providing insights based on linguistic and interactional analysis. However, Chapters 1 and 4 also reveal important information on this topic based on review of relevant research.

Chapter 1 reveals that text chat is a unique hybrid form of social written interaction, where users interact as readers and writers, not speakers and hearers, despite the multimodality of many chat tools. Chat thus deprives participants of resources which are available in face-to-face interaction, such as those which involve the body and non-verbal interactional resources. These resources are essential to children's interaction and development. The need to adapt to this bodiless environment requires users to create new language and interactional resources in the online context. For example, Chapter 2 found that emojis and emoticons are a human adaptation to text chat which attempts to fill the gap left by non-verbal, voice and contextual resources which are available to speakers in phone and face-to-face interaction. Analysis of children's online interactions showed that users deploy emojis to provide a bridge between the virtual and physical world through recontextualization. Contextual information provided by the surrounding digital text or real world context is, however, an important component to enable correct interpretations of these interactional devices.

As occurs with adults, emojis and emoticons also fulfil an important pragmatic role in children's online language and interaction in promoting politeness. They do this especially by mitigating dispreferred conversational actions. While they are widely regarded as symbols, emojis and emoticons have multiple, often overlapping, interactional functions and meanings for users across platforms. Children are able to identify their affordances for meaningful interaction, especially where the more flexible emojis are concerned. Meaning of emojis is in fact negotiated with interlocutors in interaction but is subject to (mis)interpretation, especially where their meanings are not clear-cut.

Analysis of *Club Penguin* chat indicates that the language used in large group interaction is limited mainly to requesting, ordering, naming and calling out to other avatars. It also includes well-wishing and expressing concern, excitement, support and availability to interact. Small group interactions instead permit new creative forms of interaction such as dance and ball game simulations, with accompanying textual renditions of imaginary emotions and physical actions. These simulations are linguistic and are unique to MMORG environments such as *Club Penguin*, where participants adapt to its constraints by combining text and avatar motion to express themselves playfully.

Chapter 4 focused on research which had identified various features of the language of video game interaction, where participants are gaming collaboratively rather than on their own. For example, children's out-of-game language and interaction may have somewhat restricted interactional functions which include use of directives and positive and negative evaluations. Response cries and private talk were also identified as fundamental components of video game language and interaction. These same interactional functions and response cries were also identified as recurrent features by analysis in Chapter 5. However, they were a feature not just of voice interaction but also of text chat interaction, which was publicly available asynchronously, to a YouTube audience. Chapter 5 also identifies game participants' text chat greeting exchanges and other affiliative social talk as important elements of the initial game play to promote a prosocial and reassuring gaming environment for chat participants. Furthermore, linguistic analysis in Chapter 5 identified game participants' frequent use of emoticons, African American English and colloquial positive evaluations, using adjectives such as 'cool'.

Review of previous research on video game language in Chapter 4 also identified ludolects, which are considered a creative linguistic expression of in-game, in-group text chat interaction (Ensslin, 2012). No such language was evident in the analysis conducted in this book, though the use of acronyms and abbreviations might be considered specialized in-group language across gaming and social media platforms. The review also identified swearing as a feature of the language of older children playing video games in previous research, to build rapport and save face during gaming interaction. This was not evident in this study's analytical chapters, where only euphemisms of curses such as 'Dang' for 'Damn' were present. Clearly, language is likely to vary according to gaming context and age of participants. The YouTube comments context where participants observe Ethan Gamer's gameplay provides insights on the language of an additional chat tool in Chapter 6. To start with, analysis notes children's non-standard spellings in their language on YouTube comments, which in some cases may be due to their developing ability to match spoken with written renditions of words. Repair of such language rarely occurs in substrand comments. This may be partly due to social media users' general tolerance of non-standard renditions of written language and the unique language of chat.

From a lexical and thematic point of view, participants' talk often revolves around age, especially when they use their caregivers' YouTube account. Hence, their true identities and age are unknown to other users unless they are revealed in comments. This appears necessary to facilitate connection with other young gamers. Another participant concern, which is reflected in both lexical and syntactic features of the YouTube comments context examined in Chapter 6, is participants' recounting of past experiences with Ethan Gamer's videos, which is again related to age and nostalgia. The nostalgic recounting of past experiences allows them to connect with other YouTube commenters who have had similar experiences. Given the asynchronous and disrupted nature of YouTube comments, users may sometimes select a question format to seek out other users from the current year, to connect with other gamers based on a common time of participation. This attention to time of participation is likely to increase the likelihood of a response from others, due to an additional factor in common, that is, temporal copresence.

As with other social media tools, likes or 'thumbs up' are an important feature of YouTube comments interaction and may be seen as second pair parts which are posted in response to a main strand comment, to form an adjacency pair. As noted earlier, naming of recipients is an important interactional device which unsurprisingly, is also present in YouTube comments. This promotes understanding in an environment where there are multiple participants and adjacency pairs (and recipiency) are disrupted. Questions were also often found to elicit substrand responses, thus creating a new conversation. This suggests that questions are a linguistic format that successfully projects responses even in the YouTube comments environment. The presence of linguistic play, especially puns, is also worth noting as one creative feature of substrand interaction between children.

Guiding question 3: What is the place of certain video games which isolate children and do not include interaction with human beings and language-rich environments?

Based on the video game review Chapter (4) and video game session analysis chapter (5), clearly it is best for children to avoid single player games altogether, unless they are played in the company of other children or adults. While online gaming resources appear to provide language-rich environments according to previous research, children's development is likely to be fostered through interaction with others, as described in both the review and analytical chapters. This is also likely when children play creative games like *Minecraft*, though a different type of single player interaction, only with the game, is possible. Only limited linguistic and interactional features, such as response cries and other private talk, are likely to be available when children are playing only with the game, though this requires further investigation. Supportive learning behaviours such as those identified in children's gaming interactions in previous chapters, and discussed in regard to guiding question 1, can only be fostered when interacting with other game participants.

Guiding question 4: How does children's interaction unfold in the vast array of video games and social media tools that are available on the market?

This question sought insights on how children interact online in the plethora of gaming and social media contexts available to them and has in fact already been considered in relation to previous guiding questions. Given the diversity of interactional contexts, insights were limited to this book's reviews of previous studies of children's online interaction and analysis of specific video games and social media tools. Further research would be required to be able to provide additional knowledge because interaction changes according to interactional context and how it is configured (see Tudini & Liddicoat, 2017). For example, different softwares, number of participants and availability of emojis will alter how interaction unfolds. There are, however, key findings in this book which may apply to video game and social media tools with interactionally similar contexts as those examined in this book. This was evident where analysis confirmed some of the previous research on identified learning behaviours and linguistic elements of video games (Chapters 4 and 5). For example, Chapter 5 showed that emoticons have multiple functions in text chat, but especially to add an element of playfulness and promote affiliation as part of gaming interaction. Similar pragmatic (prosocial) and playful functions were identified in social media contexts examined in Chapter 2. Additionally, Chapter 2's analysis and findings on the functions of emoticons and emojis are broadly relevant to whichever chat tool permits their use. Hence, while this guiding question has been addressed in relation to previous questions above, ongoing research is required in this broad, evolving area.

Guiding question 5: How do children manage chat's unique turn-taking system and sequence organization, given that these are developing abilities in children's younger years?

Guiding question 5 focused on children's management of turn-taking and sequence organization when they chat. This is an especially pertinent question for younger children, for whom these are developing abilities in face-to-face interaction. Based on interactional analysis of selected social media and video game platforms, children adapt to the unique turn-turning system and sequence organization of text chat interaction in the same way as adults. However, their capacity to adapt and use these resources most likely depends to some extent on the affordances and constraints of the medium they are using and on their age and interactional competence. For example, repair is a fundamental conversational resource to ensure participants understand each other, by making adjustments to the posting of turns and organizing appropriate adjacency pairs and coherent conversational sequences where needed. However, repair is not a commonly used interactional device in platforms such as YouTube comments and *Minecraft* chat, based on the analysis in this book. This may in part be due to the fact that participants are completing two tasks at the same time, so it is more difficult to pay attention to repair of their interactions. In the case of YouTube, they are posting comments and watching the video at the same time and in the case of *Minecraft* they are playing the game while submitting posts in the chat. Furthermore, only substrand comments would allow repair to be deployed clearly, as main strand comment adjacency pairs and sequences are automatically rearranged inappropriately from an interactional perspective, as discussed previously. Another conversational resource used by children in multi-party interactions, which is relevant to sequence organization, is naming addressees. This allows them to design adjacency pairs accurately, choosing intended addressees, which in turn promotes sequential coherence and understanding.

While repair and naming of addressees are visible conversational actions in the analysis, there are other implicit aspects of the various chat interactions which suggest how children best manage turn-taking and sequence organization in these constrained environments. For example, there is evidence that one-to-one or small group chat are likely to facilitate both turn-taking and sequence organization, as the taking of turns and design of adjacency pairs is more straightforward where there are fewer participants. In any case, text chat interaction is a reading and writing exercise where children need to reconstruct the conversation, as adjacency pairs may be disrupted due to delays caused by typing chat posts. The fact that participants in text chat examined in this book achieve understanding in multiple contexts, some of which are very constrained and difficult to communicate in, suggests that children adapt to this form of communication.

Guiding question 6: How can we foster quality interactional experiences for children so that their online recreation is conducive to learning and language development and is it possible to identify interactional configurations which maximize children's learning while interacting online?

Guiding question 7:

Is it possible to identify the most interactive games, not in the technical sense, but in the sense that they involve talk and interaction with human beings?

These interrelated questions relate to online interaction in general (question 6) and video game interaction specifically (question 7). They probe whether it is possible to identify the most interactive settings, not in the technical sense, but in the sense that they involve talk and interaction with human beings.

As suggested previously, the ideal environment for language learning and development is where talk and collaboration with other children (or adults) is possible. Where social media interaction is concerned, I have identified environments such as YouTube main strand comments, which do not permit the posting of appropriate adjacency pairs; hence, conversational sequences lack coherence. This is partly due to the constraints of multi-party interaction, and other factors, where addressees are not always clear. Hence, naming of addressees is required so that conversation is understandable by all participants. Alternatively, substrand comments are a suitable interaction medium for children's collaboration and linguistic development in the YouTube environment, which is one of the resources used by gamers to improve their gaming. The situation is similar in *Club Penguin* where only small group interaction, of say, no more than three children, permits understandable longer conversational sequences to be created. This is more likely to be conducive to manageable language practice and development of social and interactional competence.

A further consideration is that the language identified in video game interaction between children discussed in this book is lexically quite limited, as it relates to specific game contexts. Furthermore, the language of video game interaction is colloquial and children require exposure to a variety of text types, both formal and informal, to promote their linguistic development.

Guiding question 8: How does online interaction compromise children's safety?

Guiding question 8 focused on how children's safety is compromised in online interaction. This was considered in Chapter 3 and addressed specifically in Chapter 7. Chapter 7, in particular, noted that wherever text chat or avatars are available on social media and video games, paedophiles are able to hide their appearance and identities. There are, therefore, multiple online environments which facilitate deception and exploitation of children, who encounter ill-intentioned adults on a regular basis. The language and interactional features of online grooming, especially of unacquainted children, is an under-researched area, which could potentially lead to better education and protection of children in online environments. Single-case analysis conducted on one text chat conversation between a subsequently apprehended paedophile and his fifteen-year-old female victim in Chapter 7 indicates that paedophiles may deploy specific interactional resources to establish a relationship. These are identifiable to experts in conversation analysis and should be made available to children and caring adults. For example, paedophiles may delay responding to their target to avoid seeming eager and announce major personal troubles to provoke an emotional response. Paedophiles may also know when to retreat when their target expresses concern about excessive questioning. The analysis showed that while the conversation appeared one-sided, with the target posting most of the conversation, it was firmly in the control of the paedophile, who encouraged emotionally supportive language and asked most of the questions. Therefore, based on review of previous research and analysis of this single case in Chapter 7, online grooming trajectories may initially involve getting acquainted behaviours, small talk, troubles announcements and self-disclosures which appear benign on the surface. These trajectories, which are co-constructed between paedophiles and children, may subsequently lead to the expression of feelings and requests for information about relationships, prior to moving onto sexually exploitative interactions. Further multiple single-case analyses, involving children of a range of age groups, are required to confirm that these trajectories are widespread in these contexts.

Chapter 3 revealed that despite the linguistic restrictions imposed by *Club Penguin* software for children's safety, its language can be manipulated by users to produce altered euphemisms for banned words and other inappropriate expressions. Multiple meanings of words and expressions also provide users with scope for posting of inappropriate language. Analysis also revealed attempted exclusion of players, which is a recurrent issue in text chat and social media interactions generally.

Guiding Principles for Text Chat and Gaming Interaction

Research findings provide some guiding principles to promote children's learning and safety online, which are worth recapitulating and developing further. These are:

- Does the video game include tools which allow for collaborative interaction as part of the game?
- Are long-distance game and chat partners known to the child and adult family members?
- Have limits on screen time been negotiated with children?
- Are they collaborating and learning from each other?
- Are developmental guidelines for video games possible?
- Is multilingual online interaction an option?

Does the Video Game Include Tools Which Allow for Collaborative Interaction as Part of the Game?

In our technology-dominated world, technical language tends to prevail, even where there are alternative meanings. For example, technical versions of 'interactive' tend to be more widely used than the social definition, which denotes talk and interaction with people. These are important differentiations which are evident during children's video game play. Chapter 4 provides a starting point for selection of video games by suggesting that video games comprise two types of interaction, either through point and click, with the game system, or through language, with other gamers. And of course there is a variety of interactional configurations across games, as synthesized in Chapter 4 (Table 4.1). It should thus be possible for classification boards globally to provide potential 'social interactivity' ratings of video games for caregivers', educators' and children's use. Such ratings would reinforce the value of socially interactive video game activity and guide both users and their caregivers in understanding how social interaction through specific video games could be accomplished, before they decide to purchase. For example, classification boards or even game developers would be able to advise potential buyers on whether games have the technical capacity to be played either face-to-face with other co-present players, or long distance through text and/or voice chat. This would be especially useful if combined with information about whether and how video game users are able to control other gamers' participation, to avoid interaction with strangers.

Are Long-Distance Game and Chat Partners Known to the Child and Adult Family Members?

Given the presence of paedophiles in children's preferred online environments, children need to avoid interacting with unacquainted chat or gaming partners, who need to be known to their families. This can be achieved by blocking children's access to public servers. For assistance, families can establish contact with local government organizations and police education programs which support the community in understanding how paedophiles operate online. Caregivers and children should also be aware of sexual acronyms which children may encounter online which may reveal signs of grooming and sexual innuendo in chat. Netlingo has extensive lists of acronyms on its website (Netlingo, 2023).

Snapchat is also an application of concern, as it leaves no trace of written conversations or images, unless a screen shot is taken by the recipient. Hence, the online conversation is evanescent, as noted in analysis of *Club Penguin*. This is why it is a common strategy by paedophiles to invite children onto Snapchat when engaged in conversation elsewhere, as Snapchat conversation leaves no record. And yet it is the second most popular social media app in the UK after TikTok (Ceci, 2023, February 16).

Have Limits on Screen Time Been Negotiated with Children?

This book's findings suggest that children's online interaction in company is beneficial. However, a balanced approach is required in regard to the time they spend on screen, which needs to be negotiated with children, who also require physical activity. The Australian Bureau of Statistics' National Health Survey in 2012 found that only 60 per cent of children aged five to fourteen years of age participated in sport outside of school.[1] Data from a 2020-2021 United States government investigation indicated similar concerning statistics.[2]

Limits to screen time are also needed because entertainment games have not been devised by educators, scientists or other experts who are likely to have children's learning needs in mind. They have in fact been produced by multinational media companies, computer programmers and perhaps gamers, for commercial purposes, which requires that the games be entertaining and addictive, rather than educational, with some exceptions. Commercial interests know how to exploit the multimodality of the medium and children's interest in playing and winning the game. Educational experts generally do not have multimillion dollar budgets to produce educational games, which have difficulty competing with games which are devised for entertainment. Given the market dominance of commercial, intentionally addictive games, it is unsurprising to hear that excessive screen time may impact on children's physical, psychological and cognitive health. Preschool children are particularly vulnerable and should have little if any access to video games without adult support, given that research on the impact of video games on physical and cognitive development of young children is in its infancy (see, for example,

---

[1] www.betterhealth.vic.gov.au/health/healthyliving/sport-and-children. Accessed 15 September 2016.
[2] https://projectplay.org/youth-sports/facts/participation-rates.

Danby et al., 2018a). Time limits, negotiated with children, ensure that they are not deprived of opportunities to develop their language and promote their well-being through a range of leisure activities, including reading a variety of texts and physical activity.

Are They Collaborating and Learning from Each Other?

Adults should occasionally observe children when they play video games independently. Does it look like children are engaging in collaborative forms of teaching and learning from each other as part of their talk, online or face-to-face? This is evident when children appear to take on a teacher-like role with other players, as was sometimes evident in this book's analyses. Collaboration and learning is also evident when children ask questions and request help from other players. Depending on the game, they may show signs of helping each other to understand the game rules, solve problems, win, progress in game levels or avoid certain game figures, to name a few options which were identified in the analysis. If these kinds of behaviours are promoted by the games children are playing, this is evidence of possible ZPD and learning during the game talk. These are the most *visible* ways of identifying learning episodes, though learning may also be occurring in other ways, as children learn in multiple ways, even in highly constrained environments.

Learning behaviours are especially evident if children are new to the game and playing with more competent peers. They may teach one another how to play and solve game problems as they arise. This is an important social interaction, as 'newbies' may need assistance in negotiating and fitting into the game culture, including getting to know game characters and engaging in correct behaviour. Adult family members may also be 'newbies' to the game and are therefore suitable learning partners for children. Additionally, adults' participation in children's games provides opportunities to under-stand and connect with children and their favourite games, which is likely to be appreciated by children, as well as being good for their development, within time limits. While it focused specifically on young children's reading of various types of digital texts, Davidson et al.'s (2020) study of literacy practices involving digital tools of children from three and a half to under five years of age confirms the importance of adults' engagement in online activities with children to promote reading. Scaffolding was also evident in interactions between family members, including parents and young children, who produced spontaneous reading aloud from the screen during everyday digital technology use, including Web searching, game playing, use of the phonics program *Reading Eggs*, viewing YouTube clips and listening to music.

Are Developmental Guidelines for Video Games Possible?

Though they create convincing fictional worlds, no developmental guidelines and goals appear to be available for video games, as there are for children's books. Imagery is a fundamental component of most games, regardless of gamers' age. Hence, they need to be treated as a form of recreation, similar to films, to which children should have principled, selective exposure, as suggested earlier. Games which are based on narratives are of course more similar to books but require separate research attention. In regard to apps, Starke et al. (2021) note that even the so-called educational apps provide little evidence of educational impact, also because it is impossible to evaluate and research every one of them. Hence, multiple factors are likely to impact gaming apps' educational value, including gaming context and interactional configuration of the gaming session. The authors provide advice on how gaming and the learning experience can be blended, so that learning principles are translated into a genuine game environment to promote both first and second language learning.

In the meantime, families can expose children and their gaming partners to a larger range of vocabulary and text types by selecting a variety of suitable video game contexts, including resources related to the game.

Is Multilingual Online Interaction an Option?

Some environments are more suitable for children's practice of written conversation than others. Compared to rapid fade spoken conversation, written language has the advantage of scaffolding children's communication due to its visibility on screen, reviewability and visual saliency (Pellettieri, 2000). This is particularly useful for multilingual conversation, where children are interacting online in an additional language. However, excessive constraints related to turn-taking and sequence organization make both first language and second language writing more difficult. One-to-one or small group conversation would be more appropriate for children learning additional languages, with appropriate attention to safety considerations.

There are suitable language exchange apps, such as HelloTalk, which are suitable for children from the age of twelve and which purport to have safety features (Gupta, 2023, January 2). However, with adequate adult support, WhatsApp Messenger could be used safely. This tool signals when a user is typing their post, which assists in reducing disrupted adjacency pairs and promotes understanding of the conversation in progress. This feature should make turn-taking and sequence organization easier for children. Furthermore, children participating in chat interaction in an additional language on WhatsApp may select the option to either write, speak or record the conversation. Clearly, further research is required to fully understand affordances of this communication platform.

Further Research

Variety of Digital Contexts

One of the most difficult aspects of conducting research on children's online language and interaction is the plethora of video games, apps and social media tools which are available, many of which have vastly different affordances and constraints. Hence, findings are likely to be different according to video game and chat context and how the interaction is set up (Tudini & Liddicoat, 2017). Hence, this book started with some of the most popular digital contexts for its linguistic and interactional focus and found some commonality in research findings across gaming and social media platforms. As pointed out by Starke et al. (2021), guidelines for app developers on the creation of apps with educational, not just commercial use, may be one solution. Hence, commercial developers may benefit from linguistic and interactional research to improve devices and platforms for children of different age groups.

Further work in this area is clearly required, ideally involving multidisciplinary teams and focused on specific age groups, as is occurring at the Australian Research Council's Centre of Excellence for the Digital Child (www.digitalchild.org.au/) where research focuses on children from birth to eight years old. This international research centre also provides guidelines and works with parents and other protective adults on how to manage children's engagement with digital devices.

We also know very little about the impact of video games on attention span in activities outside the game. There is anecdotal evidence that teenagers are excellent multitaskers, a skill which may be useful in a fast-paced workforce, but more long-term scientific studies are required for this to be proven. The impact of childhood television viewing on attention was investigated by the famous Dunedin research team in a longitudinal (long-term) study of over 500 children (Landhuis et al., 2007).[3] The average time spent watching television as a child was associated with attention problems at adolescence, regardless of IQ or socio-economic status. With appropriate resourcing, it should be possible to replicate this study to focus on young gamers.

Online Grooming Language and Interaction

As noted earlier, further research on online grooming language and interaction is required to better educate and protect children. With sufficient resources and police support, further research in this area will permit identification of paedophiles in the early stages of their relationship with a child, before the conversation

---

[3] https://dunedinstudy.otago.ac.nz/.

becomes sexually exploitative. Conversation analysis is a methodology which would be able to identify details of interactional trajectories which lead to online (and in-person) abuse.

Limitations

One limitation of this study is that analytical chapters reveal only the approximate age of participants. While age is mostly clear in reviewed research, analytical chapters are based either on what children reveal during interaction, in keeping with conversation analytic principles, or on gaming and social media platforms' publicly stated age demographic. Age is also revealed indirectly through linguistic analysis, for example in Chapter 6, where participants' language reveals typical non-standard features of children's language at early stages of literacy. This book therefore provides only a snapshot of specific types of children's written online language and interaction, including video game chat. Further research requires a focus on children of specific age groups within additional single but interactionally similar, online interaction environments. Ideally, video and screen recordings of how individual children enact text chat in various contexts is required for analysis. This would permit a richer, multimodal analysis from the perspective of children, rather than entirely that of the analyst, which would provide additional insights on how online interaction is enacted by children in multiple online contexts.

Appendix: Data Table

Social media type	Interaction mode	Number of posts (including photos & other media at download)	Group or one-to-one chat	Specific context	Age	Time span	Main language/s	Acquainted or not
YouTube main strand comments: Cookie Swirl[1]	Mainly asynchronous, sometimes quasi-synchronous	903 posts	Group	Cookie Swirl (Candace) and children interested in Roblox[2]	13+	December 12 to14 2020	English	Unacquainted
YouTube Ethan Gamer (big belly substrand comments[3]	Mainly asynchronous, sometimes quasi-synchronous	104 posts (single substrand)	Group (one to one in substrand at times)	Ethan Gamer and mainly children interested in Minecraft	7–13[4]	February 16, 2020 to 1 October 2020	English	Unacquainted
YouTube Ethan Gamer Baby cow processor newest first + replies[5]	Mainly asynchronous, sometimes quasi-synchronous	957 main strand posts + 249 substrand posts (including first post)	Group (one to one in substrand at times)	Ethan Gamer and mainly children interested in Minecraft	7–13	February 16, 2020 to November 25, 2020	English	Unacquainted
YouTube Stampy Cat substrand[6]	Mainly asynchronous, sometimes quasi-synchronous	54 posts	Group	Stampy Cat (Joseph Garrett) and children interested in Minecraft	7–13	Up to 30 April 2019	English	Unacquainted

[1] Cookie Swirl: Extreme million dollar gingerbread house build https://www.youtube.com/watch?v=1bra0dXXTo0

[2] See https://www.commonsensemedia.org/blog/parents-ultimate-guide-to-roblox-0#What%20age%20is%20Roblox%20for? for description of Roblox

[3] Etham Gamer: I have a BIG BELLY 😮 https://www.youtube.com/watch?v=LLsc1bg0Exo.

[4] Official age ratings for Minecraft range from 7+ to under 13 but this may vary, YouTube's terms of service require users to be at least 13 years old, however children of all ages are permitted if "enabled by a parent or guardian". https://www.youtube.com/t/terms.

[5] Ethan Gamer: Baby cow processor; https://www.youtube.com/watch?v=wtppQX5m08g

[6] Stampy Cat https://www.youtube.com/watch?v=qbjUl2tvE3E

WhatsApp	Mainly asynchronous, sometimes quasi-synchronous	80 posts	One-to-one	Parent-child	14–16 years old	19 November 2013 to 17 January 2017	English/ Italian	Acquainted
SMS messages	Mainly asynchronous, sometimes quasi-synchronous	1206 posts	One-to-one	Parent-child	14–16 years old	3 December 2013 to 9 April 2017	English/ Italian	Acquainted
Club Penguin	Mainly quasi-synchronous	39 posts	Group	Children only	Varies	2016	English	Mixed
EthanGamerTV *Minecraft* gaming video[7]	Combination: quasi-synchronous chat; synchronous voice chat; asynchronous to public audience/ commenters	Approx 175 chat posts/636 voice turns	Group	Mostly children	Exact age unavailable but likely 7–13 (*Minecraft* target age group)	May 28, 2019 (one 31 minute episode)	English	Mostly unacquainted

[7] EthanGamer. (2019, May 28). *Ethan Gamer Fans Minecraft World 2.0!!* https://www.youtube.com/watch?v=O7xaprzRlA

References

Aarsand, P. A. & Aronsson, K. (2009a). Response cries and other gaming moves: Building intersubjectivity in gaming. *Journal of Pragmatics*, *41*(8), 1557–1575. https://doi.org/10.1016/j.pragma.2007.05.014

Aarsand, P. A. & Aronsson, K. (2009b). Gaming and territorial negotiations in family life. *Childhood*, *16*(4), 497–517. https://doi.org/10.1177/0907568209343879

Al Rashdi, F. (2018). Functions of emojis in WhatsApp interaction among Omanis. *Discourse, Context and Media*, *26*, 117–126. https://doi.org/10.1016/j.dcm.2018.07.001

Alexander, J. (2019, February 24). YouTube is disabling comments on almost all videos featuring children. *The Verge*. https://bit.ly/4eT8qDX

American Academy of Pediatrics (2017, May 4). Handheld screen time linked with speech delays in young children. *ScienceDaily*. https://bit.ly/3WhLC9V.

Anderson, M. & Jiang. J. (2018). *Teens, social media and technology*. Pew Research Center. www.pewinternet.org/2018/05/31/teens-social-media-technology-2018/

Androutsopoulos, J. (2014). Moments of sharing: Entextualization and linguistic repertoires in social networking. *Journal of Pragmatics*, *73*, 4–18.

Antonacci, P. A. (2000). Reading in the zone of proximal development: Mediating literacy development in beginner readers through guided reading. *Reading Horizons: A Journal of Literacy and Language Arts*, *41*(1), 19–33. https://scholarworks.wmich .edu/reading_horizons/vol41/iss1/2

Australian Federal Police (2022, January 30). AFP reveals top grooming tactics used by online child sex offenders. https://bit.ly/4cwzQOD

Beauvois, M. H. (1992). Computer-assisted classroom discussion in the foreign language classroom: Conversation in slow motion. *Foreign Language Annals*, *25*, 455–464.

Bennerstedt, U. & Ivarsson, J. (2010). Knowing the way: Managing epistemic topologies in virtual game worlds. *Computer Supported Cooperative Work*, *19*(2), 201–230. https://doi.org/10.1007/s10606-010-9109-8

Berglund, T. Ö. (2009). Disrupted turn adjacency and coherence maintenance in instant messaging conversations. *Language@Internet*, *6*(2), 1–25. https://bit.ly/3XYdhhd

Betz, E., Deppermann, A., Mondada, L. & Sorjonen, M. Eds. (2021). *Okay across languages: Toward a comparative approach to its use in talk-in-interaction*. John Benjamins.

Biegler, P. (2020). Pokie in your pocket. *Cosmos*, *88*, 62–69.

Black, P. J., Wollis, M., Woodworth, M., & Hancock, J. T. (2015). A linguistic analysis of grooming strategies of online child sex offenders: Implications for our understanding of predatory sexual behavior in an increasingly computer-mediated world. *Child Abuse & Neglect*, *44*, 140–149. https://doi.org/10.1016/j.chiabu.2014.12.004

Boyd, M. S. (2014). (New) participatory framework on YouTube? Commenter inter-action in US political speeches. *Journal of Pragmatics*, *72*, 46–58. http://dx.doi.org/10.1016/j.pragma.2014.03.002

Brand, J. E., Jervis, J., Huggins, P. M. & Wilson, T. (2019). *Digital Australia 2020: The power of games*. Interactive Games and Entertainment Association.

Brown, A., Shifrin, D. L. & Hill, D. L. (2015). Beyond 'turn it off': How to advise families on media use. *AAP News*, *36*(10), 54. https://bit.ly/4f0wFQT

Burley, D. (2010). Penguin life: A case study of one tween's experiences inside Club Penguin. *Journal of Virtual Worlds Research*, *3*(2), 3–13.

Cabut, S. & Santi, P. (2017, June 27). Alerte aux écrans pour les enfants. *Le Monde*. https://www.lemonde.fr/sciences/article/2017/06/26/alerte-aux-ecrans-pour-les-enfants_5151417_1650684.html

Ceci, L. (2023, February 16). *Leading social media apps used by children in the UK 2022*. www.statista.com/statistics/1124966/leading-social-media-apps-children-uk/

Chau, C. (2011). YouTube as a participatory culture. *New Directions for Youth Development*, *2011*(128), 65–74. https://doi.org/10.1002/yd.376

Chiang, E. & Grant, T. (2017). Online grooming: Moves and strategies. *Language and Law/Linguagem e Direito*, *4*(1), 103–141.

Chiang, E., & Grant, T. (2019). Deceptive identity performance: Offender moves and multiple identities in online child abuse conversations. *Applied Linguistics*, *40*(4), 675–698.

Chien, Y. (2019). The language of massively multiplayer online gamers: A study of vocabulary in Minecraft gameplay. *TESL-EJ*, *23*(3), 1–16. http://tesl-ej.org/pdf/ej91/int.pdf

Children and Media Australia (n.d.a). *Australian privacy law: Is it protecting our children when online?* https://childrenandmedia.org.au/resources/australian-privacy-law-is-it-protecting-our-children-when-online. Accessed 23 May 2023.

Children and Media Australia (n.d.b). Reviews page. https://childrenandmedia.org.au/. Accessed 23 May 2023.

Club Penguin Reunion (2016, August). *Club Penguin Glitch*. https://clubpenguin.fandom.com/wiki/Club_Penguin_Reunion

Club Penguin Rewritten (2017, November 19). https://clubpenguinsummit.wordpress.com/2017/11/19/about-club-penguin-rewritten/

Club Penguin Rewritten (2021). *Club Penguin Rewritten Wiki* https://clubpenguinrewritten.fandom.com/wiki/Cprewritten.net

Club Penguin Wiki (2018, February). *Club Penguin Wiki*. http://clubpenguin.wikia.com/wiki/Ultimate_Safe_Chat

Connelly, J. (2013). Virtual play or virtual clay? Barbiegirls.com as a space of constructive play or identity shaping. In A. M. Burke & J. Marsh (Eds.), *Children's virtual play worlds: Culture, learning, and participation* (pp. 99–118). Peter Lang.

CookieSwirlC (2020, December 13). *Extreme million dollar gingerbread house build! Christmas Roblox Tycoon* [Video]. YouTube. https://www.youtube.com/watch?v=1bra0dXXTo0

Crystal, D. (2006). *Language and the internet*. Cambridge University Press.

Crystal, D. (2011). *Internet linguistics: A student guide*. Routledge.

Curtiss, S. (1978). *Genie: A psycholinguistic study of a modern-day 'Wild Child'*. Academic Press.

Curtiss, S. (1988). Abnormal language acquisition and the modularity of language. In F. Newmeyer (Ed.), *Linguistics: The Cambridge survey* (pp. 96–116). Cambridge University Press.

Danby, S., Evaldsson, A., Melander, H. & Aarsand, P. (2018a). Situated collaboration and problem solving in young children's digital gameplay. *British Journal of Educational Technology*, *49*(5), 959–972. https://doi.org/10.1111/bjet.12636

Danby, S. J., Fleer, M., Davidson, C. & Hatzigianni, M. Eds. (2018b). *Digital childhoods: Technologies and children's everyday lives*. Springer. https://doi.org/10.1007/978-981-10-6484-5

Davidson, C. (2010). 'Click on the big red car': The social accomplishment of playing a Wiggles computer game. *Convergence: The International Journal of Research into New Technologies*, *16*(4), 375–394.

Davidson, C. (2012a). The social organisation of help during young children's use of the computer. *Contemporary Issues in Early Childhood*, *13*(3), 187–199.

Davidson, C. (2012b). When 'Yes' turns to 'no': Young children's disputes during computer game playing in the home. In S. Danby & M. Theobald (Eds.), *Disputes in everyday life: Social and moral orders of children and young people* (pp. 355–376). Emerald. https://doi.org/10.1108/S1537-4661(2012)0000015018

Davidson, C., Danby, S., Ekberg, S. & Thorpe, K. (2020). The interactional achievement of reading aloud by young children and parents during digital technology use. *Journal of Early Childhood Literacy*, *21*(4), 475–498. https://doi.org/10.1177/1468798419896040

Davidson, J., DeMarco, J., Bifulco, A., Bogaerts, S., Caretti., V., Aiken, M. & Puccia, A. (2016). *Enhancing police and industry practice*. Project Report. Middlesex University.

Din Vision. (2020, April 20). *How to use emoji on YouTube comments – Easy way* [Video]. YouTube. www.youtube.com/watch?v=YnVy1GcDgkQ

Donkin, A. (2017). Auto-netnography: First encounters as a netnographer in Minecraft. In *ANZCA Conference Proceedings*. ANZCA.

Dooly, M. & Tudini, V. (2016). 'Now we are teachers': The role of small talk in student language teachers' telecollaborative task development. *Journal of Pragmatics*, *102*, 38–53. https://doi.org/10.1016/j.pragma.2016.06.008

Dorasamy, M., Kaliannan, M., Jambulingam, M., Ramadhan, I. & Sivaji, A. (2021). Parents' awareness on online predators: Cyber grooming deterrence. *The Qualitative Report*, *26*(11), 3683–3723. https://doi.org/10.46743/2160-3715/2021.4914

Dresner, E. & Herring, S. C. (2010). Functions of the nonverbal in CMC: Emoticons and illocutionary force. *Communication Theory*, *20*(3), 249–268. https://doi.org.10.1111/j.1468-2885.2010.01362.x

Ensslin, A. (2012). *The language of gaming*. Palgrave Macmillan.

E-SafetyCommissioner (n.d.). *Roblox*. https://www.esafety.gov.au/key-issues/esafety-guide/roblox

E-Safety Commissioner (2017). *Image based abuse: National survey summary report*. Office of the e-Safety Commissioner.

EthanGamer. (2015, February 20). *EthanGamerTV fans' Minecraft world – Episode #7 – BABY COW PROCESSOR* [Video]. YouTube. https://www.youtube.com/watch?v=wtppQX5m08g

EthanGamer. (2019, May 28). *Ethan Gamer Fans Minecraft World 2.0!!* [Video] https://
www.youtube.com/watch?v=rO7xaprzRlA

EthanGamer. (2020, February 17). *I have a BIG BELLY!!* [Video]. YouTube. https://
www.youtube.com/watch?v=LLsc1bg0Exo

Farina, M. (2015). Facebook first post telling. *Journal of Pragmatics*, *90*, 1–11 http://dx
.doi.org/10.1016/j.pragma.2015.10.005

Farina, M. (2018). *Facebook and conversation analysis.* Bloomsbury.

Fewster, S. (2022, September 17). Pervert's landmark plea: Online predator abused girl
he had never met. *The Advertiser.*

Filipi, A. (2009). *Toddler and parent interaction: The organisation of gaze, pointing and
vocalisation.* John Benjamins.

Finkelhor, D., Cuevas, C. A. & Drawbridge, D. (2016). The four preconditions model:
An assessment. In D. P. Boer (Ed.), *The Wiley handbook on the theories, assessment
and treatment of sexual offending* (pp. 25–51). https://doi.org/10.1002/9781118574
003.wattso002

Fox, M. (2001). *Reading magic: How your child can learn to read before school and
other read-aloud miracles.* Sydney: Pan Macmillan.

Gale, L. (2017). Global realities of child exploitation. Seventh World Congress on
Family Law and Children's Rights. https://parlinfo.aph.gov.au/parlInfo/search/
display/display.w3p;query=Id:%22media/pressrel/5320671%22

Gandolfi, E., (2016). To watch or to play, it is in the game: The game culture on Twitch
among performers, plays and audiences. *Journal of Gaming and Virtual Worlds 8*(1),
63–82.

Garcia, A. C. & Jacobs, J. B. (1999). The eyes of the beholder: Understanding the
turn-taking system in quasi-synchronous computer-mediated communication.
Research on Language and Social Interaction, 32(4), 337–367.

Gee, J. P. (2003). *What video games have to teach us about learning and literacy.*
Palgrave Macmillan.

Gee, J. & Hayes, E. (2012). Nurturing affinity spaces and game-based learning. In
C. Steinkuehler, K. Squire & S. A. Barab (Eds.), *Games, learning, and society:
Learning and meaning in the digital age* (pp. 129–153). Cambridge University Press.

Gee, J. P. (2007). *Good video games and good learning: Collected essays on video
games, learning, and literacy.* Peter Lang.

Gibson, W., Huang, P. & Yu, Q. (2018). Emoji and communicative action: The semiot-
ics, sequence and gestural actions of 'face covering hand'. *Discourse, Context and
Media, 26*, 91–99. https://doi.org/10.1016/j.dcm.2018.05.005

Giles, D., Stommel, W., Paulus, T., Lester, J., & Reed, D. (2015). Microanalysis of
online data: The methodological development of 'digital CA'. *Discourse, Context
and Media, 7*, 45–51. https://doi.org/10.1016/j.dcm.2014.12.002

Gillen, J. (2009). Literacy practices in Schome Park: A virtual literacy ethnography. *Journal
of Research in Reading, 32*(1), 57–74. https://doi.org/10.1111/j.1467-9817.2008.01381.x

Gleason Berko, J. & Bernstein Ratner, N. (2009). *The development of language.*
Pearson.

Goffman, E. (1978). Response cries. *Language, 54,* (4), 787–815. https://doi.org/10.2
307/413235

González-Lloret, M. (2015). Conversation analysis in computer-assisted language
learning. *CALICO Journal, 32*, 569–594.

Goodwin, C. (1981). *Conversational organization: Interaction between speakers and hearers*. Academic Press.

Goodwin, M. H. (2017). Participation and embodied action in preadolescent girls' assessment activity. *Research on Language and Social Interaction*, *40*(4), 353–375. https://doi.org/10.1080/08351810701471344

Goodwin, M. H. & Kyratzis, A. (2007). Children socializing children: Practices for negotiating the social order among peers. *Research on Language and Social Interaction*, *40*(4), 279–289. https://doi.org/10.1080/08351810701471260

Gottschalk, P. (2011). A dark side of computing and information sciences: Characteristics of online groomers. *Journal of Emerging Trends in Computing and Information*, *2*(9), 447–455.

Guinness World Records. (2018, December 15). *Stampy Cat's fastest time to make 10 cakes in Minecraft – Guinness World Records* [Video]. YouTube. www.youtube.com/watch?v=qbjUl2tvE3E

Gupta, V. (2023, January 2). *HelloTalk review –Is it any good?* www.studyfrenchspanish.com/hellotalk-review/

Hanna, B. E. & de Nooy, J. (2003). A funny thing happened on the way to the forum: Electronic discussion and foreign language learning. *Language Learning and Technology*, *7*(1), 71–85.

Herring, S. C. (2013). Relevance in computer-mediated conversation. (2013). In S. C. Herring, D. Stein, & T. Virtanen (Eds.), *Handbook of pragmatics of computer-mediated communication* (pp. 245–268). Berlin: Mouton de Gruyter.

Herring, S. C., Dainas, A. R., Lopez Long, H. & Tang, Y. (2020). 'If I'm close with them, it wouldn't be weird': Social distance and animoji use. In *HCI International 2020 – Late breaking papers: Interaction, knowledge and social media* (pp. 285–304). Springer International. https://doi.org/10.1007/978-3-030-60152-2_23

Hijab Emoji Project. (2016). *The Hijab Emoji Project*. www.hijabemoji.org/

Hinchliffe, J. (2017, September 26). Too much social media could hamper your child's ability to read facial emotions, study finds. www.abc.net.au/news/2017-09-26/screen-time-could-hamper-ability-to-read-facial-emotions-study/8987512

Hjorth, L., Richardson, I., Davies, H. & Balmford, W. (2021). *Exploring Minecraft: Ethnographies of play and creativity*. Springer International Publishing AG.

Horowitz-Kraus, T. & Hutton, J. S. (2018). Brain connectivity in children is increased by the time they spend reading books and decreased by the length of exposure to screen-based media. *Acta Paediatrica*, *107*(4), 685–693. https://doi.org/10.1111/apa.14176

Howard, J. (2018, June 22). Social media and kids: What's the average age when kids get a social media account? *CNN*. https://edition.cnn.com/2018/06/22/health/social-media-for-kids-parent-curve/index.html

Hung, A. C. Y. (2011). *The work of play: Meaning-making in videogames*. Peter Lang.

Hung, A. C. Y. (2017). Hanging out on Xbox Live: How teens enter and open conversations in party chats. *Language@Internet*, *14*(3). https://scholarworks.iu.edu/journals/index.php/li/article/view/37717

Independent Inquiry Child Sexual Abuse. (2022). *The report of the independent inquiry into child sexual abuse*. London: APS Group. www.iicsa.org.uk/final-report.html

Internet Watch Foundation (2015). *Emerging patterns and trends report: Online produced sexual content*. www.iwf.org.uk/sites/default/files/inline-files/Online-produced_sexual_content_report_100315.pdf

Jefferson, G. (1987). On exposed and embedded correction in conversation. In G. Button & R. E. Lee (Eds.), *Talk and social interaction* (pp. 86–100). Multilingual Matters.

Jefferson, G. (1988). On the sequential organization of troubles talk in ordinary conversation. *Social Problems, 35*(4), 418–442. https://doi.org/10.1525/sp.1988.35 .4.03a00070

Jones, R. (2009). Dancing, skating and sex: Action and text in the digital age. *Journal of Applied Linguistics, 6*(3), 283–302. www.researchgate.net/profile/Rodney_Jones4/p ublication/264233424_Dancing_skating_and_sex_Action_and_text_in_the_digital_ age/links/53df519c0cf2a76fb6682378.pdf

Joseph, B. D. (2003). The editor's department: Reviewing our contents. *Language, 79* (3), 461–463.

Kahila, J., Tedre, M., Kahila, S., Vartiainen, H., Valtonen, T. & Mäkitalo, K. (2021). Children's gaming involves much more than the gaming itself: A study of the meta-game among 12- to 15-year-old children. *Convergence, 27*(3), 768–786. https://doi .org/10.1177/1354856520979482

Karsenti, T. (2019, April 21). Minecraft can increase problem solving, collaboration and learning – yes, at school. *The Conversation.* https://theconversation.com/minecraft-can-increase-problem-solving-collaboration-and-learning-yes-at-school-113335

Kasper, G. & Rose, K. (2001). Pragmatics in language teaching. In K. Rose & G. Kasper (Eds.), *Pragmatics in language teaching* (pp. 1–9). Cambridge University Press.

Kashian, N., Jang, J., Shin, S. Y, Dai, Y. & Walther, J. B. (2017). Self-disclosure and liking in computer-mediated communication. *Computers in Human Behavior, 71*, 275–283.

Kavanagh, B. (2016). Emoticons as a medium for channeling politeness within American and Japanese online blogging communities. *Language and Communication, 48*, 53–65. http://dx.doi.org/10.1016/j.langcom.2016.03.003

Kelly, M. (2020, May 15). Club Penguin Online shuts down after receiving copyright claim from Disney. *The Verge.* www.theverge.com/2020/5/15/21260122/club-pen guin-dmca-disney-takedown-cponline-online

Kern, R. (1995). Restructuring classroom interaction with networked computers: Effects on quantity and characteristics of language production. *Modern Language Journal, 79*(4), 457–476.

Kingsley, T. L. & Grabner-Hagen, M. M. (2015). Gamification. *Journal of Adolescent and Adult Literacy, 59*(1), 51–61. https://doi.org/10.1002/jaal.426

Kiourti, Elisavet. (2019) 'Shut the Fuck up Re! Plant the Bomb Fast!': Reconstructing Language and Identity in First-Person Shooter Games. In A. Ensslin and I. Balteiro (Eds.), *Approaches to videogame discourse: Lexis, interaction, textuality* (pp. 13–38). Bloomsbury.

Kito, M. (2005). Self-disclosure in romantic relationships and friendships among American and Japanese college students. *The Journal of Social Psychology, 145*(2), 127–140.

Kloess, J. A., Hamilton-Giachritsis, C. E. & Beech, A. R. (2019). Offense processes of online sexual grooming and abuse of children via internet communication platforms. *Sexual Abuse, 31*(1), 73–96. https://doi.org/10.1177/1079063217720927

Krohn, F. (2004). A generational approach to using emoticons as non-verbal communication. *Journal of Technical Writing and Communication*, *34*(4), 321–328. https://doi.org/10.2190/9EQH-DE81-CWG1-QLL9

Landhuis, C. E., Poulton, R., Welch, D. & Hancox, R. J. (2007). Does childhood television viewing lead to attention problems in adolescence? Results from a prospective longitudinal study. *Pediatrics*, *120*(3), 532–537. https://pubmed.ncbi.nlm.nih.gov/17766526/

Lenhart, A., Smith, A., Anderson, M., Duggan, M. & Perrin, A. (2015). *Teens, technology and friendships*. Pew Research Center. www.pewinternet.org/2015/08/06/teens-technology-and-friendships/

Lenneberg, E. H. (1967). *Biological foundations of language*. Wiley.

Liddicoat, A. J. (2010). Enacting participation: Hybrid modalities in on-line video conversation. In C. Develotte, R. Kern, M. N. Lamy (Eds.), *Décrire la conversation en ligne*. ENS Éditions.

Liddicoat, A. J. (2021). *An introduction to conversation analysis*. Bloomsbury Academic.

Liddicoat, A. J., & Tudini, V. (2013). Expert-novice orientations: Native speaker power and the didactic voice in online intercultural interaction. In F. Sharifian & M. Jamarani (Eds.), *Intercultural communication in the new era* (pp. 181–197). Routledge.

Linderoth, J., Lantz-Andersson, A. & Lindström, B. (2002). Electronic exaggerations and virtual worries: Mapping research of computer games relevant to the understanding of children's game play. *Contemporary Issues in Early Childhood*, *3*(2), 226–252. http://dx.doi.org/10.2304/ciec.2002.3.2.6

Liu, R-Y. (2022). Guiding children to respond: Prioritizing children's participation over interaction progression. *Research on Language and Social Interaction*, *55*(2), 184–202. https://doi.org/10.1080/08351813.2022.2075652

Lorenzo-Dus, N. & Kinzel, A. (2019). 'So is your mom as cute as you?': Examining patterns of language use by online sexual groomers. *Journal of Corpora and Discourse Studies*, *2*(1), 1–30.

Malinowski, D. & Kramsch, C. (2014). The ambiguous world of heteroglossic computer-mediated language learning. In A. Blackledge & A. Creese (Eds.), *Heteroglossia as practice and pedagogy* (pp. 155–178). Springer.

Marone, V. (2016). Playful constructivism: Making sense of digital games for learning and creativity through play, design, and participation. *Journal of Virtual Worlds Research*, *9*(3), 1–18.

Marsh, J. (2013). Countering chaos in *Club Penguin*. In Merchant, G., Gillen, J., March, J. & Davies (Eds.), *Virtual literacies: Interactive spaces for children and young people* (pp. 73–88). Routledge.

Marsh, J. (2014). Purposes for literacy in children's use of the online virtual world Club Penguin. *Journal of Research in Reading*, *37*(2), 179–195. https://doi.org/10.1111/j.1467-9817.2012.01530.x

Martellozzo, E. (2015). Policing online child sexual abuse – the British experience. *European Journal of Policing Studies*, *3*(1), 32–52.

McAfee (2022). *Cyberbulling in plain sight*. www.mcafee.com/content/dam/consumer/en-us/docs/reports/rp-cyberbullying-in-plain-sight-2022-global.pdf

McCormick, R. (2014, August 26). This is why people want to watch other people play video games. *The Verge*. www.theverge.com/2014/8/26/6068993/this-is-why-people-want-to-watch-other-people-play-video-games

Meredith, J. (2017). Analysing technological affordances of online interactions using conversation analysis. *Journal of Pragmatics*, *115*, 42–55.

Mitchell, K. J., Finkelhor, D., Jones, L. M. & Wolak, J. (2010). Use of social networking sites in online sex crimes against minors: An examination of national incidence and means of utilization. *Journal of Adolescent Health*, *47*(2), 183–190.

Mojang (2009). *Minecraft*. www.minecraft.net/en-us

Mondada, L. (2011). The situated organization of directives in French: Imperatives and action coordination in video games. *Nottingham French Studies*, *50*(2), 19–50.

Mondada, L. (2012). Co-ordinating action and talk-in-interaction in and out of video-games. In R. Ayaß & C. Gerhardt (Eds.), *Appropriation of media in everyday life* (pp. 231–270). John Benjamins.

Nagi, A. (2015, February 23). 11 parents who tried to use emojis and failed so hard they won. *Seventeen*. www.seventeen.com/life/friends-family/a26286/when-parents-use-emojis/

Netlingo (2023). *The Internet Dictionary*. www.netlingo.com/

Niemeyer, D. J. & Gerber, H. R. (2015). Maker culture and *Minecraft*: Implications for the future of learning. *Educational Media International*, *52*(3), 216–226. https://doi .org/10.1080/09523987.2015.1075103

Nippold, M. A., Duthie, J. K. & Larsen, J. (2005). Literacy as a leisure activity: Free-time preferences of older children and young adolescents. *Language, Speech and Hearing Services in Schools*, *36*(2), 93–102. https://doi.org/10.1044/0161-1461 (2005/009)

Nissenbaum, H. (2009). *Privacy in context: Technology, policy, and the integrity of social life*. Stanford University Press.

Official Statistics of Finland (2019). Participation in leisure activities 2017. Helsinki: Statistics Finland. www.stat.fi/til/vpa/2017/02/vpa_2017_02_2019-01-31_kat_001_fi .html

Oy, Sulake (2004). *Habbo.com*. https://www.habbo.com/

Pardes, A. (2018, February 1). The WIRED guide to emoji. *Wired*. https://www.wired .com/story/guide-emoji/

Pearce, A. M. (2017). Exploring performance of gendered identities through language in *World of Warcraft*. *International Journal of Human–Computer Interaction*, *33*(3), 180–189. https://doi.org/10.1080/10447318.2016.1230965

Pellettieri, J. (2000). Negotiation in cyberspace: The role of chatting in the development of grammatical competence. In M. Warschauer & R. Kern (Eds.), *Network-based language teaching: Concepts and practice* (pp. 59–86). Cambridge University Press.

Pellicone, A. & Ahn, J. (2018). Building worlds: A connective ethnography of play in Minecraft. *Games and Culture*, *13*(5), 440–458. https://doi.org/10.1177/ 1555412015622345

Piirainen-Marsh, A. (2012). Organizing participation in video-gaming activities. In R. Ayaß & C. Gerhardt (Eds.), *The appropriation of media in everyday life* (pp. 197–230). John Benjamins.

Piirainen-Marsh, A. & Tainio, L. (2009). Other-repetition as a resource for participation in the activity of playing a video game. *Modern Language Journal*, *93*(2), 153–169.

Piirainen-Marsh, A. & Tainio, L. (2014). Asymmetries of knowledge and epistemic change in social gaming interaction. *Modern Language Journal*, *98*(4), 1022–1038. https://doi.org/10.1111/modl.12153

Placencia, M. E. & Powell, H. (2020). 'Tu masssss ♥ te amo' Responding to compliments on Instagram among Ecuadorian teenage girls. In M. E. Placencia & Z. R. Eslami (Eds.), *Complimenting behaviour and (self-) praise across social media: New contexts and new insights* (pp. 99–117). John Benjamins.

Pomerantz, A. (1978). Compliment responses: Notes on the co-operation of multiple constraints. In J. Schenkein (Ed.), *Studies in the organization of conversational interaction* (pp. 79–112). Academic Press. www.apomerantz.com/wp-content/uploads/2015/04/Compliments_Responses.pdf

Pomerantz, A. (1985). Agreeing and disagreeing with assessments: Some features of preferred/dispreferred turn shapes. In J. M. Atkinson & J. Heritage (Eds.), *Structures of social action* (pp. 57–101). Cambridge University Press. https://doi.org/10.1017/CBO9780511665868.008

Powell, M. B., Casey, S. & Rouse, J. (2021). Online sexual offenders' language use in real-time chats. *Trends and Issues in Crime and Criminal Justice, 643*, 1–15. https://doi.org/10.52922/ti78481

Prior, M. T. (2019). Elephants in the room: An 'affective turn,' or just feeling our way? *Modern Language Journal, 103*(2), 516–527. https://doi.org/10.1111/modl.12573

Pudlinski, C. (2005). Doing empathy and sympathy: Caring responses to troubles telling on a peer support line. *Discourse Studies, 7*(3), 267–288. https://doi.org/10.1177/1461445605052177

Q+A (2008). Q+A. https://twitter.com/QandA

Quayle, E., Allegro, S., Hutton, L., Sheath, M. & Lööf, L. (2014). Rapid skill acquisition and online sexual grooming of children. *Computers in Human Behavior, 39*, 368–375. https://doi.org/10.1016/j.chb.2014.07.005

Recchia, H. W., Howe, N., Ross, H. A. & Alexander, S. (2010). Children's understanding and production of verbal irony in family conversations. *British Journal of Developmental Psychology, 28*(2), 255–274. http://doi.org/10.1348/026151008X401903

Recktenwald, D. (2017). Towards a transcription and analysis of live streaming on *Twitch*. *Journal of Pragmatics, 115*, 68–81. https://doi.org/10.1016/j.pragma.2017.01.013

Reeves, S., Greiffenhagen, C. & Laurier, E. (2017). Video gaming as practical accomplishment: Ethnomethodology, conversation analysis, and play. *Topics in Cognitive Science, 9*(2), 308–342. https://doi.org/10.1111/tops.12234

Roberts, S. (2017, July 18). MIXED EMOJIS: Here are the biggest emoji fails of all time . . . from laughing in a message of condolence to sending BOOBS on a birthday text. *The Sun.* www.thesun.co.uk/living/4041877/biggest-emoji-fails-wrong-context/

Rohlfing, K. J. & Müller-Brauers, C. Eds. (2021). *International perspectives on digital media and early literacy: The impact of digital devices on learning, language acquisition and social interaction.* Routledge. https://doi.org/10.4324/9780429321399

Rosenbaun, L., Rafaeli, S. & Kurzon, D. (2016). Participation frameworks in multiparty video chats cross-modal exchanges in public Google Hangouts. *Journal of Pragmatics, 94*, 29–46. https://doi.org/10.1016/j.pragma.2016.01.003

Sacks, H. (1992). *Lectures on conversation.* Vols. 1–2. Blackwell.

Sacks, H., Schegloff, E. A. & Jefferson, G. (1974). A simplest systematics for the organization of turn-taking for conversation. *Language, 50*(4), 696–735. https://www.researchgate.net/publication/215439057_A_Simple_Systematic_for_the_Organisation_of_Turn_Taking_in_Conversation.

Sadler, R. W. (2020). Language learning and the virtual world. In M. A. Peters and R. Heraud (Eds.), *Encyclopedia of educational innovation* (pp. 1–7). Springer. http://doi.org/10.1007/978-981-13-2262-4_88-2.

Saxton, M. (2017). *Child language: Acquisition and development.* SAGE Publications (pp. 86–117).

Schegloff, E. A. (1979). Identification and recognition in telephone conversation openings. In G. Psathas (Ed.), *Everyday language: Studies in ethnomethodology* (pp. 23–78). Irvington.

Schegloff, E. A. (1987). Analyzing single episodes of interaction: An exercise in conversation analysis. *Social Psychology Quarterly, 50*(2), 101–114. https://doi.org/10.2307/2786745

Schegloff, E. A. & Sacks, H. (1973). Opening up closings. *Semiotica, 8*, 289–327.

Schegloff, E. A., Jefferson, G. & Sacks, H. (1977). The preference for self-correction in the organization of repair in conversation. *Language, 53*(2), 361–382.

Seedhouse, P. (2005). Conversation analysis and language learning, *Language Teaching, 38*(4), 165–187

Shaban, H. (2019, February 23). YouTube axes tens of millions of comments in crackdown on child sexual exploitation. *The Washington Post.* www.washingtonpost.com/technology/2019/02/21/youtube-axes-tens-millions-comments-crackdown-child-sexual-exploitation/

Sjöblom, B. (2008). Gaming as a situated collaborative practice. *Human IT, 9*(3), 128–165.

Smith, B. (2003). Computer-mediated negotiated interaction: An expanded model. *The Modern Language Journal, 87*(1), 38–57.

Starke, A., Leinweber, J. & Ritterfeld, U. (2021). Designing apps to facilitate first and second language acquisition in children. In Rohlfing, K. J. & Müller-Brauers, C. (Eds.), *International perspectives on digital media and early literacy: The impact of digital devices on learning, language acquisition and social interaction* (pp.141–160). Routledge. https://doi.org/10.4324/9780429321399

Statista (2020). Survey on the social network usage of children and teenagers in Germany 2019. www.statista.com/statistics/422297/children-and-teenagers-social-network-usage-germany/

Statista (2021a). Hours children spent gaming weekly in the United Kingdom (UK) from 2013 to 2019, by age group. www.statista.com/statistics/274434/time-spent-gaming-weekly-among-children-in-the-uk-by-age/

Statista (2021b). Impact of COVID-19 on the frequency of playing multiplayer video games worldwide as of June 2020. www.statista.com/statistics/1188549/covid-gaming-multiplayer/

Statista (2021c). Most popular social media sites used by US teens and young adults 2020. www.statista.com/statistics/199242/social-media-and-networking-sites-used-by-us-teenagers/

Statista (2022). Number of monthly active players of Minecraft worldwide as of August 2021. www.statista.com/statistics/680139/minecraft-active-players-worldwide/

Stivers, T., Sidnell, J. & Bergen, C. (2018). Children's responses to questions in peer interaction: A window into the ontogenesis of interactional competence. *Journal of Pragmatics, 124*, 14–30. https://doi.org/10.1016/j.pragma.2017.11.013

Strambi, A. & Tudini, V. (2020). 'I'll say something about myself': Questions and self-disclosures in Italian L1–L2 online initial interactions. *Journal of Pragmatics*, *170*, 82–95. https://doi.org/10.1016/j.pragma.2020.08.006

Streeck, J., Goodwin, C. & LeBaron, C. D. (2013). *Embodied interaction: Language and body in the material world*. Cambridge University Press.

Strouse, G. (2019). Using digital media to support language learning in early childhood. In Horst, J. and von Koss, J. (Eds.), *International handbook of language acquisition* (pp.485–503). Routledge.

Suzuki, S. (2013). Private turns: A student's off-screen behaviors during synchronous online Japanese instruction. *CALICO Journal*, *30*(3), 371–392. https://doi.org/10.11139/cj.30.3.371-392.

Sydorenko, T., Thorne, S. L., Hellermann, J., Sanchez, A. & Howe, V. (2021). Localized globalization: Directives in augmented reality game interaction. *The Modern Language Journal*, *105*(3), 720–739. https://doi.org/10.1111/modl.12722

Taylor, D. C. P. J., Mwiki, H., Dehghantanha, A., Akibini, A., Choo, K. K. R., Hammoudeh, M. & Parizi, R. (2019). Forensic investigation of cross platform massively multiplayer online games: Minecraft as a case study. *Science and Justice*, *59*(3), 337–348. https://doi.org/10.1016/j.scijus.2019.01.005

Tener, D., Wolak, J. & Finkelhor, D. (2015). A typology of offenders who use online communications to commit sex crimes against minors. *Journal of Aggression, Maltreatment and Trauma*, *24*(3), 319–337.

Thorne, S. L. (2012). Gaming writing: Supervernaculars, stylization, and semiotic remediation. In Kessler, G., Oskoz, A. and Elola, I. *Technology across writing contexts and tasks* (pp. 297–316). San Marcos, TX: CALICO Monograph Series.

Thorne, S. L., Fischer, I. & Lu, X. (2012). The semiotic ecology and linguistic complexity of an online game world. *ReCALL*, *24*(3), 279–301. https://doi.org/10.1017/S0958344012000158

Thorne, S. & Hellermann, (2015). Sociocultural approaches to expert–novice relationships in second language interaction. In Markee, N. (Ed.), *The handbook of classroom discourse and interaction* (pp. 281–297). Wiley.

Tudini, V. (2007). Negotiation and intercultural learning in Italian native speaker chat rooms. *Modern Language Journal*, *91*(4), 577–601.

Tudini, V. (2010). *Online second language acquisition: Conversation analysis of online chat*. Continuum.

Tudini, V. (2013). Form-focused social repertoires in an online language learning partnership. *Journal of Pragmatics*, *50*(1), 187–202. http://dx.doi.org/10.1016/j.pragma.2012.12.005

Tudini, V. (2015). Extending prior posts in dyadic online text chat. *Discourse Processes*, *52*(8), 642–669. https://doi.org/10.1080/0163853X.2014.969138

Tudini, V. & Strambi, A. (2017). 'Siamo vicini, no?': Negotiating commonality for rapport building in Italian L1–L2 online text chat. *Australian Review of Applied Linguistics*, *40*(2), 194–211. https://doi.org/10.1075/aral.40.2.07tud

Tudini, V. (2020). Conversation analysis of computer-mediated interactions. In C. Chapelle (Ed.), *The concise encyclopedia of applied linguistics* (pp. 265–270). Wiley-Blackwell.

Tudini, V. & Liddicoat, A. J. (2017). Computer-mediated communication and conversation analysis. In S. Thorne & S. May (Eds.), *Language, education and technology: The encyclopedia of language and education* (pp. 1–12). 3rd ed. Springer International Publishing. https://doi.org/10.1007/978-3-319-02328-1_32-1

Turkle, S. (2015). *Reclaiming conversation: The power of talk in a digital age*. Penguin.

Twenge, J. M. (2017). *Why today's super-connected kids are growing up less rebellious, more tolerant, less happy, and completely unprepared for adulthood* and what that means for the rest of us*. Atria Books.

Van Dijk, C. N., van Witteloostuijn M., Vasić N., Avrutin S. & Blom E. (2016). The influence of texting language on grammar and executive functions in primary school children. *PLoS ONE 11*(3). https://doi.org/10.1371/journal.pone.0152409

Vedelago, C. (2020, June 19). More than 7.4 million images of child abuse circulating in Victoria. *The Age*. www.theage.com.au/national/victoria/more-than-7-4-million-images-of-child-abuse-circulating-in-victoria-20200619-p554dy.html

Vygotsky, L. S. (1978). *Mind in society: Development of higher psychological processes*. (M. Cole, V. John-Steiner, S. Scribner & E. Souberman, Eds.). MIT Press.

Vygotsky, L. S. (1986). *Thought and Language*. MIT Press.

Wager, N., Gallagher, B., Armitage, R., Rogerson, M., Christmann, K., Parkinson, S. & Synnott, J. (2018). *Rapid evidence assessment: Quantifying online facilitated child sexual abuse – Report for the independent inquiry into child sexual abuse*. Home Office.

Walker, G. (2017). Young children's use of laughter as a means of responding to questions. *Journal of Pragmatics*, *112*, 20–32. https://doi.org/10.1016/j.pragma.2017.02.006

Walker, S., Hatzigianni, M. & Danby, S. J. (2018). Electronic gaming: Associations with self-regulation, emotional difficulties and academic performance. In Danby, S. J., Fleer, M., Davidson, C. & Hatzigianni, M. (Eds.). *Digital childhoods: Technologies and children's everyday lives* (pp. 85–100). Springer. https://doi.org/10.1007/978-981-10-6484-5

Warschauer, M. (1996). Comparing face-to-face and electronic communication in the second language classroom. *CALICO Journal*, *13*(2–3), 7–26.

Washington, J. A. (2023). African American English dialect: What it does to the English language. webinar snippet. https://www.youtube.com/watch?v=u7Eni-QB7Lo

Webster, S., Davidson, J., Bifulco, A., Gottschalk, P., Caretti, V., Pham, T., Grove-Hills, J., Turley, C., Tompkins, C., Ciulla, S., Milazzo, V., Schimmenti, A., & Craparo G. (2012). *European Online Grooming Project*. Final report. https://europeanonlinegroomingprojectT.com/wp-content/file-uploads/European-Online-Grooming-Project-Final-Report.pdf

Webwise.ie (n.d.). A parent's guide to *Minecraft*. www.webwise.ie/parents/a-parents-guide-to-minecraft/

WeProtect Global Alliance (2019). *Global Threat Assessment 2019: Working together to end the sexual exploitation of children online*. https://www.weprotect.org/global-threat-assessment/

Wernholm, M. & Vigmo, S. (2015). Capturing children's knowledge-making dialogues in Minecraft. *International Journal of Research and Method in Education*, *38*(3), 230–246. https://doi.org/10.1080/1743727X.2015.1033392

Whittle, H., Hamilton-Giachritsis, C., Beech, A. & Collings, G. (2013). A review of online grooming: Characteristics and concerns. *Aggression and Violent Behavior*, *18* (1), 62–70. https://doi.org/10.1016/j.avb.2012.09.003

Wikimedia Commons. (2021). *Emoji/table*. https://commons.wikimedia.org/wiki/Emoji/Table

Wikitubia Fandom (2013, August 28). *Ethan Gamer*. https://youtube.fandom.com/wiki/EthanGamer#:~:text=EthanGamer%20(born%3A%20July%209%2C,Red%20Ball%204%20on%20Mobile

Williams, R., Elliott, I. A. & Beech, A. R. (2013). Identifying sexual grooming themes used by internet sex offenders. *Deviant Behavior, 34*(2), 135–152.

Wolak, J. & Finkelhor, D. (2013). Are crimes by online predators different from crimes by sex offenders who know youth in-person? *Journal of Adolescent Health, 53*(6), 736–741.

Wolak, J., Finkelhor, D., Mitchell, K. J., & Ybarra, M. L. (2010). Online 'predators' and their victims: Myths, realities, and implications for prevention and treatment. *Psychology of Violence, 1*(S), 13–35. https://doi.org/10.1037/2152-0828.1.S.13

Wolak, J., Finkelhor, D., Walsh, W. & Treitman, L. (2018). Sextortion of minors: Characteristics and dynamics. *Journal of Adolescent Health, 62*(1), 72–79.

Wootton, A. J. (1997). *Interaction and the development of mind*. Cambridge University Press. https://doi.org/10.1017/CBO9780511519895

Wootton, A. J. (2007). A puzzle about please: Repair, increments, and related matters in the speech of a young child. *Research on Language and Social Interaction, 40*(2–3), 171–198. https://doi.org/10.1080/08351810701354623

YouTube (n.d.). Learn about comment settings. https://support.google.com/youtube/answer/9483359?hl=en#zippy=%2Callow-all-comments%2Chold-potentially-inappropriate-comments-for-review

Zimmer, M. (2010). 'But the data is already public': On the ethics of research in Facebook. *Ethics and Information Technology, 12*(4), 313–325. https://doi.org/10.1007/s10676-010-9227-5

Index

For EU product safety concerns, contact us at Calle de José Abascal, 56–1°, 28003 Madrid, Spain or eugpsr@cambridge.org.

www.ingramcontent.com/pod-product-compliance
Ingram Content Group UK Ltd.
Pitfield, Milton Keynes, MK11 3LW, UK
UKHW020429240426
470322UK00017B/426